Yankees & Rebels on the Upper Missouri

Yankees & Rebels on the Upper Missouri

Steamboats, Gold and Peace

Ken Robison

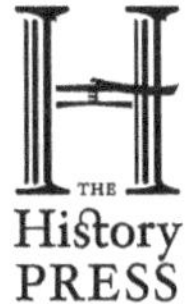
The History Press

Published by The History Press
Charleston, SC
www.historypress.net

Back cover, top: A Robert Morgan mural, *Ho! For the Gold Fields*, 1862–74, hangs in the Montana State Agricultural Museum and Center in Fort Benton, symbolizing the steamboat trade during the gold mining era. *River and Plains Society*.

First published 2016

Manufactured in the United States

ISBN 978.1.46713.562.7

Library of Congress Control Number: 2016938314

To our Upper Missouri River region, a land blessed with beauty, heritage and opportunity—a future National Heritage Area.

To Michele, a U.S. Air Force daughter and Navy wife—my partner on our life's tour.

Contents

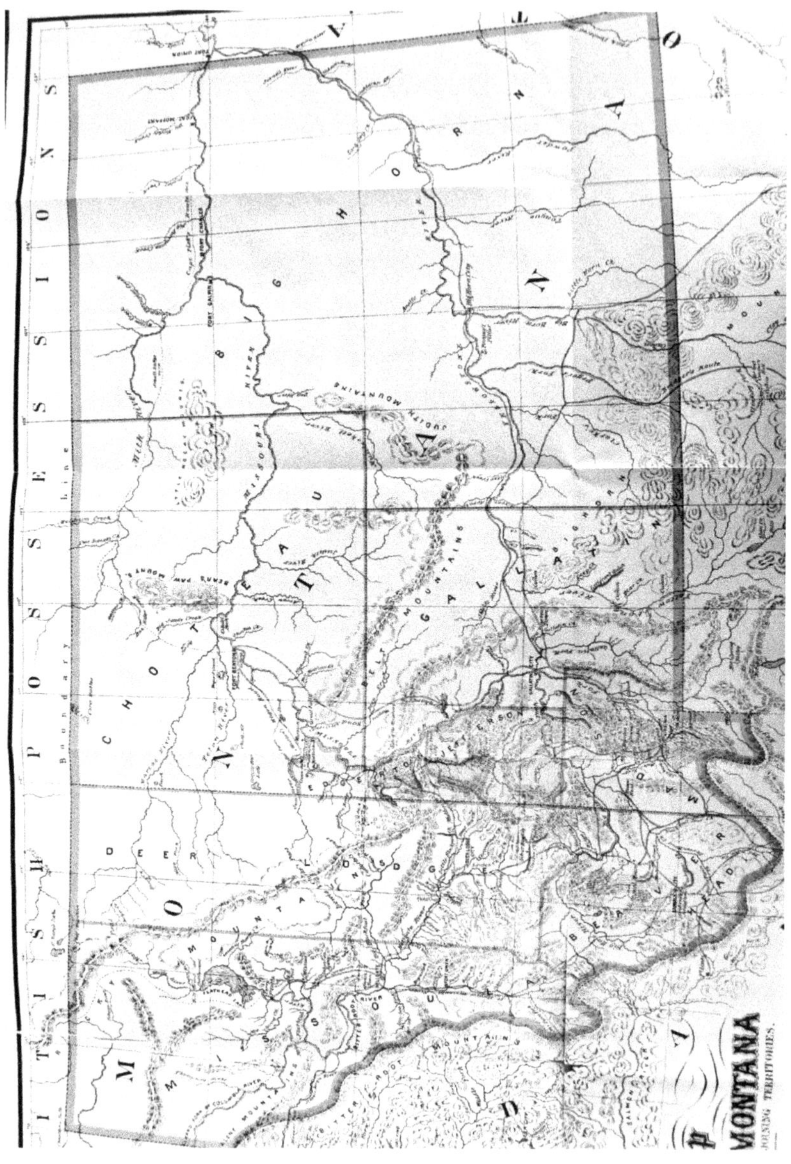

Map of the Territory of Montana in 1865. Drawn by W.W. de Lacy for the use of the first legislature of Montana. *Author's collection.*

Acknowledgements

Although the Civil War ended in 1865, the impact of that most momentous event in American history continued on the frontier of the newly formed Montana Territory. As I've roamed the state in conversation about the Civil War and its impact on Montana, I continue to find great interest in our territorial history. As we begin to celebrate the good and the bad of the post–Civil War Reconstruction era of the late 1860s and 1870s, Montana's development continued. My special thanks to those who celebrate the history of our Big Sky state, share it with others and buy books in local bookstores.

As historian at the Overholser Historical Research Center in Fort Benton, I operate in a community immersed in history. As the head of steam navigation on the Missouri River and the birthplace of Montana, Fort Benton has been making history since the mid-1840s. Today, through the River & Plains Society, we operate an impressive museums complex and research center that present the exciting history of this Upper Missouri region from the glacial lakes that formed our terrain to the era of native nations into the fur trade on to exploration and settlement, steamboating, Indian Wars, open range ranching, homesteading and on to today's agricultural environment and cultural tourism in the heart of the Golden Triangle.

A special thanks to eloquent former executive director Randy Morger of the River & Plains Society, Chairman Larry Cook and the Board of Trustees, as well as my colleagues in the Overholser Historical Research

Center for dedicating time, effort and wisdom to present our shared history to an international audience.

My thanks to Kathy Mora and the Great Falls Public Library, Megan Sanford and the History Museum and Jan Thompson and the Great Falls Genealogy Society for providing impressive research resources and working environments. Montana's Historical Society continues to make every visit an exciting adventure—many thanks. And a special thanks to Kay Strombo for sharing her impressive research into Civil War Montanans.

For friends and family, I could not have done it without you all.

Introduction

The beauty of the Upper Missouri region continues to inspire all who live or travel through its rugged grandeur. Dramatic events from 1860 to 1862 transformed the Upper Missouri River from the relative isolation of the fur and bison robe trade to the raucous gold rush days that would keep the region in turmoil throughout the Civil War. From the presence of thousands of Native Americans with several hundred white Americans clustered at several trading posts in 1860, to more than sixteen thousand miners and adventurers stampeding from gold strike to strike among the mining camps, the Upper Missouri region that became Montana Territory in 1864 was in turmoil during the Civil War years. This was a transformational moment on the Upper Missouri in the heart of native Blackfeet country.

Fort Benton, the world's innermost port at the head of steam navigation on the Missouri River, transformed from a remote fur- and robe-trading post into the heart of a growing commercial empire that, within a decade, would extend from the Dakotas to the Idaho mines and from later Wyoming northward through the British possessions that would later compose Alberta and Saskatchewan provinces.

Massive cargoes of freight and numbers of travelers bound for the gold fields of the new El Dorado would transform Fort Benton and the Upper Missouri. Still distant from the States, Fort Benton was no longer simply an extension of St. Louis as a trading outpost but the center for a commercial empire.

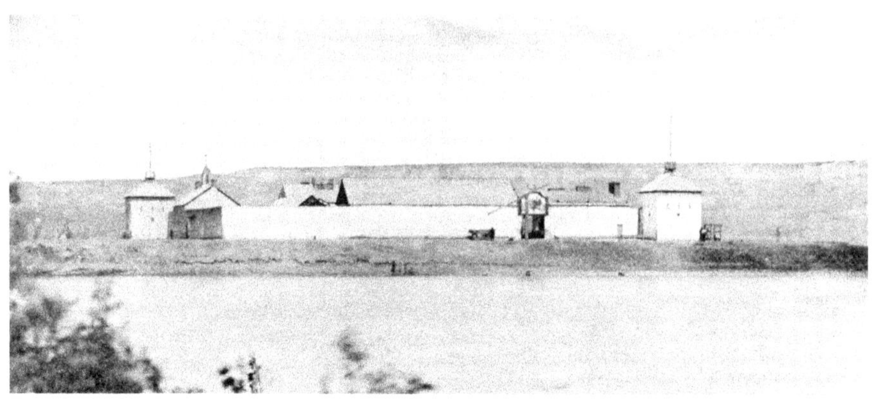

The first photograph of the American Fur Company trading post at Fort Benton, taken in 1860 by Lieutenant James Dempsey Hutton. *Overholser Historical Research Center.*

This all began in the summer of 1860. Until then, Fort Benton and nearby Fort Campbell had been the focus of white American activity on the Upper Missouri River, together with Fort Owen and a few settlements west of the continental divide. During that summer of 1860, three events occurred that set the stage for change: the first steamboats arrived at the Fort Benton levee from St. Louis with the first U.S. military unit, Major George Blake's three hundred troopers of the 1st Dragoons, onboard; the William F. Raynolds Expedition arrived after exploring the Yellowstone and Missouri Rivers; and First Lieutenant John Mullan arrived with his joint military-civilian road-building expedition, completing a 624-mile Military Wagon Road from Fort Walla Walla, Washington Territory, to Fort Benton. The native Blackfeet Indians, long dominant in the Upper Missouri region, were about to be shaken from their previous isolation from white encroachment. Steamboats from St. Louis to Fort Benton and a wagon road on to the Pacific set the stage for dramatic change in the region.[1]

Three decades earlier, fur trading posts with the Blackfeet (or Nitsitapi) and Gros Ventre (or A'aninin) had reached the Upper Missouri. In that year, the American Fur Company (after 1834 formally known as the Upper Missouri Outfit of Pierre Chouteau Jr. & Co. of St. Louis) opened a series of posts, first Fort Piegan (1831) followed by Forts MacKenzie (1832), Chardon (1844), Lewis (1845) and Benton (1846–47). In 1846, an opposition trading post, Fort Campbell, financially supported by St. Louis fur trader Robert Campbell, was established two miles upriver from Fort Benton. Mackinaws and keelboats laboriously brought upriver from Fort Union at the Dakota border served as transportation before the steamboats, bringing trade goods up and taking furs and bison robes downriver. The trading posts were more than businesses; they also served as conduits for news and ideas and as centers for exchange of customs between native Indians and white traders.[2]

In 1860, Fort Benton consisted of the trading post but no town. Civilian John Strachan, with the Mullan Expedition, described the environment in the summer of 1860 in a letter written to his brother for publication in the *Rockford* [Illinois] *Register*:

> *Fort Benton at last appeared in sight, and the prospects for home now began to brighten. Although yet distant over three thousand miles from St. Louis, the river from here is navigable, and we could now see the prospects of an outlet from this desolate region. Fort Benton belongs to the American Fur Company, is upon an extensive scale, and is worthy of the vast interest of which it is the center. Everything may be had within the Fort. They have a bakery, blacksmiths', carpenters' and coopers' shops; trade offices for buying, others for selling, for keeping accounts, and for transacting business; and also shops for retail. Goods are sold at enormous prices, the stock consisting of cotton and woolen goods, ready-made clothing, ship chandlery, tin and iron ware, fancy articles, and, in short, everything of every kind and description, including all sorts of groceries. Sugar is sold at one dollar and upward per pound, and everything else in proportion. The business here amounts to about $160,000 a year; buffalo robes the staple of the trade. All is arranged in the best order, and I should think, with great economy.*[3]

By 1860, Fort Benton served also as the outfitting post for the slowly growing colony of white Americans in Bitter Root, Deer Lodge and Missoula outposts. The first year of the Civil War brought little change on the upper river, yet as 1862 dawned, dramatic change was coming. That year brought the placer gold strikes first at Gold Creek, north of Deer Lodge, and then on Grasshopper Creek, causing the sudden formation of the mining camp of Bannack. The influences of the Civil War began to affect the Upper Missouri with the arrival of the first influx of those who had seen the war, either as participants or as observers. Many of the early arrivals came from Missouri, and the pattern quickly formed for the Upper Missouri to become the exile of choice for those who sought to avoid war or had briefly participated only to become disillusioned by defeat or paroled from capture. Most of these in the early years of the war were Southern-leaning Missourians.

The frontier town of Fort Benton sprang to life during the spring and summer steamboating season, with hundreds of freighters present to

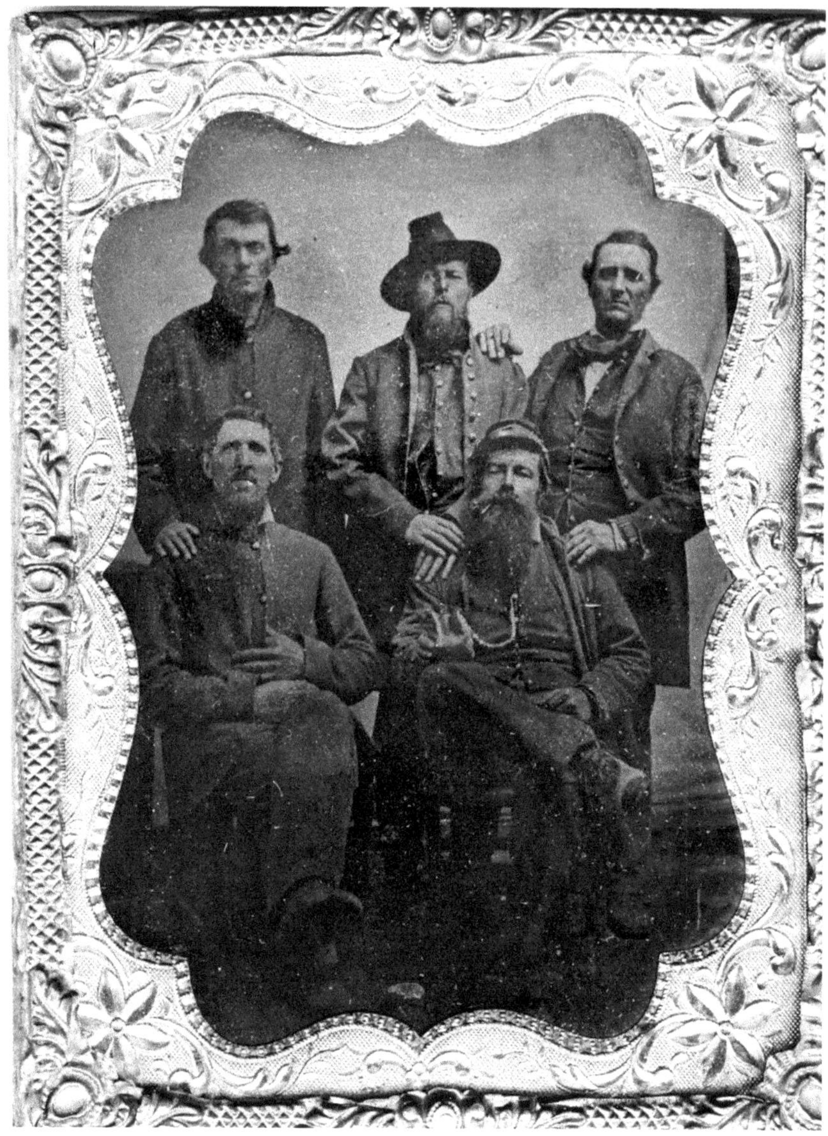

An early tintype of Confederate soldiers who flooded into Montana Territory during the Civil War. *Author's collection.*

participate in monumental overland freighting operations using mules and oxen. By 1867, miners, freighters and steamboat passengers were greeted by a daunting array of saloons, dance halls and brothels centered in one block on Front Street facing the steamboat levee. This "Bloodiest Block in the West" roared twenty-four hours a day, and everything was legal.

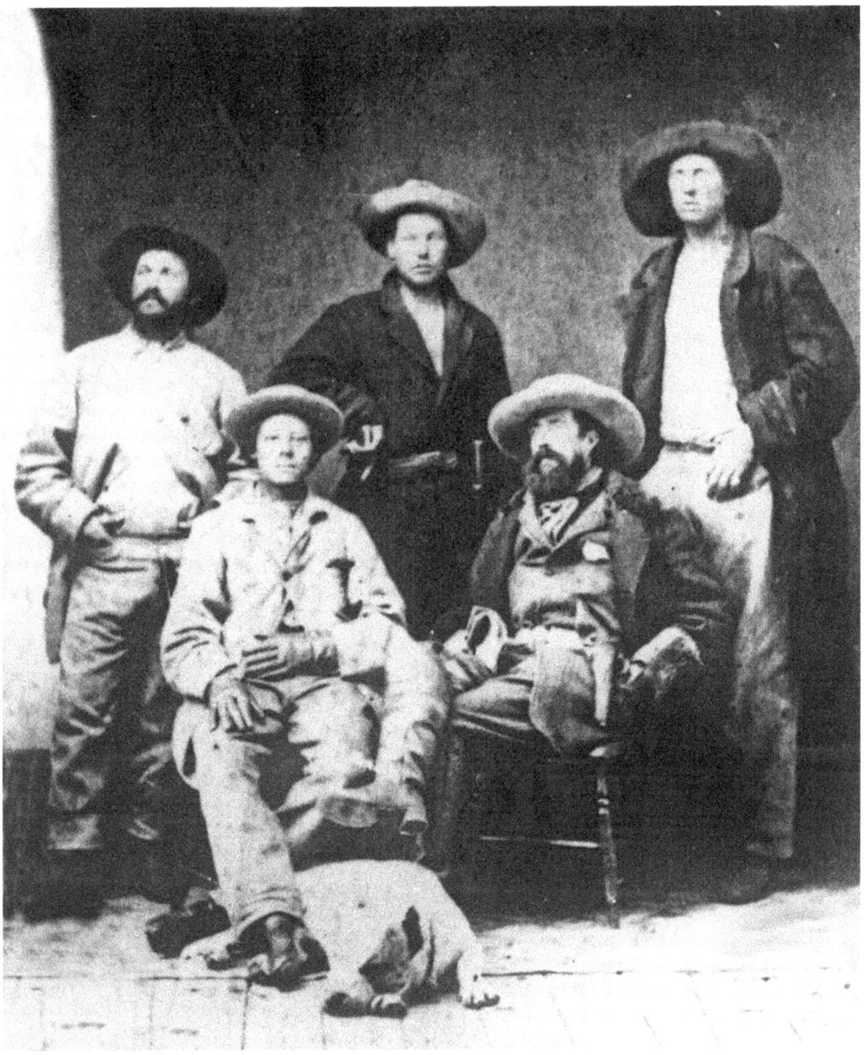

Former soldiers, North and South, became traders and miners on the Upper Missouri. *Standing, left to right*: Mose Solomon, African American Bob Mills and John Largent. *Seated, left to right*: Joe Kipp and Henry Kennerly. *Overholser Historical Research Center.*

From early spring until late fall, gambling houses with no betting limits eased the gold dust from miners. Faro, blackjack, poker and craps relieved many miners of their summer earnings before they returned to the States. Rotgut whiskey captured its share, and fancy ladies finished off what was left of a miner's poke before he boarded the boat to St. Louis. The most infamous proprietor was Eleanor Dumont, known as Madame Moustache.

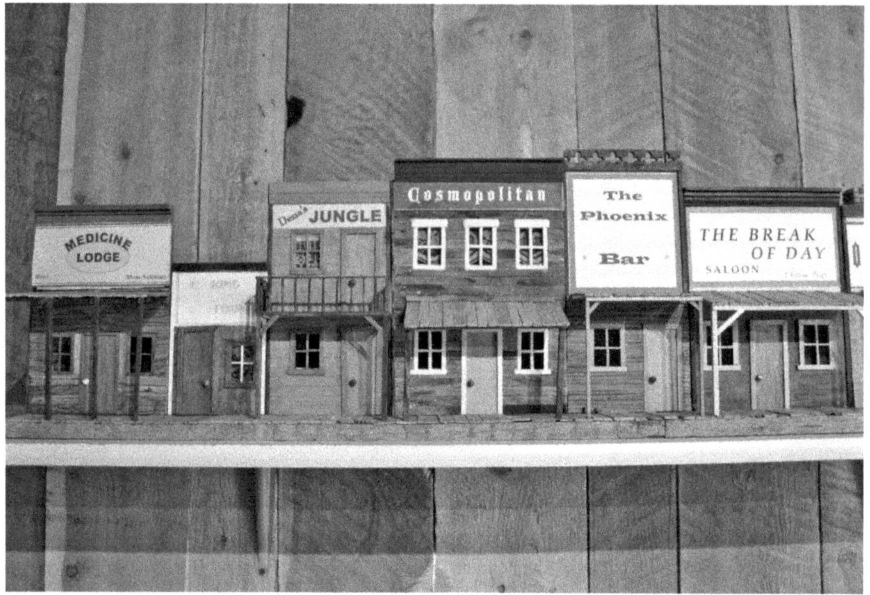

A model of Fort Benton's Bloodiest Block in the West in 1867, open twenty-four hours a day. Here, anything was legal, and infamous Madame Moustache operated the Cosmopolitan Saloon. *Author's photo.*

She packed two revolvers and chased from the levee a steamboat carrying smallpox. Dumont's Cosmopolitan was one of the most popular saloons. There, she played blackjack at a raised corner table and served booze and girls to all takers.

Other infamous institutions on the Bloodiest Block in the West on Front Street were Dena Murray's Jungle, Mose Solomon's Medicine Lodge, the Break-of-Day Saloon, the Squaw Dance and the Board of Trade. In the words of William Gladstone, a visitor from the British possessions up north:

> *One could never tell when Sunday came around as there was no distinction made between that day and any other. Drinking and gambling and whiskey-selling went on just the same. On my first Sunday there I went to hunt up some friends and opening the door of the room where they lived, found four eager-eyed gamblers hard at work.*
>
> *Each man had a bag of gold dust and a pistol on the table before him. One of the men asked me if I was one of the parties that had just arrived from the north. I said, "Yes" and he asked me about the mines.*

> *"Stranger, do you indulge?" he hospitably asked upon my admitting that now and again on rare occasions, I was known to do so, he pointed to a bucket and told me that I would find some knock-me-down in there.*
>
> *I dipped some of the liquid fire out of the bucket and asking for water was directed to another bucket which I found contained whiskey too. They all laughed at me and asked if they drank water where I came from as water in Benton was never used for that purpose.*
>
> *Oh, those were great days in Benton! Shooting and stabbing and rows of all kinds were daily occurrences and it was a wonder to me that more men were not killed.*[4]

Based on the premise that history is best when told through stories, *Yankees and Rebels on the Upper Missouri: Steamboats, Gold and Peace* is the third in my series of books exploring the lives and experiences of Montanans before, during and after the Civil War. *Montana Territory and the Civil War: A Frontier Forged on the Battlefield* overlays the events of the Civil War on the accelerated formation of Montana Territory during the war. The 1862 gold discoveries brought thousands to the mining camps, and the gold fueled the Union war effort. Yet loyalties were mixed among the miners, with a strong Southern contingent, and by 1864, the government of President Abraham Lincoln created Montana Territory to assure its loyalty to the Union. That book illustrates how Southern sympathizers and Union loyalists, deserters and veterans, freed slaves and former slaveholders, men, women and children, black and white, living side by side, made a volatile and vibrant mix that molded Montana. Fiery personalities like first territorial governor Union colonel Sidney Edgerton and General Thomas Francis Meagher fought to keep order in the newly formed frontier, while brave Confederate and Union veterans and their hardy families created an enduring legacy that shaped modern Montana.[5]

My second book, *Confederates in Montana Territory: In the Shadow of Price's Army*, focuses on the dominant early Southern-sympathizing residents who came to Montana Territory during and after the war to their "exile" of choice on the remote frontier. Confederate veterans flocked to the Upper Missouri seeking new opportunities after enduring the hardships of war. These men and their families made a lasting impact on the region. *Confederates in Montana Territory* presents fascinating characters, including guerrillas who fought with William Quantrill and Bloody Bill Anderson, as well as cavalrymen who rode with Confederate legends General Nathan Bedford Forrest and Colonel John S. Mosby. The final story features the postwar capture of steamboat *Richmond* by Quantrill guerrillas for a desperate race up the Missouri River.[6]

My goal in each book is to relate a representative sampling of how the lives of thousands of Montana's men, women and children were affected by the Civil War, the most momentous event in our nation's history. Their stories recount where they came from, why they fought or didn't fight for the North or South, what drew them to Montana Territory and how they helped shape the region. While the battles of the Civil War occurred in most instances far from Montana Territory, these future Montanans participated in those events from the war's beginning to the end, and their stories and wartime experiences are told. They came to the Montana frontier looking for hope and opportunity, bearing the scars and searing experiences of the war.

Yankees and Rebels on the Upper Missouri continues to tell this important national history through the exciting experiences of the war's impact on steamboat travel on the Missouri River—the challenges of steamboat operations during the war and after the war. Stories are presented about how Confederate raiders tried to disrupt and capture Union boats during the war. How the captains and crews battled through navigation hazards of many kinds to deliver their passengers and cargoes under trying conditions during and after the war. How steamboats were vital to operations during the Montana Indian Wars of the 1870s. What adventurous travelers saw and experienced as they passed through the wonders of scenic splendor of the Upper Missouri along the way. When participants in these stories tell their adventures well, their primary source words are presented to let their personalities shine through their narratives.

"Cradled in Dixie" presents African Americans who came up the Missouri River to seek opportunity on the Montana frontier. They brought with them their memories of survival from slavery and wartime experiences, whether shaving presidential beards or working as nurses, cooks and servants for Union soldiers and families. While their stories have been largely ignored in the general overlook of black lives, on the Upper Missouri, these men and women compiled remarkable records of achievement and serve to remind us all that black lives mattered on the frontier. Among these stories are answers to fascinating riddles through original research. Where did these newly freed black men and women spend their lives in servitude? What role did two young black women played in the household of Colonel and Mrs. George A. Custer, as well as on the Indian Wars campaign trail with Colonel Custer? What roles did they play in the newly forming communities on the frontier?

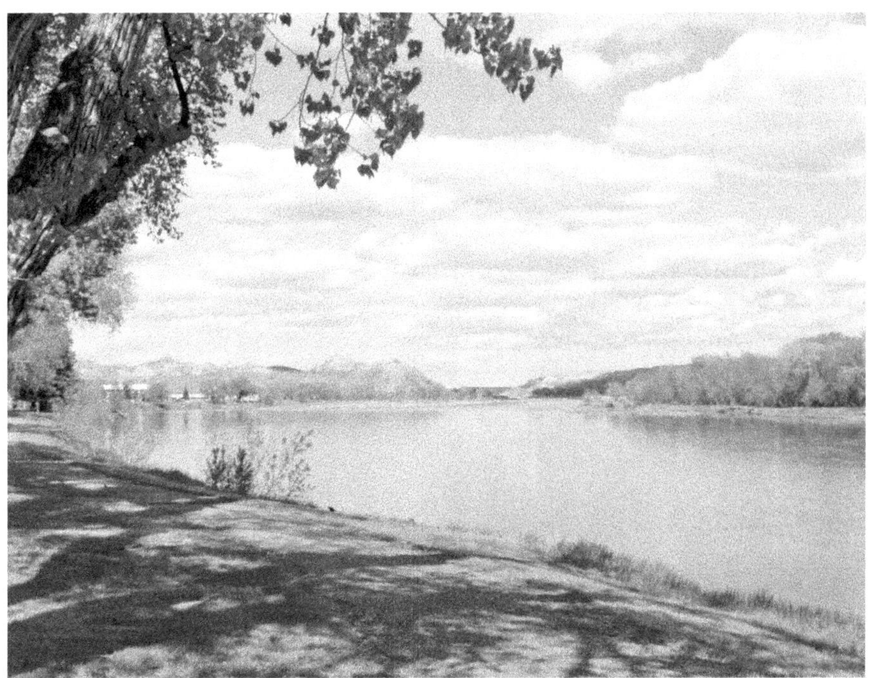

The Fort Benton steamboat levee as it appears today with Signal Point in the background just to the left of the channel of the Missouri River. *Author's photo.*

While during the 1860s about half of the cargo and many of the passengers reaching Montana Territory came up the Missouri River on steamboats, not all did. The overland routes became increasingly important by the end of the 1860s as the first transcontinental railroad, the Union Pacific, shortened the trip by many weeks. Memorable characters and outlaws share their stories in the final part of this book. The stories they bring are remarkable, ranging from major contributions during Montana's Indian Wars and in Montana politics to intriguing mysteries about events that happened during the Civil War and in Montana Territory. Among the most intriguing stories is the mystery of whether Jesse and Frank James joined the many other ex-Confederates in seeking respite in frontier Montana.

In the concluding story, the thrice-wounded veteran who tracked down the killer of President Abraham Lincoln shares the compelling story of how he and his men did it. These stories are offered in the hope you will enjoy meeting colorful men and women, learning about their wartime experiences and celebrating their role as they settled in the grandeur of the Upper Missouri frontier.

PART I

Steamboat Operations on the Missouri River:

Civil War Challenges

Chapter 1

Steamboat Operations on the Upper Missouri

The Civil War Years and Beyond

The pre–Civil War years from 1855 to 1860 formed the zenith of the golden age of Missouri River steamboating. From the St. Louis gateway, the Missouri River rose as a natural highway to the West. Settlements along the Missouri's banks moved higher and higher until by 1852, Sioux City, Iowa, was settled, and eight years later, steamboats began to moor at the Fort Benton levee, head of navigation on the river. By the end of the decade, more steamboats left St. Louis for Missouri River ports than the entire Mississippi River trade.

Steamboat operations on the Missouri River during the Civil War years reflected the ebb and flow of the war in Missouri and the western theater. Trade on the river from St. Louis to Kansas City was disrupted early in the war by the military campaigns as pro-Union forces struggled to control the state of Missouri and the river. Missouri was a slave state, and along the Missouri River through Little Dixie, sympathy for the South was strong. Almost all steamboat captains and pilots, many of them slaveholders, sympathized with the South. In contrast, many steamboat owners were loyal to the Union from the war's beginning. In the words of Hiram Chittenden, biographer of famed Missouri River Captain Joseph La Barge:

> *The steamboat business on the river felt the weight of the war almost immediately upon its breaking out. Most of the business was with loyal people and was, of course, considered by the Confederates as a*

> *legitimate subject of confiscation. Guerrilla bands infested the country along the river, fired into the boats, and did all they could to break up the business.*[7]

Harassment by pro-Confederate raiding parties, such as the attack and capture of the steamboat *New Sam Gaty* in 1863, disrupted the river trade. (The story of the *Sam Gaty* incident follows in Chapter 2.) President Abraham Lincoln's strategy from the beginning placed iron-willed emphasis on retaining the state of Missouri in the Union, controlling St. Louis as the gateway to the West and seizing and maintaining control of strategic western rivers—the Missouri, Ohio, Tennessee, Cumberland and Mississippi.[8]

On the middle Missouri River from Kansas City to Sioux City, river traffic increased during the early war years, fueled by overland freighting demands from Leavenworth, Kansas, and other towns leading to the western territories. Above Sioux City, as the war progressed, the discovery of gold on the Upper Missouri and increasing warfare with the Sioux Indians in the Dakotas greatly increased demands for steamboat operations all the way to Fort Benton. This dramatic growth in Upper Missouri steamboating did not come quickly but by the mid-1860s was booming.

In February 1861, the Confederate States of America formed, and on April 12, the Civil War began with the attack on Fort Sumter, South Carolina. All through the spring of 1861, Missouri was in turmoil, with pro-secession governor Claiborne Jackson determined to lead the state into the Confederacy. The Camp Jackson affair in St. Louis occurred on May 10, when Captain Nathaniel Lyon, with loyal Union regiments, surrounded and captured the pro-secession Missouri Militia. This incident kept St. Louis as the Union stronghold in Missouri. The war for the state and the rivers continued for another year until Union forces controlled most of the Missouri and pro-Confederate troops were forced to retreat into Arkansas.[9]

On April 25, 1861, the American Fur Company steamboat *Chippewa*, commanded by Captain William H. Humphreys, followed one week later by the larger steamer *Spread Eagle*, commanded by Joe La Barge's brother John, got underway from St. Louis for the Upper Missouri carrying Indian annuity goods, their own Indian trade goods for the Fort Benton post and other freight, including $7,000 stock of merchandise for Frank Worden's new post at Hell Gate, near today's Missoula. After reaching Fort Union, the larger *Spread Eagle* offloaded its cargo, loaded eighteen thousand bison robes and got underway for return downriver.[10]

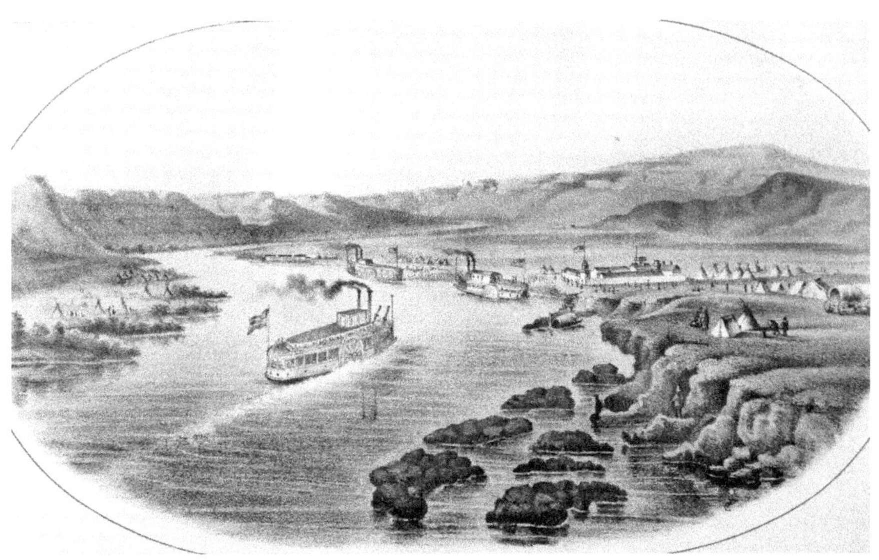

Gustav Sohon painted this scene of the first arrival of steamboats at the Fort Benton levee in 1860. Lithograph by Bowen & Co. *Author's collection.*

Heavily loaded with about 250 tons and crowded with crew, company employees and about fifty adventurers, *Chippewa* departed Fort Union for Fort Benton on a trip that would end in disaster (as told later in Chapter 7, the story of adventurer John Mason Brown with friends artist William Cary and Major William H. Schieffelin). Although the cargo was quickly offloaded before the *Chippewa* exploded, this was a blow to both the American Fur Company and the white settlements on the Upper Missouri.[11]

In St. Louis and the lower Missouri River, the summer of 1861 proved difficult from guerrilla harassment and doubts about the loyalty of rivermen. Federal authorities knew the Southern sympathies of men like Captain Joe La Barge and the Chouteaus, and these and other powerful St. Louis men had to prove their allegiance—and most did with time. In the case of La Barge, he encountered incidents early that summer that caused his steamer *Emilie* to be confiscated, and for the rest of that summer, La Barge was ordered not to command his boat. In his absence, Captain Nicholas Wall assumed command of the *Emilie*. Ironically, Wall just months before had been captured as major of commissary at Camp Jackson, held as a prisoner of war and only released on parole that required him to remain in St. Louis or banished him to the western territories.[12]

During the winter of 1861–62, Captain La Barge formed a new firm, La Barge, Harkness & Company, to challenge the Chouteaus for control of the Upper Missouri trade. On April 30, 1862, the steamboat *Shreveport*, commanded by John La Barge, steamed from St. Louis, and two weeks later, the *Emilie* departed with Captain Joe La Barge in command. The two side-wheel steamboats together were packed with about five hundred tons and three hundred deck and cabin passengers, lured by "gold fever" in the St. Louis press and bound for the Idaho Salmon River mines. News of the strikes by James and Granville Stuart and others early that spring at Gold Creek in later Montana had not then reached St. Louis. Captain Nick Wall, leading an organized group, the American Exploring and Mining Company, was on board the *Emilie*, and Wall served additionally as the clerk of the boat on the *Emilie* for the trip up the Missouri.[13]

In the face of its new competition, on May 10, the American Fur Company sent the *Key West* and *Spread Eagle* with trade goods for its trading post, Indian annuities and wagons and supplies for the gold seekers. Between the La Barge and Chouteau steamers, about 1,300 tons and six hundred passengers were delivered to the Upper Missouri that season. Fueling excitement back in the States was the cargo of $100,000 in gold dust brought downriver from Fort Benton by the *Shreveport*. Thus, the year 1862 marked the beginning of potentially dramatic growth in the steamboat trade on the Upper Missouri fueled by the new gold discoveries.[14]

Upon the arrival of prospective miners and their supplies at Fort Benton, they learned of the Gold Creek strikes in the Deer Lodge Valley. The newly completed Mullan Military Wagon Road carried a large number of travelers heading southwest to the mines. Captain Wall and James Harkness set up trading posts near Gold Creek to supply the miners, and Fort La Barge was constructed two miles upriver from the Fort Benton post. After modest success at Gold Creek, in the summer of 1862, major quantities of placer gold were discovered 140 miles south at Grasshopper Creek, fostering the boomtown of Bannack.

With the *Emilie*'s return to St. Louis, Captain La Barge continued to operate on the Missouri into the fall. In October, his steamer was seized by guerrillas and required to offload his cargo and ferry 175 Rebels and their horses across the Missouri River, with Union cavalry hot on their heels.[15]

As the navigation season dawned in the spring of 1863, prospects for Upper Missouri trade appeared promising. Placer mining on Grasshopper Creek was booming, followed later in the summer by even greater strikes along Alder Gulch, with thousands of miners from Colorado and the East flooding into Virginia City and the other camps. Yet this would be a year of great frustration on the river.

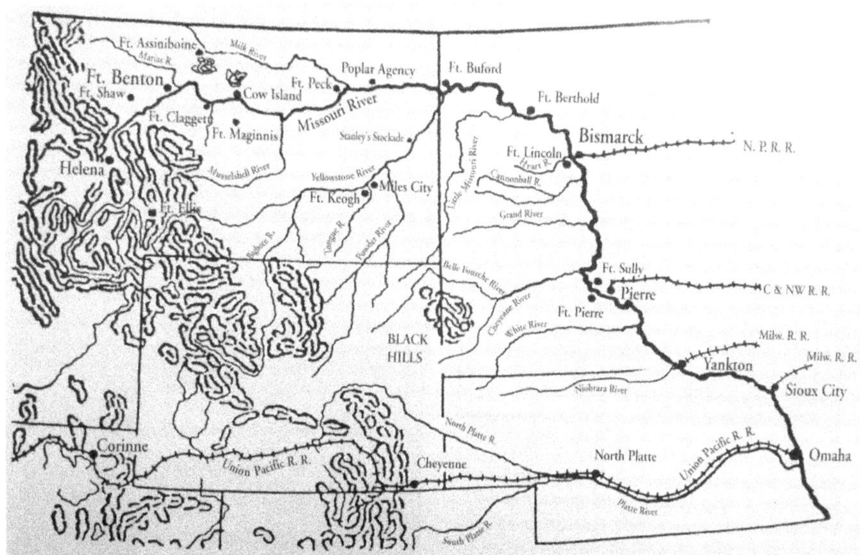

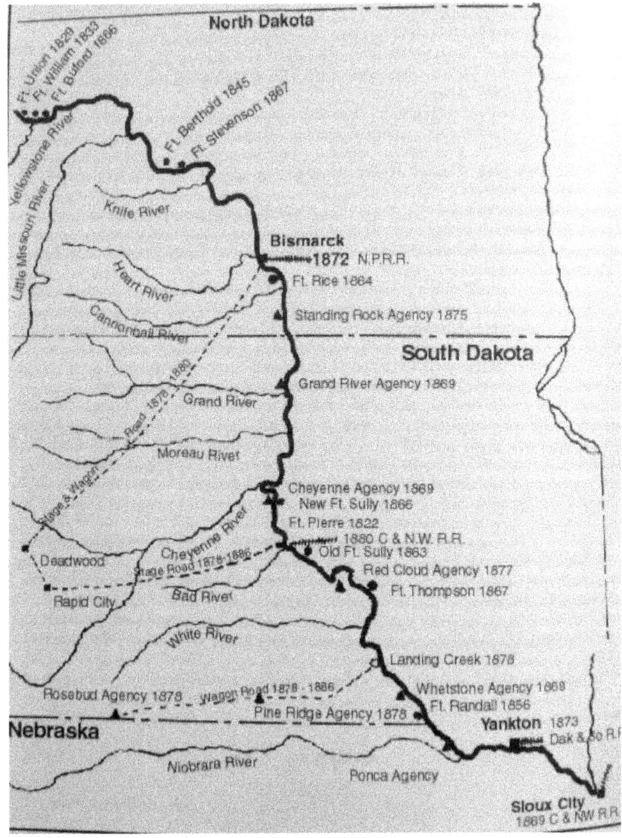

Above: Map of the Upper Missouri River within Montana Territory. *Overholser Historical Research Center.*

Right: Map of the Upper Missouri River from Sioux City, Iowa, to the border of Montana Territory. *Overholser Historical Research Center.*

La Barge, Harkness & Company underbid Chouteau for the government contract to deliver Indian annuity goods, and the firm sent the *Shreveport*, under Captain John La Barge, and the larger *Robert Campbell*, under Joe La Barge. The American Fur Company dispatched the *Nellie Rogers* and the *Alone*. All four boats faced extreme low water conditions on the Upper Missouri, and all were fired upon by Sioux Indians, an indication that the Sioux Uprising or Dakota Conflict was erupting to endanger river travel. During this disastrous steamboating year, not a single boat reached Fort Benton.

The *Robert Campbell* could not even reach Fort Union, so the *Shreveport* made five trips lightering 500 tons of cargo to Fort Union. Even worse, through the extreme bad judgment of Captain John La Barge, the *Shreveport* offloaded its 250 tons and eighty-five passengers at Snake Point, a landing almost inaccessible for freight wagons by land. Adding to La Barge's problems was an attack on his boats by the Sioux at Tobacco Gardens, about eighty-eight miles downriver from Fort Union. The American Fur Company boats fared little better—*Nellie Rogers* left 250 tons and eighty passengers at the Milk River, while the *Alone* reached Fort Charles, just above Poplar River, leaving 250 tons of freight. Overall, about five hundred passengers and 1,250 tons of cargo arrived, but it would take many months, and even up to a year, for all the freight to reach Fort Benton and the mining camps. In addition, as the *Alone* and *Shreveport* descended the Missouri, they were impressed by Brigadier General Alfred Sully to support his Sioux campaign.[16]

The steamboating season in 1864 presented great opportunities mixed with concerns. Despite the dangers and hazards, the "Mountain" steamboat trade could be enormous, with profits on some of the long, slow, risky trips so great that the cost of the steamer could be paid by a single trip "to the mountains." The Bannack and Alder Gulch gold mines fueled a boom that produced about $8 million worth of placer gold in 1863. Virginia City and the other camps were booming, and by May 1864, Montana Territory was formed. In September, the territorial census recorded more than eleven thousand nonnative males in Madison County and almost sixteen thousand throughout the new territory.

La Barge, Harkness & Company had gone bankrupt, a result of poor management and the ruinous costs of recovering the cargo left at Snake Point, followed by loss of court suits. Steamboats bound for the Upper Missouri were now outfitted with boilerplate offering some protection of pilothouses from Indian attack. Charles Chouteau also had problems; he had

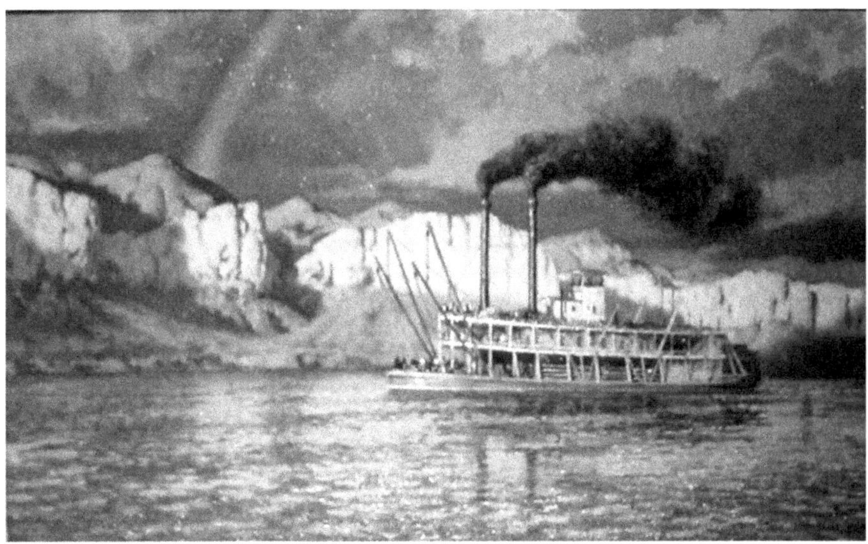

A Charles Fritz painting of the steamboat *Benton II* fighting its way up the Missouri through the White Cliffs on its way to Fort Benton. *Author's photo, River & Plains Society.*

lost the lucrative Indian annuity contract and was under further suspicion of Confederate sympathies and faced loss of government freight contracts.

Into this mix a new company emerged out of the ashes of La Barge, Harkness & Company—the Fort Benton and Idaho Transportation Company, funded by St. Louis pork packer Captain John J. Roe, operated by Roe's son-in-law Captain John G. Copelin and managed by Captain Nick Wall, their partner in Montana Territory. Roe company steamboats would bring cargo to Fort Benton, where Roe company freight wagons would haul the cargo to the mining camps, where Roe company retail stores would sell the merchandise. For the next five years, John J. Roe & Company would dominate the commercial scene on the Upper Missouri, with one outgrowth being the famed Diamond R (for Roe) Overland Freighting Company. Despite another low-water navigation year in 1864, eight steamboats brought 1,660 tons of cargo and 650 passengers upriver and 400 passengers and 250 tons down, including twenty thousand bison robes.[17]

During 1865, placer mining was booming in Alder Gulch and newly opened Last Chance Gulch, today's Helena. Demand for cargo and passenger traffic was immense, yet this proved to be the third low-water year in a row, and of twenty steamers bound for Fort Benton, six had to offload downriver—and one other, the *Bertrand*, a Copelin boat, snagged and sunk

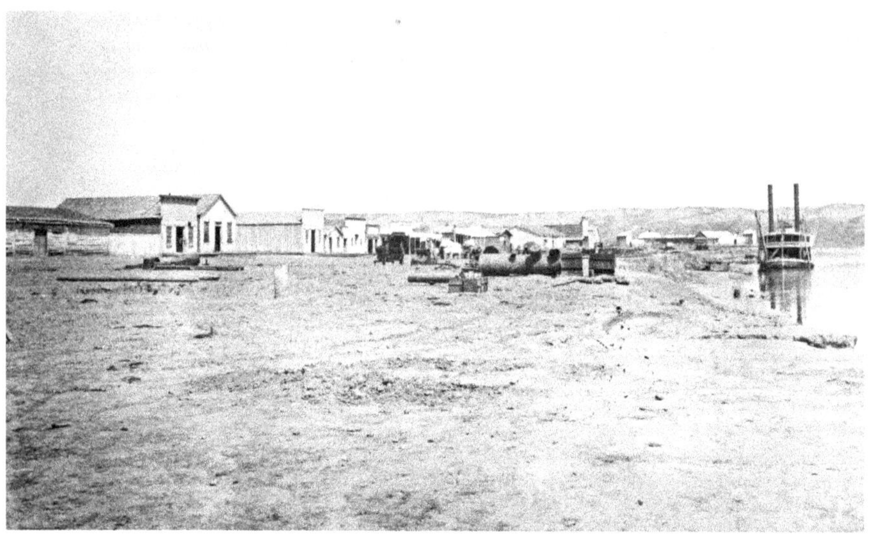

The town of Fort Benton with the steamboat *Success* at the levee in this photograph by Salt Lake photographer C.R. Savage in August 1868. *Author's collection.*

in DeSoto Bend, north of Omaha, with its cargo lost. Over one hundred years later, the *Bertrand* was located under a cornfield in 1968 and its cargo recovered. Today, the *Bertrand*'s astonishing array of essential mining supplies and luxury goods, bound for the Montana gold rush, is on display at DeSoto National Wildlife Refuge.[18]

The year 1865 marked the end of the American Fur Company on the Upper Missouri when Charles Chouteau arrived on the company steamboat *Yellowstone* to turn over the old Fort Benton trading post to Hubbell and Hawley of the North West Fur Company. On Chouteau's trip down, the *Yellowstone* carried twenty-nine thousand bison robes and furs (worth about $145,000 at that time) and a shipment of gold dust worth up to $400,000—not a bad way for the American Fur Company to bow out from the Upper Missouri.

For this last year of the Civil War, nineteen steamboats arrived on the Upper Missouri, bringing 3,700 tons of cargo and more than 1,850 passengers upriver, while 800 returning miners and families and 365 tons of cargo went downriver.[19]

In the four postwar years from 1866 to 1869, until placer mining played out in Montana Territory, during the four-month navigation season from May into August, and bolstered by high water in the river each year, an average of fifty-one steamboats reached the Upper Missouri, with thirty-

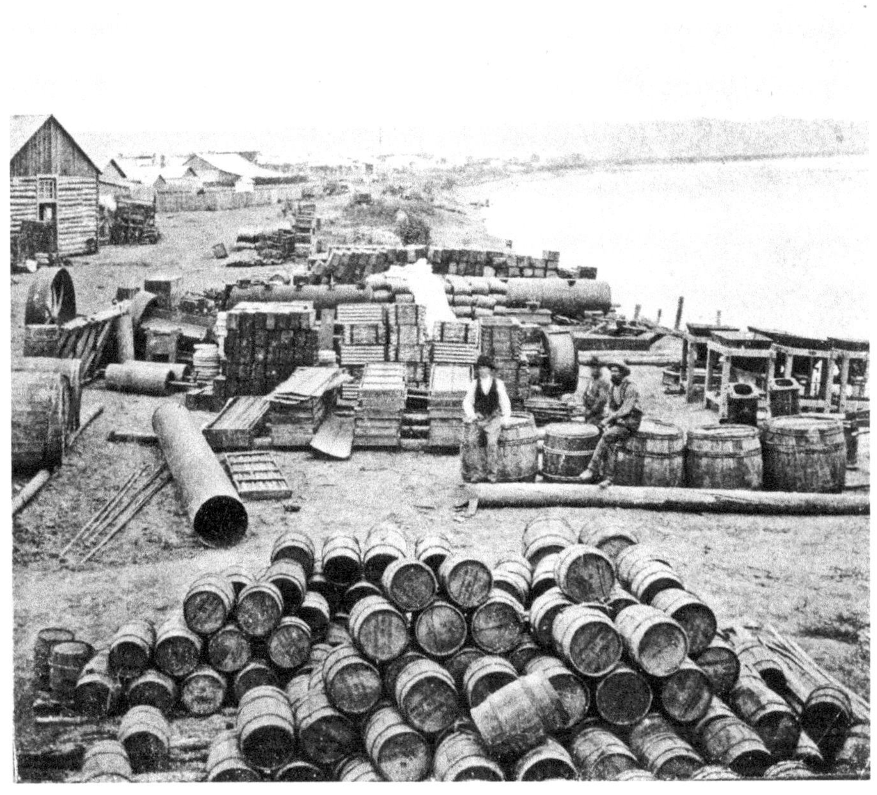

Massive freight being offloaded by Coulson Line steamboats on the upper levee at Fort Benton. *Overholser Historical Research Center.*

eight moored at Fort Benton annually. These boats each year delivered 7,714 tons of freight and 5,575 passengers to Fort Benton. During these boom years, on occasion, as many as six or eight steamboats moored along the lower and upper levees at Fort Benton at a time. Passengers and supplies for the growing territory arrived and exceptional cargoes of gold dust and valuable bison robes returned downriver. On a single trip in 1866, the steamer *Louella* delivered 2.5 tons of Confederate Gulch gold dust, valued at an astonishing $1,250,000. Granville Stuart was in Fort Benton on August 29, 1866, to record the arrival of this gold dust by a freight wagon drawn by four mules and escorted by fourteen armed miners. This was the richest cargo ever to go down the Missouri.[20]

With the end of the Civil War and in response to increasing incidents along the river and on the Benton to Helena wagon road, the U.S. Army

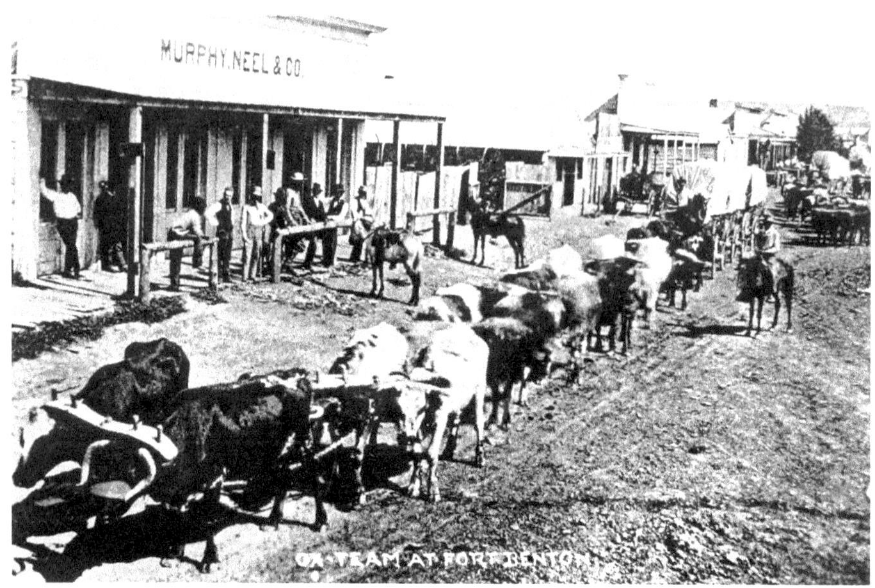

The levee or Front Street in the 1860s during freighting season with ox teams by Murphy Neel and Carroll and Steell stores, loaded and ready to move out on trails leading every direction from Fort Benton. *Overholser Historical Research Center.*

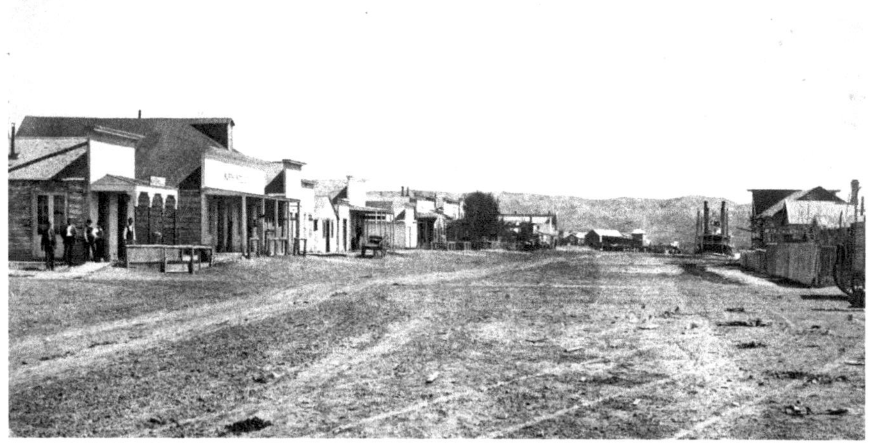

A quiet day in Fort Benton in the 1870s with a steamboat at the levee and the Fort Benton trading post in the background. *Author's collection.*

constructed its first military post in Montana Territory. Some thirteen steamboats carried the 13th Infantry Regiment and construction material and supplies for the new post, Camp Cooke, at the mouth of the Judith River, ninety miles downriver from Fort Benton. This marked the beginning of major new military business for steamboat lines bringing recruits and supplies upriver. Camp Cooke proved immediately that it was at the wrong location and was moved shortly to Fort Shaw (1867) in the Sun River Valley. After the Nez Perce War of 1877, Fort Asinniboine (1879), near today's Havre, was established using troops and supplies offloaded at Coal Banks Landing.

Through these years, business in Fort Benton was booming. Equal in excitement to the river traffic arriving at Fort Benton was the overland transportation industry required to carry this massive cargo and passenger flow. Stage lines, bull trains and mule trains of all kinds were available for points beyond Fort Benton. "All trails lead out of Fort Benton" was a familiar term, and the trails and roads radiated from the town like spokes on a wagon wheel. Fort Benton was the anchor of the Mullan Road to Fort Walla Walla, which quickly evolved into the Benton to Helena and Benton to Virginia City roads; the Northern Overland and Fisk Wagon Roads to Minnesota through northern Montana into Dakota; the Whoop-Up Trail and Fort Walsh Trail leading into Canada; and the Cow Island Trail to downriver landings where freight was dropped off when the boats could not reach Fort Benton. The combination of steamboats and freighting kept Fort Benton prosperous for two decades until railroads eventually arrived. During this period, merchant princes like T.C. and John Power, Isaac G. Baker, William G. and Charles Conrad and the men who worked for them ranged throughout Montana Territory, as well as southwestern Canada.

Chapter 2

Quantrill Guerrillas on the Missouri River

Capturing the Sam Gaty

Throughout the early years of the Civil War, steamboats plying the lower Missouri trade from St. Louis encountered harassment by pro-Confederate raiding guerrilla parties. These incidents ranged from isolated rifle fire to occasional capture in order to ferry Rebels across the river. The most serious attack occurred in the spring of 1863 when the steamer *New Sam Gaty* was targeted.

The steamboat *New Sam Gaty*, under Captain John McCloy, departed the St. Louis levee late in the afternoon on March 17, 1863, bound for the Upper Missouri, with a heavy load of freight and passengers on a trip that descended into hell. On board was considerable government freight, paroled Union soldiers, seventy-six contrabands (slaves freed by the war) and several wealthy passengers on their way to the newly discovered gold fields of what would become Montana Territory the next year.[21]

From the onset of the Civil War, steamboats quickly became important wartime transportation resources on the Mississippi and Missouri Rivers. The Union immediately began to militarize boats with arms and armor for use as gunboats in its campaign to seize control of the vital rivers of Missouri, Kentucky and Tennessee. Construction of armored gunboats commenced in Union shipyards, and they were used for many different missions. The Union and Confederacy both relied on steamboats as gunboats, troop and prisoner transports and for hauling food, livestock and supplies of all kinds, including medical.

As the war progressed, the Union used steamboats to transfer freed slaves and return prisoners freed from Confederate prisons. Because of their important military tasks in the early years of the war, Confederate guerrillas along the Mississippi and Missouri Rivers routinely engaged in hostile actions against Union steamboats as well as plantations and towns under Union control.

The steamboat *New Sam Gaty* was named for Samuel Gaty (1811–1887), the first manufacturer of steamboat machinery west of the Mississippi. It was built in 1853 at a St. Louis yard at a cost of $32,000. The *Sam Gaty*, a side-wheeler, was 215 feet in length with a width of 30 feet, 6 inches. Through the course of the Civil War, it saw considerable service on both the Missouri and Mississippi Rivers, yet this trip would bring lasting infamy.[22]

Four days after *Sam Gaty*'s departure from St. Louis, news arrived that the steamer had met with an accident near Hermann and had burst out both cylinder heads. New cylinder heads were sent by railroad, and repairs were made so that the steamer could be underway by March 23. For the next three weeks, no news came of the overdue steamer. Finally, on April 15, the *Sam Gaty* returned to St. Louis with a good cargo of produce and its cabin full of passengers. Without explanation for its long delay, newspapers reported only that it "had an adventurous trip, but came out all right."[23]

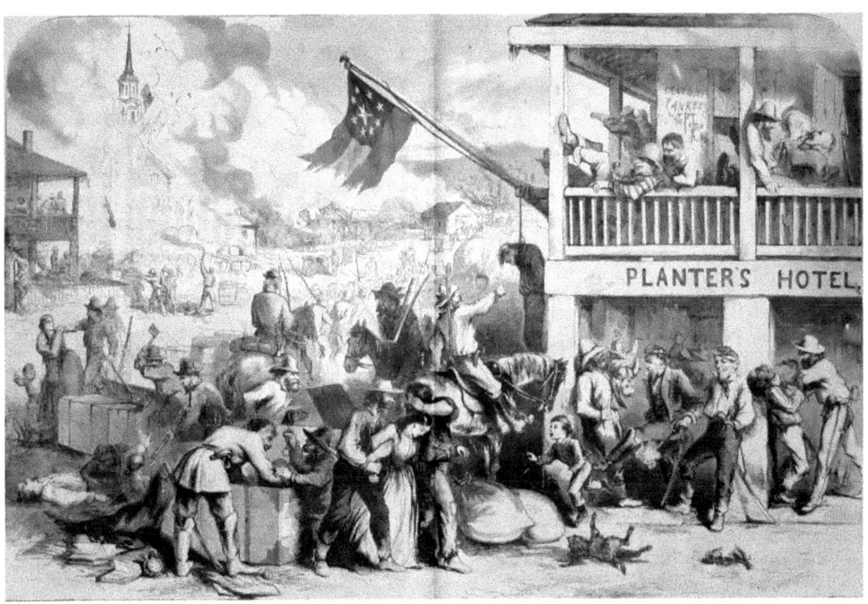

This illustration by Thomas Nast captures the confusion and panic during one of Quantrill's guerrilla lightning-fast raids. Harper's Weekly, *1862*.

Eventually, the mysterious delay became clear—the *Sam Gaty* had been fired upon and captured by Confederate guerrillas in one of the worst Missouri River incidents of the war. In the early morning hours of March 28, Quantrill guerrillas led by William H. Gregg with eleven other men attacked the *Sam Gaty* at Sibley Landing in northeast Jackson County in western Missouri. Sibley provided an ideal location for an ambush since the channel of the river ran close to a wooded bluff edge and the high bluff formed a perfect angle to fire down on boats as they neared the landing. Various accounts in the Liberty, Leavenworth and Jefferson City newspapers varied in the details of the number of African Americans on board and those killed, the number of bushwhackers and even the identify of guerrilla leader Bill Gregg.[24]

On Saturday morning, March 28, at 2:00 a.m., the steamboat *Sam Gaty* neared Sibley Landing, about thirty miles below Independence, Missouri. It was coming up from St. Louis and had on board, besides its government freight, seventy-six contrabands sent by Major General Samuel R. Curtis to Major General James G. Blunt. These contrabands were freed slaves liberated by Kansas abolitionists from Missouri plantations downriver and being transported to Kansas and freedom.

At Sibley, the river runs within thirty feet of the bank, and it was at this point that Captain John McCloy of the *Sam Gaty* reported that Gregg's guerrillas fired into his boat and ordered the steamer to stop. Gregg and his heavily armed men coerced the pilot into pulling the boat to the landing by threatening to burn the vessel, and the boat was moving too slow against the current and too close to the landing for the pilot to refuse. Only a few persons on the boat were awake at the time. Among Gregg's men was believed to be Cole Younger, destined for fame in the postwar James-Younger gang.

As soon as the *Gaty* landed, the bushwhackers rushed onto the boat, took the captain prisoner and began to search and rob the boat. They knew that the contrabands were on board and also knew the names of many passengers. How they obtained this intelligence was never determined. Gregg's men searched for a "Mr. Wilson" of the 5th Kansas Cavalry Regiment, who they believed had charge of the contrabands. One of Colonel William R. Penick's soldiers of the 5th Missouri State Militia was mistaken for Wilson and was immediately killed, while a second soldier from Penick's regiment was shot and apparently killed. Wilson was never found, apparently safely hidden by the contrabands.

Gregg and his men were inexperienced in capturing steamboats, and they lacked the numbers to properly control the large number of terrified

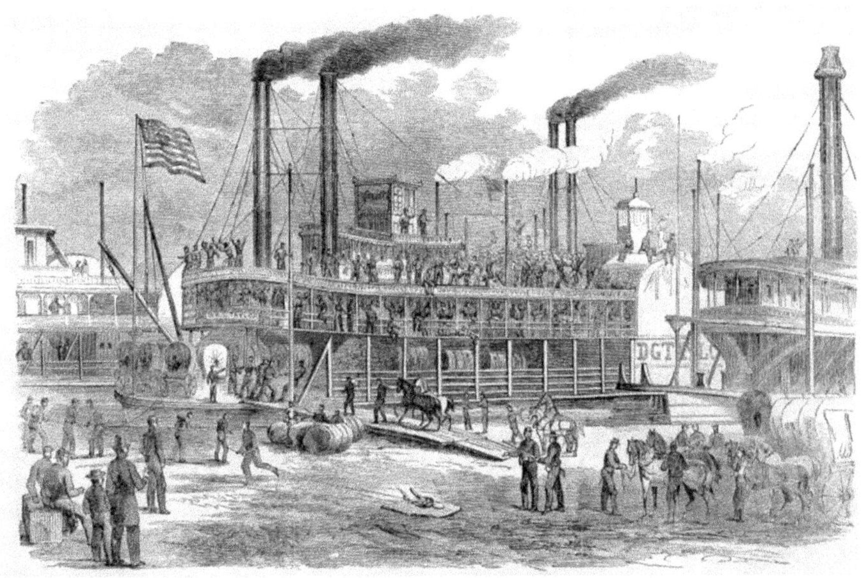

A steamboat loading Union troops in St. Louis during the Civil War. *Author's collection.*

former slaves as they tried to move them off the boat. All but twenty of the contrabands immediately bolted into the darkness. Enraged at this turn of events, Gregg's men, under lantern light, lined up the remaining former slaves and executed nine of them with pistol shots to the head within full view of many of the *Sam Gaty* passengers. A tenth black man survived his head wound. Shocked that the guerrillas would commit mass executions in front of witnesses, the passengers and crew offered no resistance.

Gregg and his men searched the boat and forced the crew to open the safe and empty it. The guerrillas searched every passenger who could be found and robbed them of money, watches, arms and such clothing as the Rebels wanted. About $3,000 worth of government freight—including forty-eight U.S. Army wagon beds and sacks of flour, bacon, sugar, coffee and other foodstuffs—was thrown into the river by the guerrillas, assisted by some of the thirty-five passengers who had been coerced into helping.[25]

Captain McCloy, with difficulty, persuaded the gang not to burn the boat, and the raiders did not molest the privately owned cargo after the captain explained much of it and many of the passengers were destined for the Montana gold fields. Gregg and his raiders held the boat at the landing from two o'clock in the morning until almost daylight before they released it and rode away. The Union military reaction over the next several days was massive and relentless.

The covert and sudden nature of guerrilla warfare lent itself to "the fog of war," or a scarcity and uncertainty of facts even long afterward, and the March 28 attack on the *Sam Gaty* exemplified this lack of clarity. Gregg and his guerrillas had been told that famed Kansas jayhawker and "slave stealer" Parson Hugh Fisher was aboard the *Gaty* with three hundred "stolen" slaves, but in fact, Wilson, with only seventy-six blacks, was actually on board. Wilson survived when passengers hid him under the cargo and the bushwhackers failed to find him. Yet Wilson's survival cost the lives of two of Colonel Penick's soldiers.

Other guerrilla attacks and seizures of steamboats occurred on the Missouri River throughout the war, but no other incident would result in such a loss of life as Gregg's March 1863 attack on the *New Sam Gaty*.

Chapter 3

Capturing a Steamboat during the Civil War

Private John C. Lilly Reveals the Plan

Young German immigrant John C. Lilly fought with the Confederacy in the Civil War, serving in Forrest's Old Regiment, the 1st Kentucky Cavalry, under Colonel Nathan Bedford Forrest. Born John Carl Lillie in 1844 in Prussia (now Germany), he immigrated to the United States in 1858 and found work on a farm in Shelby County, north central Kentucky. When the Civil War began, Lilly joined with his friends, local secessionists, to serve the Confederacy. Private Lilly rode off to war. After the war, Lilly migrated to Fort Benton, where he became active in business and fought during Montana's Indian Wars.

Private John C. Lilly left an account of his experiences riding with Lieutenant Colonel Nathan Bedford Forrest, the "Wizard of the Saddle," and much of his fascinating story is published in *Confederates in Montana Territory: In the Shadow of Price's Army*. Not previously published is Lilly's story of an attempt by Colonel Forrest to capture a Union gunboat on the Cumberland River. In the early war years, the name "Nathan Bedford Forrest" struck terror among Union forces and the loyal civilian population—his innovative tactics led to victory after victory early in the war. His attempt to capture a Union steamboat affords a fine example of Colonel Forrest's "outside the box" thinking.[26]

Colonel Forrest and his newly formed cavalry had scored their first significant victory in late December 1861. With this first taste of victory, morale soared as the regiment returned to its winter quarters near

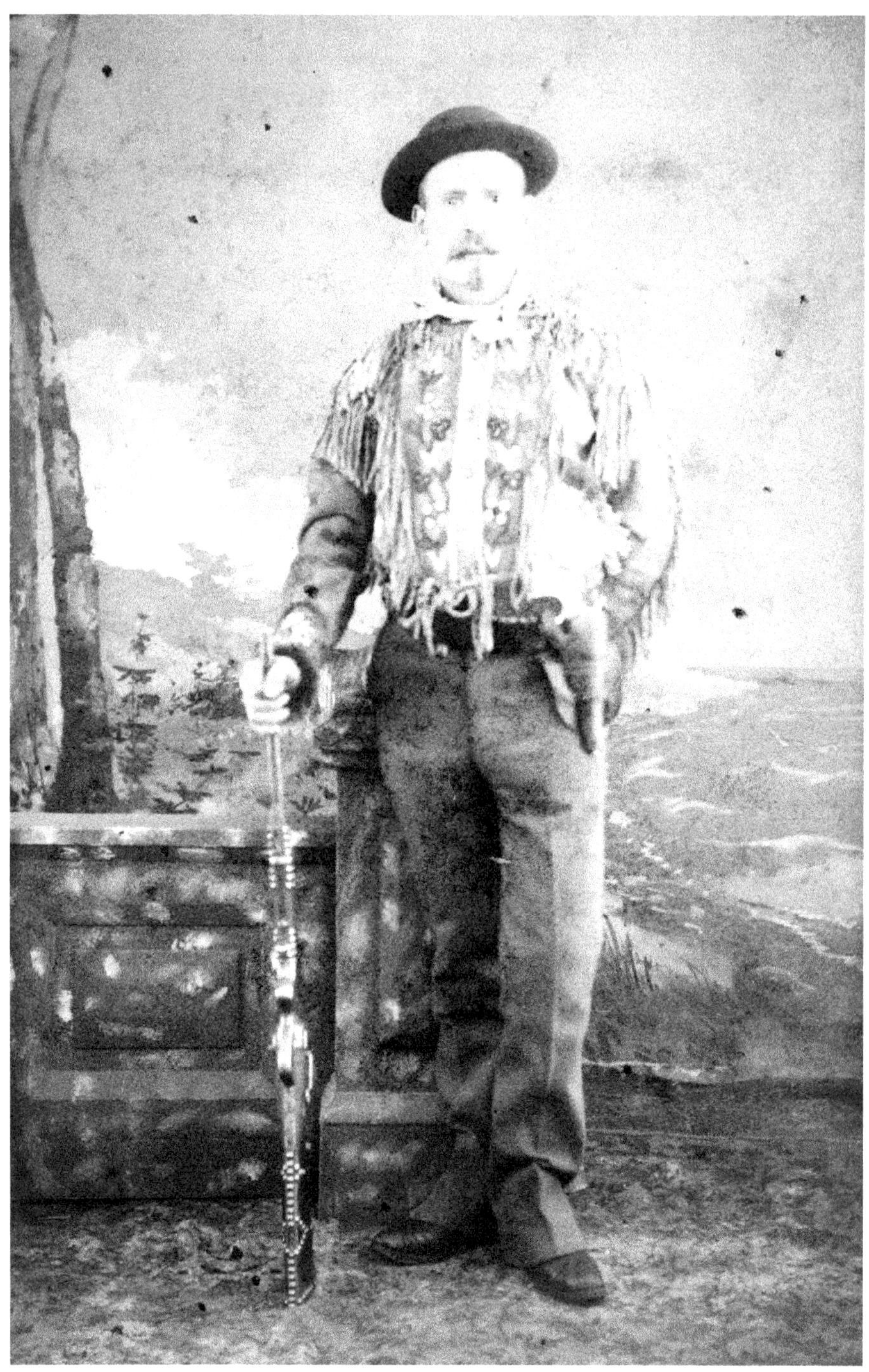

Private John C. Lilly, in his later years along the Upper Missouri frontier. *Author's collection.*

Hopkinsville, in western Kentucky near the Cumberland and Ohio Rivers, in January 1862. Private Lilly provides the narrative for this colorful attempt to capture a Union gunboat:

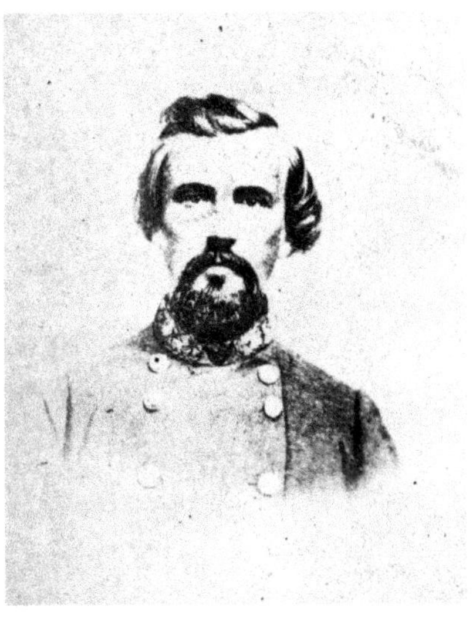
Colonel Nathan Bedford Forrest, the "Wizard of the Saddle." *Author's collection.*

> *When we got back to our winter quarters the first news was that there was a gunboat going up the Cumberland River. Confederate* [Brigadier] *General* [Charles] *Clark had some infantry camping at the Hopkinsville Fairgrounds with a few pieces of artillery. Now I will give the reader a plan of Col. Forrest's scheme. Col. Forrest wanted to capture that gunboat with his cavalry. His idea was to capture that boat and then go down the river under the U.S. flag and destroy the whole Yankee fleet at Paducka* [Paducah, Kentucky], *and at Cairo, Illinois which I believe he would have done if we could have got away with the Yankee gunboat.*
>
> *We left Camp in January* [1862], *I forgot the date, and marched for the Cumberland River. At Edayville the Col. found out that the boat had passed up. When we got to Caseyville the boat had passed up to Fort Donaldson. Here the Col. prepared for battle, a half mile or little more below Caseyville we were put in position. Our Company* [A] *was put behind an old fence pretty close to the River and two old brass cannons right below us where there was an old slue, and a pretty good landing could be made for the boat. Company B was stationed below and the balance were stationed behind the guns in the timber and the orders were to lay low and keep out of sight. Our Horses were back a mile from the River in our rear. The two old brass pieces were loaded and covered with a blanket. There were a few old boats men in our Company. They were to take charge of the boat.*
>
> *The scheme was so planned that as soon as the boat would come in a hundred yards of our guns. They should be turned loose and the men behind the guns should remain hidden. Then the boat would land and take the two old guns as trophies and while they were trying to do so then our companies should board the boats and take possession and the company below was to*

come to our assistance . . . Everything was well planned and everyone was agreed for the work. We waited a long time and got out of patience.

At last the black smoke was seen and she was coming down the River. In a short time she was in sight moving very slow and when she got in front of the town of Caseyville she anchored in the middle of the River. By this movement of her we thought that there was something wrong and this was actually the case. The Capt. of the boat was posted that Forrest was laying for him. This was done by a shoemaker of the town who had gone down the River and informed the Captain of the boat. So the crew of the gunboat knew all about Forrest and his plans.

With the boat lying anchored in the middle of the River she was making all the preparation for battle of which we were not aware at that time. At last she drew her anchor and the black smoke was rolling out of her. Slowly she came on down close to the other bank of the River. Every one of us was lying close to the ground. The boat was right in front of us and in a few seconds the silence was broken by bang of our cannon and bang again of the other cannon, and then our cannoneers retired to the rear.

We were still lying close to the ground when all at once the portholes opened and solid shot and shells were whistling through the air. Then she

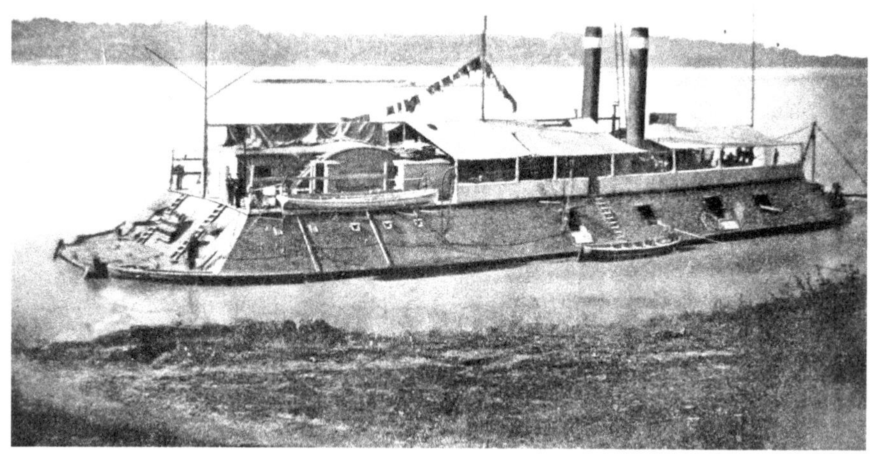

Union gunboats were used as mobile artillery and troop transports in the war along the rivers. *From* The Photographic History of the Civil War, *vol. 1.*

> *turned around broadside and commenced to shell the town. We could hear the women and children scream. As Forrest concluded that they would not land he ordered us to fire and do as much damage thru the portholes as possible. Both companies over and the one below opened fire thru the portholes which was too much for her. When she quit shelling the town and commenced loading her guns with grape and canister and turned loose on us, but the position that he had she could not see us.* [The gunboat] *found that out and swung around and left us and steamed down the river.*
>
> *All we lost was one old gray horse belonging to our preacher that had gone up on a key point where there was an old log cabin and left his horse outside as he was watching the battle. It was supposed that the Captain of the boat thought that it was the Col.'s Head Quarters, and they sent a five shot up there and happened to kill the horse and our man of the Gospel got sick. The boys of course were making fun of the good man.*
>
> *We camped on the battlefield. The next day we were making for our winter quarters at Hopkinsville. At Eadyville we found out the gunboat had lost 12 men in killed and wounded and the Capt. of the boat lost a fine Newfoundland dog, which if it is so or not I am unable to swear to that he did not care for the men but he was scared of losing his dog. Also one of our cannon shots had bored a hole thru the boat. So that ended the charge of Cavalry charging a gunboat on the Cumberland River where we* [did] *not lose a man.*
>
> *We landed again with triumph in our camp. The people of the surrounding country and of Hopkinsville would visit our Camp and thought that Col. Forrest and his Cavalry were the heroes of the Southern Confederacy. Then we had a good time in camp* [with] *plenty of good rations and fat and slick horses* [with only] *a little camp duties and drilling to do and get passes to go out in the Country and see the girls whom thought more of Forrest's Cavalry than they would of themselves. Who would not be a soldier under such circumstances as that but God knows we saw some hard times afterwards.*[27]

Colonel Forrest and Private Lilly went on to hard fighting and increasingly hard times to the end of the Civil War. Shortly after, Lilly migrated up the Missouri River to Fort Benton, where he quickly established a reputation as one of the toughest, most colorful characters in a frontier filled with war veterans, adventurers and desperadoes. Whether running dance halls in the "Bloodiest Block in the West" or fighting the Nez Perce with Donnelly's Mounted Civilian Volunteers, John Lilly left an indelible mark on frontier Montana.[28]

Chapter 4

King of the Upper Missouri River

The Legend of Captain Grant Marsh

A new generation of rivermen gained experience and power during the Civil War and would soon replace the prewar stalwarts like Captain Joseph La Barge. Young Grant Marsh rose in the ranks from mate to pilot to captain on steamboats during the Civil War and emerged from his wartime experiences as a leader in the new wave on the Upper Missouri—none would rise to greater fame.

One of the new northern rivermen, Grant P. Marsh, was born in 1834 in Rochester, Pennsylvania. He began his career as a cabin boy at age twelve, and six years later, he was based at St. Louis and a deckhand on Missouri River boats. By 1858, Marsh had been promoted to first mate on the *A.B. Chambers No. 2*, with Samuel L. Clemens as second mate.

During the Civil War, Grant Marsh earned a stellar reputation as a pilot on the western rivers until he assumed command of the steamer *Louella* in 1866. Over the next sixteen years, his reputation on the Upper Missouri and Yellowstone Rivers assumed legendary status.

After growing up in Hannibal, Missouri, Sam Clemens worked as a riverboat pilot on the Mississippi River. A "cub" or novice pilot, Clemens showed talent both in navigating through treacherous river waters and in leadership of men. High praise of Clemens's ability came in later years from Missouri River captain and pilot Grant Marsh in an account Marsh wrote about an earlier time on the Missouri River when Sam Clemens saved the lives of Marsh and his men:

I picked up a Sunday magazine of the Minneapolis Journal *of Nov. 10th* [1907], *containing the autobiography of Mark Twain, paying tribute to his wife and daughter. I have never met either but I know Sam Clemens well. I first met him in 1858 when he was "cub" pilot on the steamer* John J. Roe, *running between St. Louis and New Orleans. . . . This was in the fall. The next fall, I was mate on the steamboat* A.B. Chambers, *a big, fine Missouri river, wide wheel boat. Those days the Missouri river would get low in the fall.*

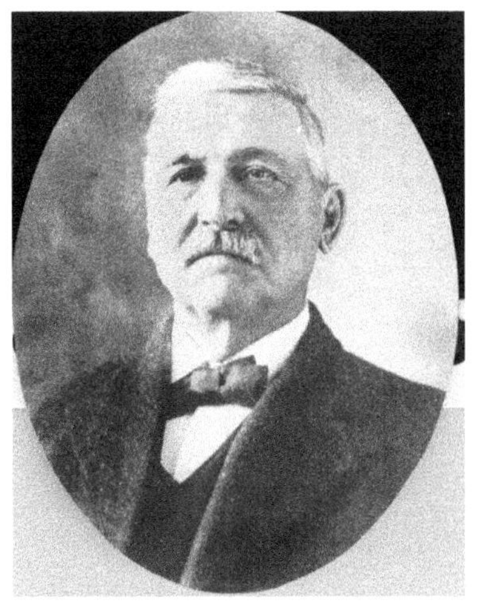

The legendary steamboat captain Grant Marsh, king of Montana's rivers. *Overholser Historical Research Center.*

The big Missouri river boats would stop in St. Louis and be put in order to load, and when flour would get $1 per barrel they would load for New Orleans. We did not have long to wait to get a load. For this trip we got Jim DeLancy and Sam Clemens as pilots. We loaded and had lots of trouble in getting aground between St. Louis and Cairo, but it was always on Jim DeLancy's watch that we would get on ground.

When we arrived at New Orleans the captain discharged Jim and hired Joe Bryan to take his place. During the winter Joe and Sam were with us. Two nicer or better behaved men never turned the wheel on the steamboat. During one of our trips we left St. Louis in heavy running ice. After we left we made good headway till we arrived at Power's Island, two miles below Commerce and thirty-five miles from Cairo [Illinois], *and we ran in an ice gorge. We had a big load, lots of livestock and many passengers. In those days boats burned all wood, no coal. It was loaded in small, flat boats. Going up stream we would take them in tow, take the wood out of them, then turn them adrift with the man who owned them, and he would fill them again. Going down stream we would land and take it off the bank. The weather moderated, and the ice moved out, but left us aground where we got out of fuel. Our case was desperate. Out on the river in the winter without fuel. So the captain ordered me to get the yawl with a crew of men to go up to Commerce and get a flat boatload of wood. He put Sam Clemens in charge of the party. We had to cross over to the Illinois side and go up the right of Barnam's island, past Santa Fe, to escape the floating ice.*

> *We went up above Commerce to what is known as Chain-of-Rocks, about a mile and a half, before we could start over to the Commerce side where the wood boat was. The weather had moderated and the ice was soft. It would stop a few minutes at the rocks then the pressure above would start it again which would leave an opening in the ice below the rocks.*
>
> *It was not long until Sam saw an opening in the ice, and he gave me orders to go ahead with all speed. We had not gone far when the opening commenced to close ahead of us, we were all excited. I called to Sam to let us turn back quick, or the ice would crush us. He said, "No, pull for your life," which we did. It so happened that the opening ahead of us got larger. If we had gone back we would have all been lost, as the opening closed behind us. It was Sam's cool, good judgment that saved all of our lives. We arrived at Commerce all right, with the yawl, slept there that night and got the wood boat. Next morning we went to the boat, got off the bar and made the best trip of the winter. . . . I think Sam Clemens and I are the only ones living that were on the boat. At that time I was twenty-four and Sam was about the same age. The last letter I had from him was dated Wellington Court, Prince Albert Gate, London. Mr.* [Joseph Mills] *Hanson, the author of my book (*Conquest of the Missouri*) received a letter in answer to one written by him to Mr. Clemens. In referring to the above incident he said that the way I had it was about the way he remembered it.*[29]

Early in the Civil War, Grant Marsh served on boats in the Union fleet on the lower Mississippi until 1864. He then joined one of the steamers in General Alfred Sully's fleet on the Upper Missouri during the Sioux Indian Wars.

The end of the Civil War saw Grant Marsh serving as captain and pilot on St. Louis to Fort Benton steamboats during the postwar rush to the Upper Missouri. In 1873, Marsh relocated to Yankton, Dakota Territory, serving as captain for Coulson Line steamers. By the mid-1870s, Captain Marsh was already a legend on the Upper Missouri, taking chances others would not in government service exploring the Yellowstone River. In 1876, with Captain Marsh in command, his steamboat *Far West* was leased to the army at $360 per day for service in the Sioux campaign for the duration. Marsh was able to navigate his shallow-draught steamboat to the mouth of the Big Horn River to ferry Brigadier General John Gibbon's Montana Column command across the Yellowstone. He then navigated the *Far West* up the Big Horn River as a command support and supply boat several miles upstream above the mouth of the Little Big Horn.

There on June 30, Captain Marsh ferried the surviving members of the 7th Cavalry to the north bank of the Yellowstone River, loaded the wounded and in a remarkable feat steamed down the Yellowstone 710 miles in just fifty-four hours. Arriving at Bismarck on July 5 with *Far West* draped in black and flying its flag at half-mast, Captain Marsh delivered the shocking news of the loss of Lieutenant Colonel Custer and his men.[30]

Captain Grant Marsh continued to operate on the Upper Missouri and serve the army on occasion. In 1881, on the *Eclipse*, he commanded a flotilla of five boats ferrying about 1,500 Lakota Sioux captives from Montana to Indian agencies in the Dakotas.

On his last trip to Fort Benton in July 1908, two decades after the end of steamboat service to the head of navigation, Captain Grant Marsh arrived by Great Northern train to meet the government steamboat *Mandan*. The *Great Falls Leader* of July 17 covered this historic visit by the legendary king of Upper Missouri steamboating, drawing memories of the old days of steamboating on the Upper Missouri:

> *The sound of a steamboat whistle which is familiar to old-time residents of this city, brought a large crowd to the lower levee about 8 o'clock Thursday morning* [July 15] *to welcome the government boat* Mandan, *says yesterday's* Fort Benton River Press. *Her trip up the Missouri river from Sioux City has occupied several weeks, part of the time being occupied in removing snags, and making new charts of localities in which the course of the river has been changed.*
>
> *Captain* [William H.] *Gould, who is in charge of the* Mandan, *made several visits here in steamboating days, and is renewing acquaintance with many of his old time Fort Benton friends. The* Mandan *is a strongly built boat, constructed especially for river work, the hull and lower deck being covered with steel sheathing. Her bow is fitted with a derrick, from which is suspended a mammoth snag-lifting apparatus with iron jaws that will accommodate any obstacle that it is desired to lift.*
>
> *Among the visitors who are in town to meet the* Mandan *is Captain* [Grant] *Marsh, one of the pioneers of the Upper Missouri river steamboat traffic, who made frequent trips to this point in the 70's, his last visit dating back to 1879. Captain Marsh relates many interesting stories of steamboating in early days, one of them relating to a business transaction with W.G. Conrad, the well known Montana banker, who was at that time employed by I.G. Baker.*

> *Captain Marsh was in charge of the steamboat* Josephine, *which was loaded with a cargo of freight from Sioux City to Fort Benton, and as it was late in the season it seemed probable that the boat could not go further up the river than Cow Island. Upon his arrival at that point, Captain Marsh found Mr. Conrad camped with three bull teams, and was informed that the low stage of water would prevent his reaching Fort Benton. He* [Captain Marsh] *inquired the rate for hauling from Cow Island to this city, and as it appeared to be exorbitant* [he] *decided to proceed up the river, and the* Josephine *being of light draft managed to reach Fort Benton.*
>
> *Two larger boats were scheduled to follow the* Josephine, *and in the meantime Mr. Conrad had tested the depth of the water at various places between Dauphin rapids and Cow island by wading into the river and using a sounding stick. He discovered that the larger boats could not possibly pull through some of the shallow places, and patiently awaited their coming. When they arrived and the question of freighting the merchandise to this city was discussed, Mr. Conrad quoted a rate three or four times the steamboat rate from Sioux City.*
>
> *The steamboat men refused to pay the price, and attempted to continue their trip up the river, but they soon encountered trouble and concluded to accept Mr. Conrad's terms.*
>
> *Captain Marsh will go down the Missouri river with the* Mandan *in the interest of the Benton Packet company, to inspect the conditions and report to Captain I.P. Baker, manager of that line, with a view of running a steamboat between this point and the mouth of Milk river. It is proposed to inaugurate this business the present season if possible.*[31]

Captain Grant Marsh's record of achievement on the rivers of Montana is stunning in terms of the number of trips, late season operations and path-breaking events. Captain Marsh earned the honor of "King of Montana's Rivers" (the Missouri and the Yellowstone), as demonstrated in this remarkable record of his trips to the Upper Missouri:

1866, *Luella*: In 1866, during the height of the Montana gold rush, Captain Marsh received his first command, the *Luella*, and both the boat and Captain Marsh earned accolades that year. Captain Marsh, acting both as master and chief pilot, arrived at Fort Benton on June 17 from St. Louis. Keeping *Luella* on the Upper Missouri throughout the summer, Captain Marsh returned to Fort Benton on July 11 from Fort Union with cargo for the North West Fur Company. Captain Marsh arrived Fort Benton for the third time on August 10 with cargo and machinery salvaged from the steamer *Marion* at Pablo's Rapids. The first to remain so late on the Upper Missouri,

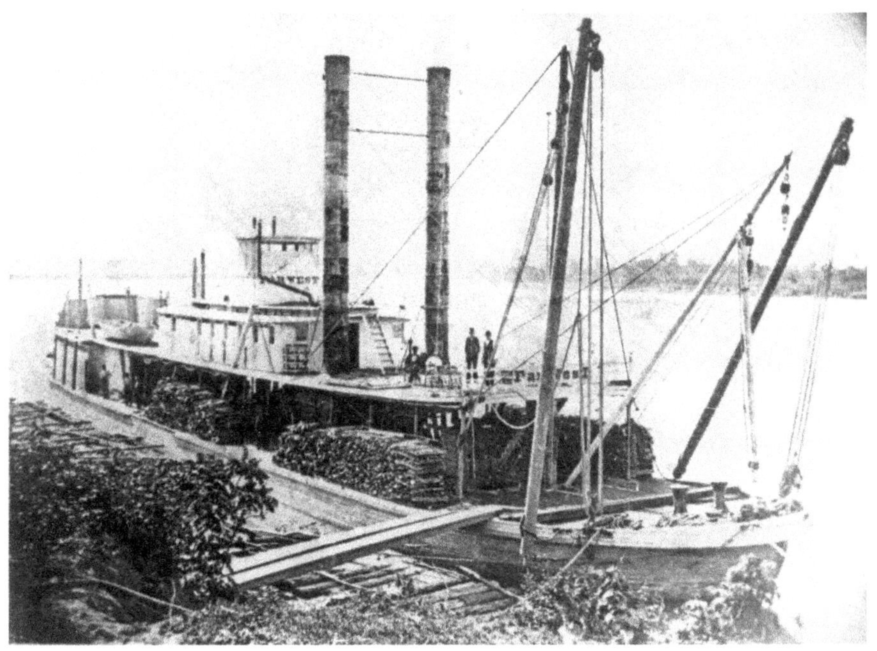

Famed steamboat *Far West* made twenty-three trips to the Upper Missouri. During the Terry/Custer Expedition in June 1876, the *Far West,* under Captain Marsh, brought Custer's wounded men 710 miles downriver to Fort Abraham Lincoln in just fifty-four hours, an astonishing feat. *Overholser Historical Research Center.*

Luella departed Fort Benton on August 16, and dropped down to Cow Island for a September 3 departure after boarding 230 miners returning to the States. Captain Marsh piloted *Luella* down the river through water barely two feet deep with a cargo of two and a half tons of Confederate Gulch gold dust, conservatively valued at $1,250,000—the richest cargo ever to go down the Missouri River from the Montana mines.

1867, *Ida Stockdale*: Captain Marsh brought this new-construction boat from Pittsburgh to Fort Benton, arriving on June 16. After bringing a second load, including passengers and cargo from the wrecked steamer *James H. Trover*, to Fort Benton on June 29, the *Ida Stockdale* took the *Trover*'s machinery down to Fort Buford. Passing downriver, the *Ida Stockdale* was hailed 220 miles below Fort Buford by the military, which wanted Captain Marsh to return to Fort Benton for a third time to convey Major General Alfred Terry, commanding the Department of the Dakota, and his staff. Stopping at the new Camp Cooke for one day, the *Ida Stockdale* arrived at Fort Benton on August 5 and began a slow low-water return to St. Louis.

1868, *Nile*: Departing St. Louis, the *Nile* steamed up the Missouri River, arriving at Fort Benton on May 21 and then double-tripped back to Fort Hawley for the balance of its cargo. Returning to St. Louis too late for a second trip to Fort Benton, the *Nile* engaged in trade on the Lower Missouri. In October, the army quartermaster insisted that Captain Marsh take a load to three small agencies to satisfy provisions of a new Indian Commission Treaty with Red Cloud and the Oglala Lakota Sioux. Although Captain Marsh was convinced that he would not be able to deliver this late in the season, the *Nile* departed St. Louis on October 15 for the Upper Missouri, facing low water and impending icing. Captain Marsh skillfully took the *Nile* up the Missouri to a point 140 miles above Fort Randall, where much of the cargo was offloaded and stored. *Nile* then steamed on another 150 miles to the Cheyenne River Agency before heavy flowing ice stopped progress. The remaining cargo was unloaded, and the *Nile* turned southward as Captain Marsh tried to escape the winter elements. At a point 25 miles below Fort Thompson, *Nile* became imbedded in ice for the winter.

1869, *Nile*: Captain Marsh began the year by extricating the *Nile* from its winter shelter without damage from breaking ice and bringing it down to St. Louis. This marked the first time a steamer had wintered on the Upper Missouri and returned downriver in the spring undamaged. After a quick turnaround, the *Nile* departed on April 25 for a trip to Fort Benton, arriving on May 27 with colorful frontier characters Marshal "X" Beidler and "Liver-Eatin'" Johnston aboard and returning to St. Louis by mid-July.

1869, *Tempest*: In St. Louis, Captain Marsh contracted to travel overland by rail and stage to Fort Benton, then down the Missouri River by mackinaw boat to Cow Island and there take command of the steamer *Tempest*, being held by a mutinous crew. Upon arrival, Captain Marsh immediately shut down the bar and its supply of whiskey, brought the crew in line and got the boat underway, steaming slowly down to St. Louis.

1869, *North Alabama*: Late in the season in October 1869, Captain Marsh successfully steamed the *North Alabama* northward up the icy river to deliver supplies to forts in the Dakotas up to Fort Buford. Twenty-five miles short of its destination, ice closed in solid around the *North Alabama*. The supply of vegetables aboard was transferred overland to Fort Buford. Ten days later, the temperature moderated, and the *North Alabama* broke free to return to Sioux City on November 15.

1870, *Kate Kearney*: The St. Louis trade with the Upper Missouri changed with the arrival of the railroad at Sioux City, Iowa, so Captain Marsh engaged in commerce between St. Louis and Lower Missouri ports.

1870, *Ida Reese No. 2*: Late in the season, Captain Marsh assumed command of the *Ida Reese No. 2*, a Durfee & Peck steamer, from Sioux City to Fort Buford.

1871, *Nellie Peck*: During this season, Captain Marsh supervised construction and then operated the new *Nellie Peck* on the Lower Missouri.

1871, *Silver Lake*: Late in the season in November 1871, post traders at Fort Buford, Leighton & Jordan, asked Captain Marsh to take command of the old, slow *Silver Lake* for a successful trip to Fort Buford. On the down trip, Indians fired into the *Silver Lake* forty miles above Fort Rice, and pilot Joe Todd was painfully wounded. The steamer was frozen up for the winter near Fort Thompson.

1872, *Nellie Peck*: During this season, Captain Marsh brought *Nellie Peck* from Sioux City to Fort Benton on two trips, arriving on May 18, the first boat in, and on June 30. During the second trip, the *Nellie Peck*, with a larger cargo, and the *Far West* raced each other from Sioux City to Fort Benton. The *Far West* overhauled and passed the *Nellie Peck*, beating it to the Benton levee by several hours. This trip set a new record from Sioux City to Fort Benton, just seventeen days, twenty hours.

1873, *Josephine*: By early 1873, Captain Marsh joined other investors in forming the Coulson Packet Line, with major contracts with the military to carry troops and supplies to the upper river. Captain Marsh moved his family upriver from Sioux City to Yankton and began this season with his first trip from St. Louis up the Yellowstone River.

1873, *Key West*: Captain Marsh then took command of the steamer *Key West*, and on orders from General Phil Sheridan, Marsh was selected by the army to explore navigation on the Upper Yellowstone. This began Captain Marsh's long period of exploration and contract support for the army on the Upper Yellowstone. On his first trip from Fort Buford, the *Key West* entered the Yellowstone on May 6, steamed to a point two hundred miles up the river and was stopped by a reef of rocks two miles short of the mouth of the Powder River with General Sheridan and General George A. Forsyth and staff on board. Their mission was to explore the Yellowstone and select army posts on the Upper Missouri. *Key West* departed Fort Buford again on June 25 to act as transport and patrol for General David S. Stanley of the 22nd Infantry Regiment during the Yellowstone Expedition. This path-breaking season ended with the return of the *Key West* to Bismarck.

1874, *Josephine*: During this season, Captain Marsh returned to Missouri River navigation, making three trips from Yankton and Bismarck to Fort Benton, arriving on June 1, June 22 and July 22, respectively. *Josephine* made a late-season fourth trip up the Missouri to Cow Island, arriving on August 28.

1875, *Josephine*: Captain Marsh began this season with a trip from Yankton to the new port of Carroll at the mouth of the Judith River, arriving on May 10 as the Coulson Line tried to break Fort Benton's role as head of navigation on the Missouri River. Captain Marsh then returned to Yellowstone exploration, taking the *Josephine* with General James W. Forsyth aboard 483 miles up the Yellowstone River, some 75 miles above the Big Horn. They stopped on June 7 just below "Hell Roaring Rapids." The *Josephine* reached within 60 miles of the northeastern corner of Yellowstone National Park; no other steamer ever went that far up the Yellowstone River.

1875, *Far West*: Captain Marsh departed Yankton on September 24, 1875, for a late-season trip with army freight and recruits up the Missouri River to Carroll. At Carroll, he left the *Far West* to take command of the *Josephine* for a return trip to see his family at Yankton.

1876, *Far West*: Under army contract, Captain Marsh departed Bismarck in support of General Terry and the Custer Expedition against the Lakota. During this season, *Far West* remained between the Powder and Big Horn Rivers. Captain Marsh steamed and warped the *Far West* up the uncharted Big Horn River to resupply and rescue the survivors of the Battle of the Little Big Horn. In a navigation feat never equaled on western waters, Captain Marsh brought more than fifty wounded survivors from Major Reno's command seven hundred miles down the Yellowstone and Missouri Rivers to Fort Abraham Lincoln in just fifty-four hours, arriving at 11:00 p.m. on July 5, 1876. This was one of the most remarkable exploits in Missouri River steamboating annals. It was Captain Marsh and those he brought with him who relayed the fate of the 7th Cavalry to the rest of the nation, then celebrating its centennial year.

1877, *Rose Bud*: In early spring, Captain Marsh met this new construction Coulson Line boat *Rose Bud* at St. Louis and brought it to Bismarck. Once more, Captain Marsh was selected to move a high-level army delegation and supplies up the Yellowstone River. William T. Sherman, commanding general of the army, and his party were on an inspection tour of Montana military posts. With General Sherman's party on board, Captain Marsh proceeded from the Yellowstone up the Big Horn and then the Little Big Horn to a new post under construction, Fort Custer. For the rest of the summer, the *Rose Bud* remained on the Upper Yellowstone, shuttling army supplies between the Tongue and Big Horn Rivers.

1878, *F.Y. Batchelor*: In early spring, Captain Marsh went east to take command of a new construction boat, *F.Y. Batchelor*, and steam it from Pittsburgh to Fort Custer. After five more trips up the Yellowstone moving supplies to Forts Keogh and Custer during this long season, Captain Marsh finally returned to Bismarck in early November.

1879, *F.Y. Batchelor*: During this long season, Captain Marsh made eight trips up the Yellowstone with army supplies. In late September, he departed Bismarck on a late-season trip up the Missouri River to Coal Banks Landing with one hundred army recruits for a new army post, Fort Assinniboine.

1880, *F.Y. Batchelor*: This demanding season for Captain Marsh began with five trips up the Yellowstone with army supplies. He then made two trips to Fort Peck Reservation at Poplar River on the Missouri River. Even though it was very late in the season, the army insisted that Captain Marsh make a final trip up the Missouri to the mouth of the Musselshell River with a cargo of grain to support operations by General Nelson A. Miles. Departing Fort Buford in early November, Captain Marsh navigated through extremely low water conditions to arrive at the army depot on the Musselshell on November 12. By November 16, snow had begun to fall and winter conditions set in as the *Batchelor* became imprisoned in ice near the mouth of the Milk River. Leaving the boat under guard, Captain Marsh and part of the crew went overland to Yankton, suffering severely from the winter conditions.

1881, *F.Y. Batchelor*: This year began with major flooding on the Missouri River at Yankton. Captain Marsh departed early to the Milk River to extricate the *F.Y. Batchelor* and bring it down to Fort Buford. With the *Batchelor*, Captain Marsh made one trip up the Yellowstone, returning from Fort Keogh with a cargo of robes and furs valued at an exceptional $106,000.

1881, *Eclipse*: Taking command of a new steamer, Captain Marsh operated the *Eclipse* for the rest of the season. Again under army contract, he steamed up the Yellowstone as flagship of a five-boat fleet to Fort Keogh to bring three thousand captive Indians held by General Miles for transfer to Standing Rock Agency.

1882, *W.J. Behan*: In the spring, Captain Marsh bought the packet *W.J. Behan*, the last Upper Missouri River boat he would operate. With the *W.J. Behan*, Captain Marsh participated in one more notable event in late April 1882, transporting Sitting Bull and his remaining 171 followers from Fort Randall, where they had been detained after their return from Canada, to Fort Yates.

For a decade and a half, from 1866 to 1881, Captain Grant Marsh plied the difficult waters of the high Upper Missouri and the Upper Yellowstone Rivers without ever losing a steamboat. He was a great captain not least because he was a great pilot and master of low-water operations. His reputation for achievement and professional skill became legendary. Grant Marsh earned the honor of "King of Montana's Rivers."[32]

Chapter 5

A Trip to the Gold Regions of Montana

Impressions of Rosalie Ruthren

During the height of steamboat travel on the Missouri during the Montana gold rush in the mid-1860s, relatively few of the travelers were women, and even fewer wrote accounts of their travel to the Upper Missouri. Miss Rosalie Ruthren, an educated, unmarried and opinionated young woman, was a notable exception. Rosalie joined the passengers on the steamboat *Favorite*, departing St. Louis on April 1 bound for Fort Benton. She was the rare adventuress, traveling alone to the head of navigation on the Missouri River, all the while sending letters to the editor of the *Missouri Daily Republican* in St. Louis. Here is a portion of her adventure in her words:

> *I am going thirty-one hundred and twelve miles in search of information. . . .*
>
> *First. What has education done for me?*
>
> *Second. How many degrees are we removed from barbarism? . . .*
>
> *To give you an idea of the delights of travelling up the "Big Muddy," the association that surrounds us, and the pleasure of steamboat traveling in general, I must bring to your notice the principal features of our boat, as the comfort of passengers depends greatly upon the cast and style of them.*
>
> *Enter Captain H.* [Asa Hutchinson], *with the style of a Minnesotan. The case, very much the gentleman, and I really believe, judging from personal observation, one of the greatest drivers in existence, and takes the greatest delights in finding abundance of work for his crew; never swears when there are ladies about, can make the most eloquent speeches at short notice, and dance like a Frenchman. Who would not travel with Captain H.?*

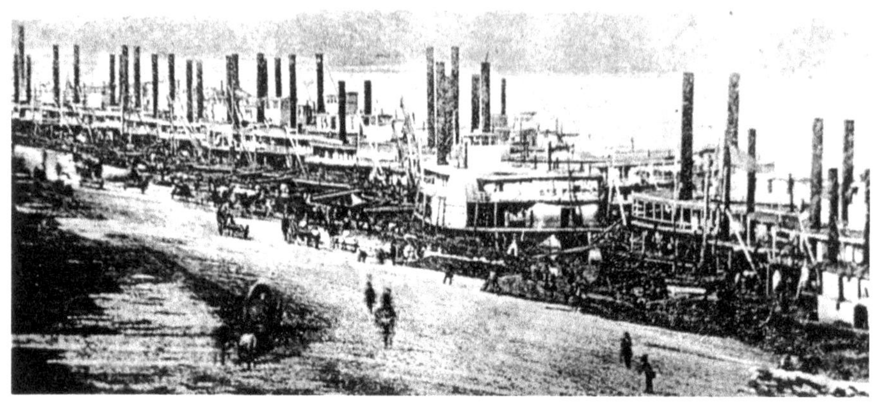

The vast St. Louis steamboat levee was crowded with steamers heading for the Ohio, Mississippi and Upper Missouri Rivers in this photo by R. Goebel. *Author's collection.*

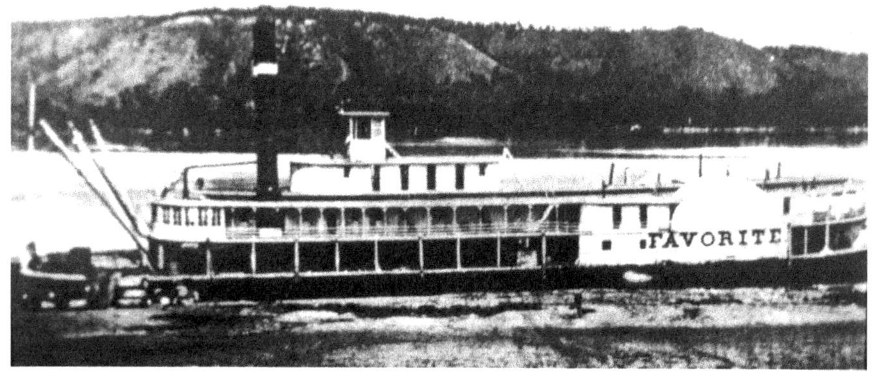

The steamboat *Favorite* under Captain Asa Hutchinson completed a trip from St. Louis to Fort Benton in 1866. *Overholser Historical Research Center.*

Enter Mr. T., the gentleman in the office. A man of few words indeed, but can tell eel stories like a Waterman—rather given to sarcasm, but withal a very pleasant gent, considering that he does not take to ladies.

Exit Mr. T. Enter pilot, who is in delicate health, and has a sublime temper.

Enter Mr. M., mate. Nice man; never swears only on special occasions; should judge him to be an excellent person, as he keeps a dog.

Passengers we have of all variety, each in themselves a bound edition of human nature, put up to suit all tastes. Children, the dear little wretches, are

> *at par, without discount or premium. Now, I have a fondness for darlings, and can manage very well with a moderate supply.*
>
> *. . . People are going up here to pick up nuggets of gold. Fathers of no very small families are leaving a country where they had but a small* certainty *for no very large* uncertainty, *and take their little ones with them to share the profits, be it starvation or gold dust. 'Tis certainly very novel to see the fond affection these men have for their wives; cannot be parted from them long enough to make sure of prospering, should they find employment, or have a hut ready to shelter them when he should wish their presence.*
>
> *I like to see the devotion that will subject the* dear *ones, I know not what, in a strange country, especially when they expect to make a fortune and have but a few dollars to make it with.*
>
> *Wives, give your husbands an opportunity "to do" what man can "do"; lighten his shoulder that he may feel free to take hold of any implement that presents itself in their new field for men who are not afraid to work. Many say, "I am afraid to trust my husband alone out there, men get so wild." Tush! If your husband is a man of honor, he may get rough, but wild never! If he is not a man above temptation, you being with him will not save him, and your power and influence will be greater at a distance until obstacles are overcome.*[33]

Throughout Rosalie's trip up the Missouri on the *Favorite*, she shared her opinions and observations of her fellow passengers, especially unruly children. She paid special attention to the towns and villages along the way. As the *Favorite* reached the military forts and native Indian settlements in the Dakotas, she observed the customs and "civilization" in very judgmental fashion, on the one hand sympathetic to the plight of Indian men, women and children yet quick to criticize customs and hygiene.

Finally, after seventy-four days, the *Favorite* fought its way past the final rapids, rounded the bend and arrived at the Fort Benton levee on June 14 with forty-seven passengers and a full load of cargo. Rosalie's narrative continued:

> *Fort Benton at last! . . . I gather the following incontrovertible facts:*
>
> *That the Missouri river is the dirtiest river in the world.*
>
> *That the Missouri river is the most fickle river in the world.*
>
> *That the Missouri river has the most pertinacious sand bars of all sand bars.*

That it is an awful sin to force circumstances, and therefore it is an awful sin to force a passage through the Missouri river.

Sum total—That the creator never intended the Missouri river for the exercise of material science during the present age, or until an infant has been born that will bring with it a bottle that won't blow up, a spade that will remove sand bars, a saw that will cut snags, and a boat that will climb a twenty-five mile an hour current, without warping. Oh! To mother THAT child! Yea, verily!

Such rejoicing as there was when we came in sight of Fort Benton, although the place is a sad disappointment to those who expect to see anything more than a few log huts—to be sure there are two or three very commodious large ones, where any amount of freight can be stored away, and there are some well-supplied stores, where every thing in the shape of clothing and groceries are to be had. I noticed more woolen shirts than any thing else, however. Then there is a tailor shop, a meat shop, and two very excellent Forts [Benton and Campbell]. *Accommodations, in the shape of hotels, there are none. Passengers generally remain on board the steamer until they find wagons or teams of some kind to take themselves and baggage to the mining district, or Helena, which is a hundred and sixty miles from Benton. Helena is, I am told, a very flourishing town, and is said to be quite as "fast" a place as St. Louis, and equal to California in its infancy for wickedness. Everybody steals, everybody gambles, everybody lies, with the exception of the one who informs us of this, they being so strictly orthodox, and sound at the core, that the rascality of the populace caused them to smite their breasts and exclaim with the publican of old, "Oh Lord, I thank thee that I am" better than those other fellers. Just so!*

. . . *"Did you hear about that unfortunate affair at the Fort* [Campbell].[234] *A woman shot herself!"*

"No. What for?"

"Well, she had been sick, incurably so, for nearly a year, and her husband was unkind to her. That is all I could hear about it. Let's go over and see."

Oh, what a sad miserable sight! a comfortless stifling little room in the Fort—a dead woman—three poor little children, the youngest four months, the eldest four years old—a dirty squaw, a gun, a few wooden chairs, an old table and a rusty old stove.

Great God! (with all reverence I say it), why are thy gifts so unequally distributed? When we look upon such things, give us faith to trust in thy everlasting goodness. Why hast thou permitted this? A woman, thy tenderest, thy best work; a mother! The holiest name on earth amongst creatures. It

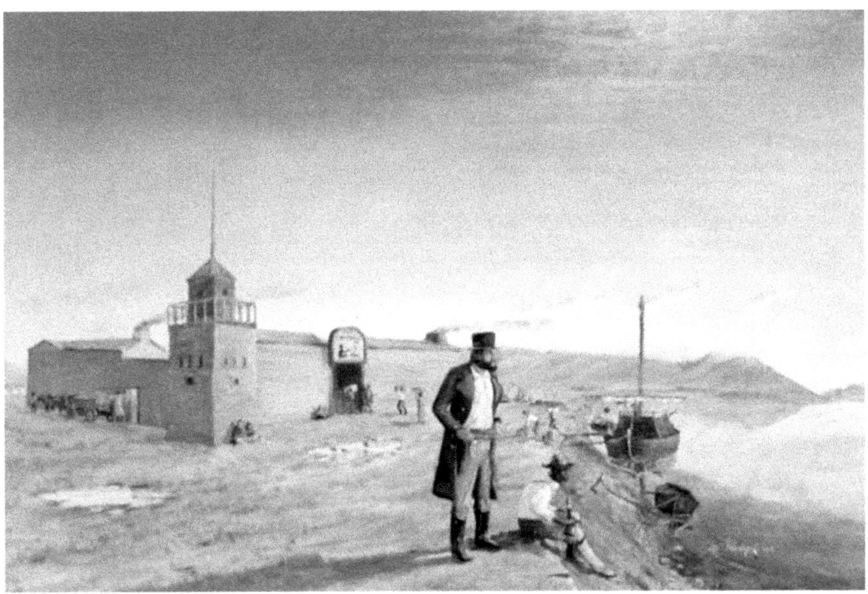

This painting by David Parchen of Fort Campbell depicts the "Opposition" trading post on the upper levee at Fort Benton. *Author's collection.*

lies there, a senseless, almost disgusting mass, driven beyond the bounds of human endurance, her sufferings so great that mother love *is overcome by them, beyond the friendly hope of home friends, abused, neglected by him who promised to love and cherish while life lasts, poverty and sickness her only companions. Was not her burden more than she could bear? If not, why did this wretched mortal put a gun to her head, and in countless torments, send her soul before the judgment throne, while three little helpless babes are left to cry vainly for a mother's care? Who can replace their loss? These little motherless ones, you, oh God! will protect. But do not we the orphans neglect? God forgive us, if we cry to thee in doubt, and say, "Is this as Thou hast willed it?" We need faith to say, "Thy will be done."*

They buried her deep, deep, beneath the ground; and when, a few days after, we passed her grave, wild beasts and cattle had trampled over it, until nothing but a sinking in the earth could be seen to mark it. Poor children! what a father they have, who does not even protect their mother's grave!

They have frightful wind and hail storms up here; they come at a moment's warning, and are over again as suddenly. Just before sunset we had a terrible one. Mr. Wind made all bow before him, while the hail pelted one right smartly, if one dared his fury. In ten minutes after, the atmosphere was as clear as the most transparent glass; a magnificent rainbow adorned the sky, and the old tyrant, Sol, was just nodding behind the monstrous heaving of mother earth, leaving; a dazzling radiance of bright coloring upon a beautiful blue canopy, as we stood upon the hurricane deck of the Favorite. *She seemed to lie on a perfect lake of fire—there was not a ripple on the water, and looking about me, I certainly could not help but exclaim, "Is it possible, that in so grandly beautiful a world there is so much misery?" What a lovely picture this was! Talk about Italian skies and landscapes! You moneyed fools! pass the heavenly beauties of your own country, to say you have seen that of others, but you will never behold anything more beautiful than this.*

A green velvet carpet on each side of a golden river, above you fanciful pictures in brilliant colors, on a deep blue back-ground, and this enclosed by blue black mountains capped with silvery snow, just trees and wild flowers enough to be seen to give the picture a paradisiacal look, and you have just precisely what we saw that evening.

. . . [I] *had an invitation from Captain W.* [John A. Williams], *of the steamer* Peter Balen, *to visit the Falls of Missouri River on his boat, which was willingly accepted. Started at 9 a.m. from Benton, had very tolerable water for ten miles, and then the current became so swift that as it rushed over the rapids it foamed and boiled fearfully. Of course no boat would defy that and survive; so the Captain concluded that he had arrived at the end of navigation on the Missouri, at all events, and contented himself with the knowledge that he had taken his boat farther than any one else ever attempted in safety; so he landed at a very lovely valley, where we remained making bouquets of wild roses, eating a very nice dinner, and otherwise entertaining ourselves until evening, when we made the return to Benton, ten miles, in less than thirty minutes.*[35]

[I] *did not visit the gold mines or Helena, as the courage was wanting to brave a broiling sun a distance of nearly two hundred miles in a closed stage or an open ox team. A great many people are leaving there, a failure; others again, are doing well. Those who have the wherewithal, can double it, when the less fortunate ones return poorer than ever. If more will "trust to luck," they have every chance to become independent, where there are as many chances to fail. But never would it be best to take families with them, on an uncertainty, to such a country. Let them make the trial alone. If success attend them—and any man who has perseverance and energy can succeed—then let them prepare a nook for their family, and have them come. There are many now returning who would have been wealthy had they not*

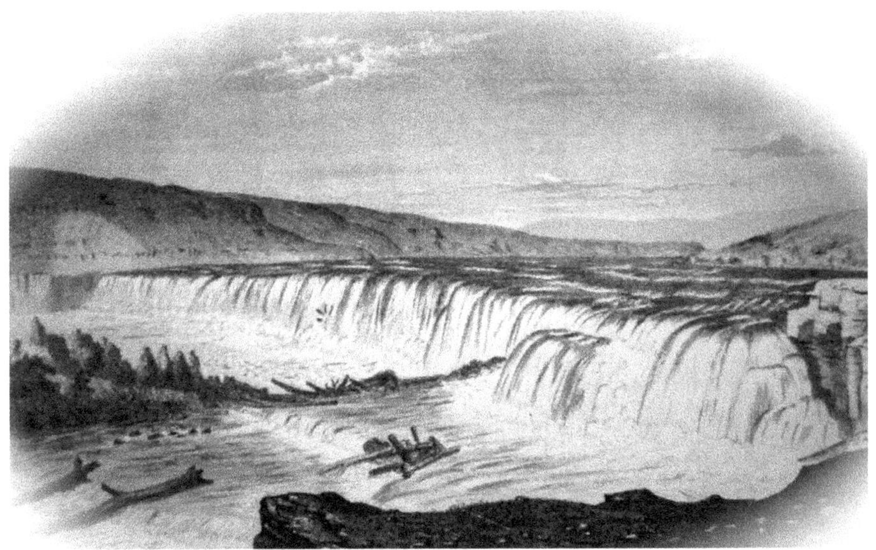

The legendary Great Falls of the Missouri River in an 1860s sketch by A.E. Mathews. *Overholser Historical Research Center.*

been obliged to use their little capital to take care of their "olive branches," while they were on the look-out for "something to turn up," perhaps, at last, take up with any kind of labor to supply their necessities, thereby losing opportunities that might have paid well in the end. They would call it "bad luck," where I rather think it is bad management.

The scenery along the upper portion of the Missouri is, verily, something wonderful. At one place, called the "Citadel," there is an immense rock, which nature has given the exact shape of a steamboat, a monster thing; looks as though it was just puffing up over the mountain in great haste. The place is well named "Citadel," for it is an almost perfect fortress of white rock. The hand of man could not have formed it more perfect than this freak of nature has done. Further on, there are the same kind of rock in the shape of churches, quaint looking old castles, dark dismal convents, where pale-faced nuns were petrified while at their devotions. Here is an assembly listening to some fanatic standing on a delicate vase, where the flowers are tumbling from the sides, as if their tender nerves had become mad with the frantic eloquence of their destroyer. Here is a beautiful citadel, with a very large Bishop standing in front. At one side is what appears to be a graveyard with the most perfect tombstones, which would be an envious sight to a marble-cutter. It does not require imagination to see all this, it is

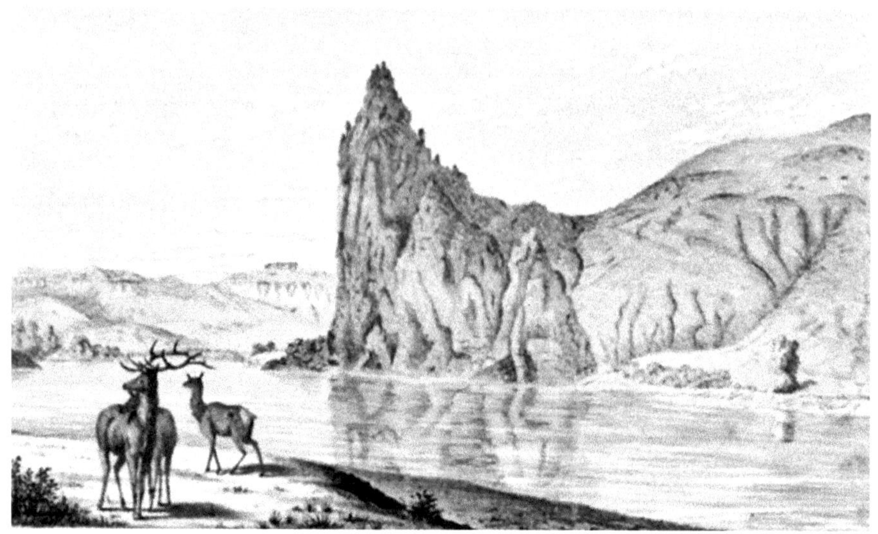

Citadel Rock in the spectacular White Cliffs of the Missouri in this sketch by Alfred E. Mathews. *Overholser Historical Research Center.*

> *plain to every eye. It is something for geologist to go mad over, and sculptors to steal their models from, and a real feast for those who love the actual beauties of most perfect nature.*

After eight days in port, on June 22, the *Favorite* departed the levee at Fort Benton with sixty-seven passengers, including Rosalie Ruthren. She concluded her final letter to the *Missouri Daily Republican* with these words:

> *We turn our faces towards "home again," with what boatmen term "a good trip," and fly down the river at the rate of twenty miles an hour. Oh, how sweet sounds the name of home! Haste, the faithful old boat, for, though the time be ever so short, it is still too long for hearts that long for home. Absence and home have a tender cord between them, and when there is too much strain upon it, the vibration too strong, it may give for a while, but eventually it will snap and break with extreme pain and leave but a vacant space, or a broken article to connect the bond of absence and home.*
>
> *What has civilization done for us?*
>
> *It has given us a refined intellect, wherewith we may manufacture material to cover our savage propensities.*
>
> *What has education done for you?*

> *It has given to each an individual labyrinth wherein prudence, selfishness, love, hate, politic and money, are so inextricably entangled, that* policy *is the only thing that can undo the knot, or loosen the strings for the others to get a slight airing. Policy is a* big *man, for he rules the world. ROSALIE RUTHREN.*[36]

Just two weeks after leaving Fort Benton, the steamer *Favorite* arrived on July 7 at St. Joseph, Missouri, with fifty-seven passengers and an aggregate among the passengers of $125,000 in gold dust. Along the way on the trip down, the *Favorite* met eighteen steamboats, including the steamer *Louella* with its $1,250,000 gold dust cargo from the Montana mines. Rosalie Ruthren's adventure trip to the mountains ended several days later in St. Louis.

Chapter 6

Going "to the States" on the Legendary Steamboat *Far West*

Travels with Martha Edgerton Rolfe

Most steamboat travel up the Missouri River in the early years featured miners and adventurers, and their diaries offer insight into the trip up or down the river, wildlife and scenery and incidents along the way. Only later did women and children join the migration up the Missouri. Diaries and accounts by female travelers are far fewer in number. In this account, Martha Edgerton Rolfe, the daughter of Montana's first territorial governor, Sidney Edgerton, traveled down the Missouri, sharing her impressions along the way.

Martha Edgerton was born on May 14, 1850, on her grandparents' farm at Tallmadge, Ohio, the eldest child of Sidney and Mary Wright Edgerton. When the Civil War began, Sidney Edgerton served as Republican congressman from Ohio. In 1863, President Lincoln appointed him chief justice for the new Idaho Territory. Unable to reach the territorial capital in Lewiston because of winter's approach, the Edgerton family found a home in the booming mining camp of Bannack in eastern Idaho Territory.

When Montana Territory was created the next year, Edgerton became the first territorial governor. His daughter, precocious young Martha, became a passionate observer of Civil War Montana.

In 1876, she returned to Montana Territory with her husband, Herbert P. Rolfe, and together they became exceptional achievers in those frontier days. Years later, Martha Edgerton Rolfe Plassmann wrote prolifically for the Montana Newspaper Association, a service for weekly newspapers in the 1920s and '30s. In this story, Martha presents her

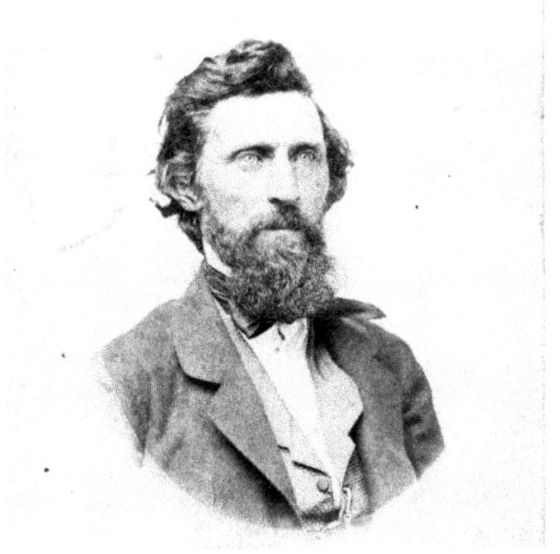

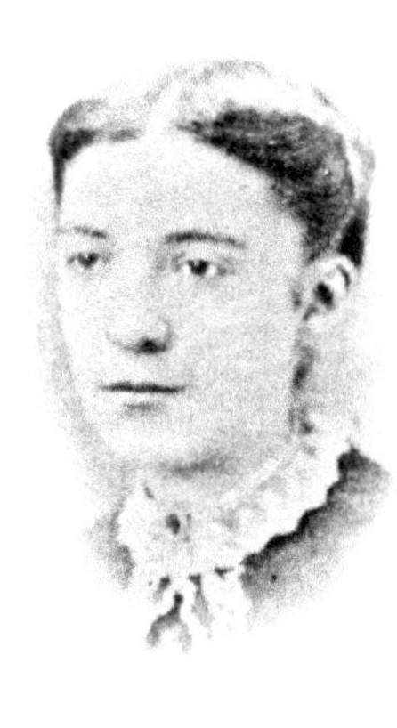

Left: Martha's father, Montana's first territorial governor, Sidney Edgerton. *Thomas Minckler Collection.*

Right: Young Martha, daughter of Governor Sidney Edgerton, on the early Montana frontier. *Author's collection.*

experiences in 1881 traveling down the Missouri River from Fort Benton on the steamboat *Far West.*

> *After five years in Montana, I decided to spend the summer of 1881 at the home of my parents in Akron, Ohio, taking with me my two little girls* [Mary Pauline, born 1877, and Harriet Louise, born 1879], *the oldest not quite four. Had my home been elsewhere than at Fort Benton, in order to reach the railroad, a long stage journey, with its attendant discomforts, would have been necessary.*
>
> *Navigation of the Upper Missouri had not then been abandoned and every season saw many steamboats tied to the levee at Fort Benton, where, in fur trading days, mackinaws and keel boats came and went, fetching supplies and bearing to St. Louis their loads of furs and dried buffalo tongues, that much prized delicacy.*
>
> *Only during the brief period of high water could steamboats ascend so far. For this reason there were many applications for passage down river on the first boat that should arrive and which one that would be was always problematical. In 1881 the* Far West, *the most famous boat on the river, led the rest of the fleet and on it I obtained passage to Bismarck, hoping by doing so to prolong my visit east by a few days.*

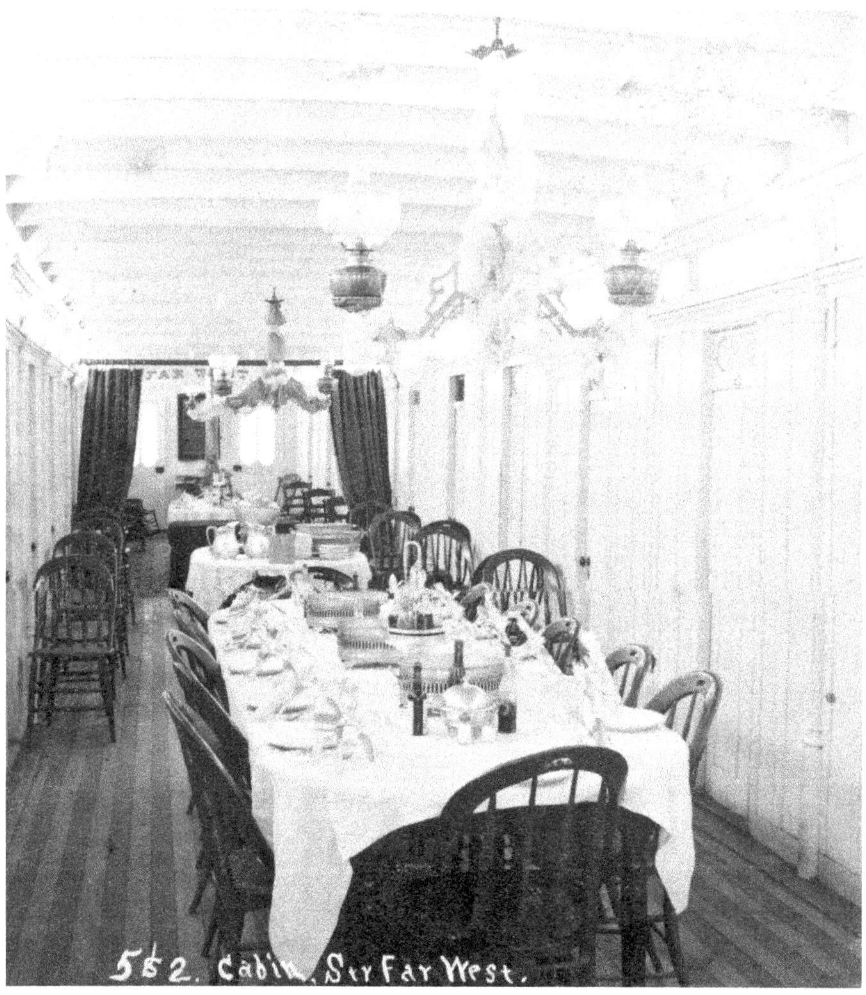

The salon or cabin of the steamer *Far West*, typical of the simplicity of accommodations among the "mountain boats." *Author's collection.*

Hardly was I fully established on board and ready for the journey when the mule drawn ambulance from Fort Assinniboine drew up at the levee to discharge officers and their families, who had also engaged passage on the Far West. *Among the passengers who were booked on the* Far West *were a large number of officers and their families from Fort Assinniboine, Col.* [W.H.] *Brown, post commander with his wife and son; Captain Cass Durham and family; Mrs. Hoyt, whose husband, Capt.* [George S.] *Hoyt, superintended the building of Fort Harrison; Mrs. Wood, who with her son had been visiting her sister, Mrs. Hoyt; Mrs. Baldwin, wife of Maj. Baldwin, and Major* [William] *Arthur, brother of President* [Chester A.] *Arthur, who was then an Army paymaster. The remainder were civilians, including myself and my two children, the younger a little more than a baby.*

All the listed passengers were aboard; the work of taking on freight was ended; and still we did not leave the levee. Then the Helena*'s whistle was heard around the bend below the town, and soon it steamed up to the landing. Our delay in starting could not be explained, boats rivaled one another in making record runs to and from Fort Benton. We began to think we had made a mistake in going on the* Far West, *but at length the boat started down the river, closely followed by the* Helena, *which finally passed us.*

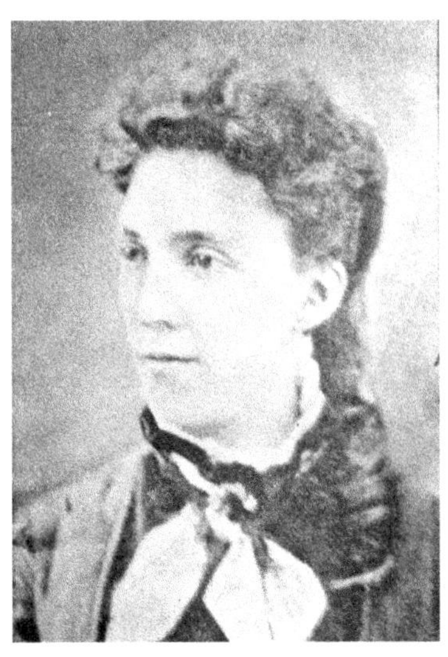

Martha Edgerton Rolfe and her two children visited the "States" on the steamer *Far West* in 1881. *Overholser Historical Research Center.*

Had I known the history of the gallant little craft on which we then were on, as I do now, I should have considered it a privilege to be one of her passengers.

Built in Pittsburg in 1870, the Far West *possessed the desirable qualifications for upper river navigation, of being light, sturdy and speedy, and because of these it was engaged in government service during the tragic summer of 1876, when occurred the Custer massacre.*

At Yankton it took on food supplies for Fort [Abraham] *Lincoln; but arriving there found the fort nearly empty, an expedition having started for the scene of some Indian disturbances on the Yellowstone, ten days before, and the* Far West *was ordered to follow, which it did, arriving at Powder River June 7th. Here General* [Alfred] *Terry came on board and there established his headquarters. The next day, the boat reached a point fifteen miles below the mouth of the Tongue river, where General* [John] *Gibbon joined Terry, and they went up a few miles to Gibbon's camp, where the* Far West *remained a couple of hours. When Gibbon took leave, the boat returned to Powder River, arriving there June 8th. General Terry then left for the camp of General* [Lieutenant Colonel George A.] *Custer.*

From that date until the fifteenth of June the Far West *was engaged in transfer work. Early on the 15th, General Custer set out for the Tongue* [River], *with six troops of cavalry, and carrying his supplies on pack mules. General Terry and his staff followed on the boat, which carried additional supplies. At the Tongue River, news awaited from Major* [Marcus] *Reno. This came on the evening of the 19th. A large Indian trail had been discovered, leading, it was thought, towards the Big Horn. The time for decisive action had arrived now that the position of the enemy was known, and the cavalry marched to the Rosebud, arriving there about noon of June 21st, to find General Terry and the* Far West, *had reached there first.*

It was in the cabin of this boat that the three generals, Terry, Gibbon, and Custer, held council, and mapped out the following campaign, which ended so disastrously. This meeting ended, General Terry gave to General Custer his written orders. Whether the latter obeyed them, is still a matter of controversy outside of army circles, but not within them.

On the morning of the 22nd, Custer's command began its march. The Far West *did not immediately follow, as it remained to rescue a mail sack containing the last letters of the departed cavalry men, which had fallen into the river from an overturned skiff. On the 24th the* Far West *passed the mouth of the Big Horn, and went two miles above it, where it gave out eight days' rations to the troops. All that day, this boat crossed and re-crossed the river carrying over Crow scouts, and finally the troops. General Gibbon, being ill, remained on board. Then came General Terry's order to Captain Marsh, of the* Far West, *that he was to ascend the Big Horn, for the purpose of bringing supplies to the soldiers.*

This seemed almost impossible to undertake, as the river was rapid, shallow and full of islands. In some places it was necessary to draw the boat along by cables around large trees and worked by the boat's capstans. In this way June 25th was passed. The next morning came further orders, that the boat should try to reach the mouth of the Little Big Horn, which it succeeded in doing by the aid of the soldiers, and passed beyond it, returning to the Little Big Horn on June 27th, and tied up at an island.

That evening, officers and men spent fishing from the shore of the island, until a mounted Indian startled them by breaking through the nearby willows of the mainland. It proved to be "Curley," one of Custer's Crow scouts. He seemed greatly excited, and anxious to deliver information he did not know how to convey, as there was no interpreter there, and he could not speak English.

The officers took him with them on board the boat, where he threw himself down weeping and groaning. When he could be quieted, Captain [Stephen] *Baker* [of 6th Infantry Company onboard the *Far West*] *gave him paper and a pencil, indicating that the Crow should tell his story by drawing. Quickly comprehending what was wanted of him, he took the pencil and paper, while about him stood a circle of the officers watching his every movement with intense interest. As Joseph Mills Hanson describes the scene:*

The Crow drew first a circle and then, outside of it another. Then between the inner and outer circles he began making numerous dots, repeating as he did so in despairing accents:

"Sioux! Sioux!"

When he had quite filled the intervening space with dots, he glanced up at the intent faces around him and then slowly commenced filling the interior circle with similar marks, while his voice arose to a yet more dismal tone as he reiterated:

"Absaroka! Absaroka!"

"By Scotts!" exclaimed Captain Marsh, "I know what that means. It means soldiers." . . .

He was interrupted by Curley, who suddenly sprang to his feet, faced the listeners and flung his arms wide. Then, swinging them back, he struck his breast repeatedly with his fingers, exclaiming at each blow, in imitation of rifle shots:

"Poof! Poof! Poof! Poof! Absaroka!"

The white men stood in tense silence, searching each other's faces. For a moment no one dared to confess that he understood. Captain Baker was the first to speak:

"We're whipped!" he said hoarsely. "That's what's the matter" and he turned away.

A few days after this dramatic incident, the Far West *was converted into a hospital ship, to receive the wounded, and its captain was instructed to go down the Big Horn to the Yellowstone. There it was detained by military necessity for a short time, and then set out for its sad trip to Bismarck, and Fort Lincoln.*

[As we steamed down the Missouri in 1881,] *I overheard one of the army contingent inquire, "I wonder if we are to take on those Indians?" "What Indians?" said I. "Why Sitting Bull's band that is to be sent to Standing Rock agency. Had you not heard?"*

When this conversation took place, we were out of sight of Fort Benton, well on our way down the river, with the Helena *a close companion by day and when we tied up to the shore at night. The army folk worried. I heard them talking about the situation. By special favor due to my army connections, I was admitted into their circle. Evidence of my singular good fortune appeared at the table, where my seat was next to a captain's wife.*

At that time the government gave large contracts to the river craft for carrying supplies to posts along the way and for those further inland in the Dakotas and Montana, where railroads had not yet penetrated. It naturally followed that the army received first consideration from those in command of the boats and there were rules of etiquette, as on ocean steamers, regarding the precedence to be accorded passengers, with army officers always given first place.

The trip would have been delightful but for the growing fear that our boat was to be one of those to take the Indians to Standing Rock. The weather favored us and the season was not far enough advanced for mosquitoes and buffalo gnats to be troublesome. From early morning until late at night we sped down the river, tying up at the bank generally at a woodyard, when it became unsafe to travel because of the difficulty of determining the channel and danger of sand bars and snags.

In the deepening twilight, the passengers sat on deck idly watching as the roustabouts went and came over the plank extending to the shore, fetching in wood or going for more, their work hastened by the reiterated commands of the mate watching them from the deck.

Now and then during the day, a visit was made by an occasional passenger to the lofty pilot house from which a magnificent view could be obtained of the country for a long distance east and west, cleft by the sparkling Missouri. One could converse with the pilot, but his replies were given with his eyes straight ahead, noting every peculiarity in the treacherous current.

We passed the mouths of the Judith, Musselshell and Milk rivers, streams still bearing names given them by Lewis and Clark. In all that long distance where twenty years earlier herds of buffaloes crossing the river often impeded the progress of the boats, now but one was seen.

This, an ancient bull, wandered to the sheltering willows close to the water and became the target for every gun on board. When killed, the boat drew alongside, where, with the aid of a donkey engine, the crew hauled it aboard, to the consternation of at least one of the army ladies, who anxiously inquired, "Do you think they are going to feed us on that?"

The sight of it certainly was not appetizing. For days afterward, whenever meat appeared at the table, the woman referred to would ask the waiters, who well understood her squeamishness, "What kind of meat is that?" With a broad grin, displayed a faultless set of teeth, the reply was always the same "Buffalo steak, ma'am." That woman became a vegetarian for the rest of the journey.

We had not been long on our way, before the rumor was afloat, but not credited, that our boat was again under military orders to assist in transporting Sitting Bull's people to the Standing Rock Agency.

With every day the rumor grew, and we began to question if it might not be true, when we reached the mouth of the Yellowstone, where another boat joined us. Then all doubt was dissipated, and we knew our fate.

We civilians were not greatly alarmed at the prospect; but the army group wore an air of settled gloom. Undoubtedly our unconcern arose from our ignorance. Certain it was that the officers on our boat were no more worried over the prospect than were their brother officers at Fort Buford where the Indians came on board. They enlarged on the danger we were about to face, and besought our army officers to leave their wives and children at Fort Buford if they themselves must go on. After due consideration, our officers decided that not only they but their families would run the risk. . . .

That evening, one of the army officers said, "That band of Indians of Sitting Bull is to be taken from Buford to Standing Rock Agency. It is possible that the Far West *is to assist in their transportation." The next day the* Helena *overhauled us, and kept near us until we reached the mouth of the Yellowstone.*

As we came in sight of the latter river, we saw a steamboat [General Sherman] descending it. That was all the army officers needed to assure them that they were right in their surmise regarding the mission of the three boats, and they were greatly worried. Two at least of the boats carried women and children. Their safety might be endangered by having on board a lot of wild Indians, who had overcome and slaughtered the flower of our cavalry.

At Fort Buford, the officers of that post besought the army men on our boat to leave their wives and children at Buford, until another boat came down. They declared we were all running a great risk if we went to Bismarck with the Indians. We civilians had no choice in the matter; we must go, Indians or no Indians, or lose our fare. In the end, all decided to take the chance of being scalped, the army group and civilians alike.

That night the Indians had a parting feast to which their remaining dogs contributed the principal dish. Many of the passengers from the three boats watched the festivities. I was prevented from joining them, because of my two children.

One woman from Helena took her little girl with her—a beautiful child, with long golden curls. The squaws crowded around her, and uttered in Sioux exclamations their admiration of the fair maid with the golden locks.

The next morning began the embarkation. The wind was blowing a stiff gale, as the Indians came down to the landing, and from our boat we watched the scene. Dignified old men in brightly colored blankets strolled leisurely along, apparently unconcerned at being exiled. Several of these carried pipes with long stems, set with knife blades in the form of a wide inverted "V" the blades varying in length from four to six inches. I could not but think that they might prove effective weapons. All ages and both sexes were represented. Some of the squaws wore capes reaching to the waist, made of alternate rows of blue cloth, and elks' teeth, the latter placed closely together. . . .

Old and young, all were in festal attire. They laughed and chattered as though about to go on an excursion, instead of leaving their homeland forever. Nor was it the homeland of any but the younger generation. The Sioux had made this region theirs, as we had made it ours, by conquest. Driven from Minnesota before the all-powerful white race, they journeyed west, where they wrested the land from the weaker tribes. Their title to this region was as good as ours; but they, like those they supplanted, did not have sufficient strength to maintain it. They made their last effective stand at the time of the battle of the Little Big Horn, where the Custer Massacre was staged. . . .

As the Indians went on board the boats, they were assigned the front of the lower decks, where they were closely packed. The leading men, however, were permitted to stay on the rear of the second decks, and to take their meals there. The reason for granting this privilege to the chiefs, may have arisen from a desire to separate them from their followers; but the passengers did not enjoy their proximity.

It is said that there were but 187 Indians taken to Standing Rock at this time. This may be a true estimate of the number, but it seemed like there were over a hundred on our boat alone. There were not more than thirteen soldiers allotted for the protection of each group of passengers—that is to say, about forty for the three boats. I am not certain that this is the correct number, but it is the one given by the officers in our company. It seemed much too small for the purpose designated.

While the Indians were embarking great stores of provisions for them were taken on board. This work took several hours, and it was close to noon before we left Fort Buford, the boats following one after the other, and not far apart. The brilliant coloring of the Indians dress resembling bunting displayed by ships on gala occasions, and giving the scene a festal appearance.

The passengers had a fine opportunity to study Indian domestic life, as they looked down on them from their vantage point on the upper deck. The Indians conducted themselves as if in their tepees. They made their toilets and nursed their children; carried on their love affairs unabashed by onlookers; and the squaws sewed and embroidered. One elderly gentleman from Philadelphia after spending half a day watching the activities on the front lower deck exclaimed: "When I reach home, if I were to tell my folks half of what I have seen today, they would not believe me."

It was sunset as we approached Fort Berthold. Before us spread a gorgeous red sky down to the horizon, towards which the boat was headed. "Come up to the Texas," said one of my friends, "and hear the Indians sing." I gladly followed her aloft, where half a dozen [men] . . . *were singing and indulging in some primitive dance steps, wholly oblivious to the audience surrounding them.*

They swayed gently side to side, now and then half turning round, and meanwhile chanting what sounded like "Hi-yi-yi," repeated again and again. Their voices were good, and I discovered there was a real melody to what they sang. Some one said they sang because they were approaching an enemy's country. There they stood, their splendid, almost naked forms outlined against the glowing sunset. As they sang, shrill boys' voices from the lower deck took up the burden of the song in another key, but with similar intervals. It was a concert never to be forgotten, on a stage impossible of reproduction, and hung with curtains of a celestial hue.

That night, having arrived at Fort Berthold, the boats tied up side by side, with planks connecting the decks one with the other. Never during our journey was so much fear expressed by our passengers. The army group showed greatest apprehension, for they knew the Indians best. Few retired before midnight, and some of them sat up much later. My children were asleep in our cabin, and I took the philosophical view that if we were attacked the children would be killed before they awakened, and as for myself, nothing would be gained by being scalped in imagination, and then in reality. One such an ordeal was sufficient. So I went to bed and slept peacefully all night, not awakening once.

In the morning I learned that an Indian child having fallen into the river, while trying to pass from one boat to another, a chief's daughter had been drowned while attempting to save it. Then the Indians raised their death wail; and those of the passengers who heard it believed their hour had come. Their apprehension was not quieted until they learned for those lugubrious ululations, so like the cry of the coyote.

Nothing else startling happened on our way to Bismarck; but fear of the Indians was not allayed while we were on the boat, and it was with a distinct feeling of relief that we left it for the train.

The rail journey was exceedingly tiresome. Father and mother met me in Cleveland. It was a great relief to me to have their assistance in the care of the children, as I was utterly exhausted. My delight at seeing them once more, was tempered on noting that they had aged, and mother, especially, was not very strong.

Long unused to the heat of an Eastern summer, I found it hard to endure. It almost counterbalanced my pleasure at meeting friends and relatives, and I did not altogether regret leaving Akron when the time came for me to return to Montana.[37]

After spending the summer with her Edgerton family in Ohio, Martha and her girls boarded the steamboat *Dakotah* at Bismarck on August 18 for the trip up the Missouri River to return to Fort Benton. Though short in distance, the lateness of the navigation season presented problems as the steamer proceeded up the river. Martha continues her narrative:

My Army companions of the downward trip again took the same boat with me at Bismarck, as did also two Army doctors, a lieutenant, and a few soldiers. The river ascent was enjoyable, but without incident, except that one night Pauline had the croup. I called one of the Army doctors to attend her, and he did his best, with a lighted candle under a cup of water to generate steam, and she recovered. At night, after the boat tied up, no hot water could be obtained. Hence, the cup and candle. . . .

One evening when the boat "wooded up" at one of the wood yards along the river, several of the soldiers seized the opportunity to go in swimming. Most of the passengers were sitting on the front deck watching the long line of roust-a-bouts going and coming over the gang plank, when suddenly the cry of "Help" was heard. This happened twice, and it was suggested to the lieutenant that one of his men might be in need of assistance.

"Oh no!" he returned, "that fellow is only trying to attract attention." He discovered his error later. The swimmer never again rose to the surface.

Because of the rapid falling of the water, the boat could not complete the journey, and its captain unceremoniously dumped us all at Cow Island,

> *a hundred miles from Fort Benton* [on about August 23]. *This is the island where the Nez Perces crossed the river, and from here the boat put out down stream to make known the fact to General* [Nelson A.] *Miles, who still believed he was ahead of the Indians. It was chance, not military science, that enabled him to learn their whereabouts; catch up with them, and complete their subjugation. It was consideration for the women and children, the old and the wounded that led Chief Joseph to surrender* [at the Bear's Paw Mountains]. *From that day he became a sad and broken man.*
>
> *The captain telegraphed our predicament to Fort Benton and Fort Assinniboine, and the army ambulance awaited its passengers when we landed, as did a "dead axe" wagon* [without springs] *and driver for another woman, Mrs.* [Winfield Scott] *Wetzel, and myself, our four children, our trunks and other baggage.*
>
> *I rode on the front seat that would have been comfortable but for the trunks stored beneath that rendering the springs inoperative. We cooked by a campfire, and slept in the covered wagon, with no mattress to soften the boards of the wagon bed. Plenty of food was sent us, but neither dishes, nor knives and forks. We ate from cans as we could, fingers coming prominently into play, and I shared the frying pan with the driver, a division line being marked through the center. The driver brought along a supply of potatoes, and I then discovered they are never so good as when cooked out of doors.*

Mrs. Martha Edgerton Rolfe rejoined her husband, Herbert P. Rolfe, in Fort Benton in the late summer of 1881. Remarkable Herbert Rolfe, a lawyer and surveyor, had led the organization of the Republican Party in the old riverport community that had long been dominated by the Irish and southern Democrats. In 1884, the Rolfes became early settlers in the new town of Great Falls, where Herbert served as surveyor and lawyer for founder Paris Gibson before starting the *Great Falls Leader*, in opposition to the Democratic *Tribune*. When Herbert died at age forty-five, Martha assumed editorship of the *Daily Leader* while also raising their family of seven small children.

Part II
Adventurers on the Upper Missouri:

Going to the Mountains

Chapter 7

From Adventures on the Upper Missouri to Combat in Civil War Kentucky

John Mason Brown

John Mason Brown journeyed twice to the Upper Missouri during 1861–62 before becoming embroiled in the Civil War in his native Kentucky, where he joined the Union army and led his Kentucky cavalry regiment into combat against notorious Confederate general John Hunt Morgan. On his first trip up the Missouri River on the steamboats *Chippewa* and *Spread Eagle* in 1861, Brown became friends with Andrew Dawson, chief factor of the American Fur Company. Brown, with other adventurous travelers during that two-month river trip, also met Charles P. Chouteau, head of company operations, and colorful trader Malcolm Clarke. The trip fueled Brown's interest in the Upper Missouri in his quest for knowledge and adventure.[38]

John Mason Brown was born in Frankfort, the capital of Kentucky, on April 26, 1837, in imposing Liberty Hall, built for his grandfather John Brown, a leading lawyer and one of Kentucky's first two senators. John Mason Brown's father, Mason, was a substantial landowner and slaveholder, holding fifty-one slaves in 1860 and wielding considerable political influence. Young John Mason graduated from Yale College in 1856 and returned to Frankfort, where he taught school and studied law. In April 1860, he opened a law practice in St. Louis, Missouri.[39]

During Brown's first trip up the Missouri in the spring of 1861 on the American Fur Company's *Spread Eagle* steamboat, traveling in company with the *Chippewa*, he had long conversations with new friend Andrew Dawson, as well as other frontiersmen. During this trip, Dawson wrote,

"In St. Louis there was not a pistol to be had for love or money. Nothing is talked of but soldiering and even here on the S[team] Boat the passengers have formed themselves into a Company and go through daily drill" organized by John Mason Brown. The fifteen "Spread Eagle Guards" were armed with government annuity rifles provided by Charles Chouteau—arms being taken upriver for distribution under treaty obligation to the various Indian nations.[40]

Throughout this trip, Brown kept a remarkable diary that contained daily entries describing the many hazards of the trip up the Missouri River, his travels throughout what later became Montana Territory and geographical features of the Rocky Mountains.

Boarding the smaller steamer *Chippewa* at Fort Union, the travelers soon faced disaster. A careless crewman striving to imbibe liquor stored in the dark hold dropped a candle, igniting the alcohol and eventually spreading to two hundred kegs of gunpowder, and the boat blew up. Before then, quick action by the crew beached the *Chippewa* long enough for Brown; his friends, artist William de la Montaigne Cary and William H. Schieffelin; and the other passengers to scramble ashore. Brown described the disaster as it unfolded:

> *We were smoking our after-supper pipes when the cry of* Fire! *was raised below. The rush and excitement was terrifying but the boat being near shore a hawser was gotten out ahead and after some delay the human freight safely landed. I managed to save my gun, pistol, overcoat, valise and*

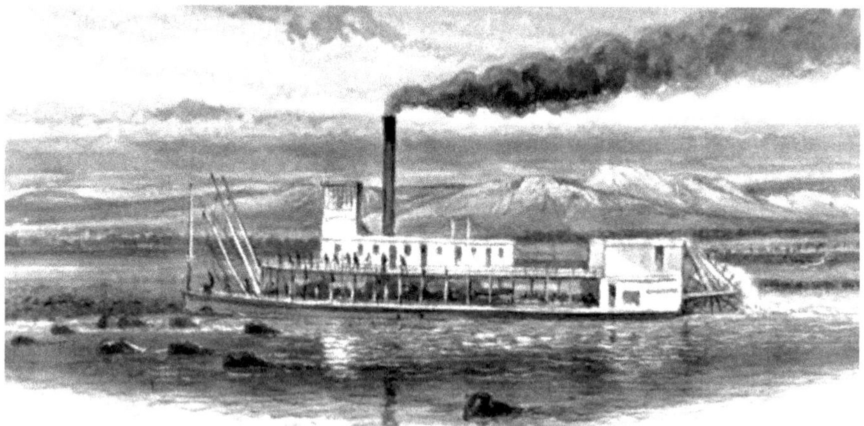

The steamboat *Chippewa* encountered a herd of bison crossing the Missouri River as every man with a rifle took aim at the herd. Sketch by William Cary in *Recreation Magazine*, 1905. *Author's collection.*

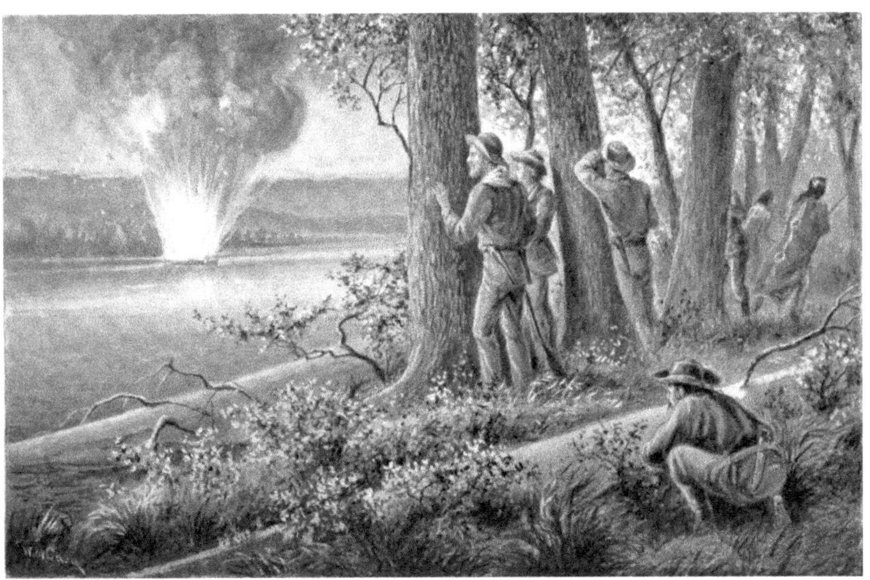

Chippewa blew up when fire reached the powder magazine in the hold. By then, the passengers had reached the banks of the Missouri River and observed the loss of their transportation to Fort Benton. Sketch by William Cary in *Recreation Magazine*, 1905. *Author's collection.*

> *blankets, besides various property of others. . . . The boat floated down after the hawser burned and the powder exploded with a tremendous noise. Boat and cargo total loss.*[41]

This appeared to be just the sort of adventure John Mason Brown craved, and after locating horses, he and his companions started overland to Fort Benton, arriving after a series of incidents during the seventeen days. After being entertained at Fort Benton by Factor Andrew Dawson, Brown traveled along the Mullan Military Wagon Road via the Blackfeet Government Farm at Sun River, describing it as "the most beautiful stream that I have ever seen, large, bold, cold as ice, fed from the Rocky Mt. snows and swarming with Trout."[42]

Along the way, Brown wrote extensively of his travels along the Mullan Road, meeting and riding with Captain John Mullan at St. Regis de Borgia, describing conditions along the road, observing the Indians, the violence, the quest for gold and the deeply divided loyalties of white residents as news arrived about the war. He continued on the Mullan Road to Fort Walla Walla and then to San Francisco and home via the California overland route.

On his second trip up the Missouri, Brown departed St. Louis on May 10, 1862, on the company steamer *Spread Eagle*, renewed his friendship with Dawson and Clarke and met the legendary trader Alexander Culbertson and his Blackfeet wife, Natawista. Again Brown kept a diary with daily entries describing the trip up the Missouri River from St. Joseph, Missouri, to Fort Benton; his encounters with traders, miners and hunters; and various Indian tribes in the Northern Plains, Rocky Mountains and Alberta, then Rupert's Land, and the return trip down the Missouri.[43]

A highlight of Brown's second trip occurred when he joined a prospecting expedition with a party of Bentonites consisting of Matthew Carroll, James M. Arnoux, Dr. Atkinson, Paul Longleine, Henry Bostwick, Edward Williamson, David Carafel, George Magnum and John Munroe. They proceeded north of Chief Mountain in July 1862, searching for gold that they had learned about from a man named La Rue. La Rue, who had lived among the Blackfeet for several years as a self-appointed priest, had sent a package to Dawson with word that it was gold-bearing sand. The sand was washed and found to contain an exceptional amount of gold. The party formed quickly at Fort Benton and prospected along every stream from the Marias River to the Willows, a point about twenty-five miles south of the Hudson Bay Company's Fort Edmonton.[44]

The prospectors found light gold colors along the way but nothing to warrant working. La Rue could not be found, and the frustrated prospectors concluded that he had deceived them, so in September, they returned to Fort Benton. His sense of adventure satisfied, John Mason Brown joined a party of miners returning downriver to St. Louis by mackinaw boat.

Brown's return to Missouri and Kentucky and the reality of the Civil War must have presented a dilemma to the young man. The border states were deeply polarized into Union and Confederate camps, largely over the issue of slavery. In the war, nowhere were the divisions more acute than in Kentucky and Tennessee, since slaves made up about 20 percent of the population in the former and 25 percent in the latter. Tennessee seceded, while Kentucky did not. By comparison, slaves in Missouri formed just 10 percent of the total population. Despite the slave-owning background of the Brown family, John Mason never wavered, no doubt influenced by his years at Yale College and St. Louis, as well as the two summers on the Upper Missouri.

Within five days of his return from the second trip to the Upper Missouri in October 1862, Brown was commissioned major in the Union 10th Kentucky Cavalry Regiment. On March 15, 1863, from the camp of the 10th Kentucky Cavalry, Major Brown wrote to Andrew Dawson, known to friends for his copper-red hair as "Sorrell Top":

My very esteemed old friend "Sorrell Top."

I have this day caused to be shipped to "Andy Dawson, care of P Chouteau Jr & Co St. Louis" by Adams Express, in a sea-worthy keg, a small portion of good whiskey which I hope you will find awaiting you on your arrival from Ft Benton—And in case it arrives all right I hope that you will condescend to touch it to the good luck of your young Ky. friend, who owes so much of the pleasant life he led in the Far North West to your kindness and friendship—If [Malcolm] *Clarke ever departs from his ascetic rule of cider and ale I trust he will join you in the glass—*

I wrote you, via Walla Walla, in [Frank L.] *Worden's care, immediately after reaching St. Louis—Even if that letter miscarried you heard I presume of our progress from Hotchkiss and Gerard* [likely William D. Hodgkiss of Fort Union and J.J. Gerard of Fort Berthold]—*Suffice it to say now that we got down safe, and in 5 days after my return to Kentucky I found myself Major of the 10th Regiment of Kentucky cavalry, busily engaged in drilling my men—This position I have held ever since but am now (I am informed by the Genl. Comdy* [general commanding]*) to be put in command of a regiment of my own—the immediate cause being the fact that I got my clothes badly torn in some recent fights—The Lord in his mercy Grant that the promotion may come!*

. . . I most sincerely hope that your health is greatly improved and that your legs are again fully up to their duty—[Dawson had been badly crippled in an earlier fall at Fort Benton.] *Let me have a short letter from you, if you can find the time, directed to Frankfort Kentucky—whence it will be forwarded to me.*

Please do not fail to remember me most sincerely to Clarke, Carroll and Geo Steele [Steell]*—friends whom, with yourself I can never forget—and whose numerous kindnesses make Fort Benton seem a home to me—If it were possible that I could be in Frankfort, at my own home I would insist on you and Clarke spending a day or two with me if the time could possibly be squeezed out of your short allowances, but I am as I told you a cavalry officer and one day in Kentucky, the next probably in Tennessee—uncertain as to times and places . . .*

Most truly & sincerely yr friend
Jno Mason Brown

Do me the favor to express to me at Frankfort a couple dozen buffalo tongues if any have come down—and send bill collectable on deliver of freight.[45]

The 10th Kentucky Cavalry was raised by Colonel Joshua Tevis, a veteran of the Mexican War, and organized at Maysville, in northeastern Kentucky, during the summer of 1862. During July to September, Confederates invaded Kentucky, and the Union 10th Kentucky encountered the enemy at the Battle of Perryville. After that battle on October 8, the Confederates retreated from Kentucky, and the 10th participated in the pursuit, following General Humphrey Marshall's men through the mountains, capturing prisoners, horses and arms. The 10th remained on duty in Kentucky during the principal part of its service, with occasional excursions into Tennessee and (what is now West) Virginia.

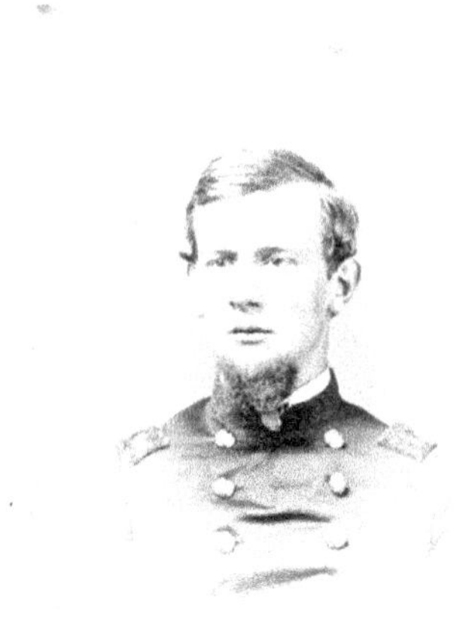

Major John Mason Brown of the 10th Kentucky Cavalry. *Author's collection.*

Major John Mason Brown joined the 10th Kentucky on October 27, 1862, and assumed command of two companies, forming a battalion for a two-month scouting expedition. On December 25, Major Brown's battalion moved through London and Barboursville to Big Creek Gap and engaged in numerous skirmishes along the way.[46]

Major Brown's battalion rejoined the regiment in central Kentucky and remained on active service through the winter and spring of 1863, operating from the borders of Virginia to Somerset in south-central Kentucky. During this time, Colonel Charles J. Walker and Lieutenant Colonel R.R. Maltby commanded the 10th while Major Brown led the battalion.

In the spring of 1863, Confederate cavalry returned to raid Kentucky. On March 5, Confederate colonel R.S. Cluke's 8th Kentucky Cavalry crossed the Cumberland River at Stigall's Ferry below Somerset and made its way to Richmond, Winchester, Mount Sterling and other points. Major Brown's battalion opposed Colonel Cluke, advanced from Crab Orchard and skirmished at Lancaster. Pushing on, it encountered Cluke's men at many points. Among them was a fight about halfway from Winchester to Mount Sterling where Major Brown's men checked a fierce attack, and with the 44th Ohio Infantry coming up in support, the Confederates fled some 135 miles, with Major Brown's cavalry in pursuit. On March 28, cooperating with the 5th Kentucky Cavalry, the 10th succeeded in driving Colonel Cluke out of Kentucky and into Virginia.

On June 30, 1863, Major John Mason Brown assumed command of the 10th for a month. In July, a portion of the 10th under Major Brown captured Confederate general Humphrey Marshall's artillery. Throughout this period, the 10th Cavalry protected eastern Kentucky and had numerous engagements with the enemy in which it suffered casualties. Among its battles were Elk Fork, Tennessee; Gladesville, (West) Virginia; and Mount Sterling, Triplet's Bridge and Lancaster, Kentucky. It participated in the pursuit and rout of Brigadier General John Pegram. In the course of the 10th's service, it was rarely at rest, being active all over eastern Kentucky and into east Tennessee and West Virginia. The depleted 10th was mustered out of service on September 17, 1863, at Maysville.

In the fall of 1863, Brown was promoted to colonel to recruit and assume command of the 45th Kentucky Mounted Rifles. Mustered in on October 10, the 45th served at Mount Sterling and covered the front from Cumberland Gap to Louisa until March 1864. At that time, Colonel Brown was appointed commander of the 4th Brigade, 1st Division, District of Kentucky.[47]

In May 1864, Confederate general John Hunt Morgan rode into Kentucky through Pound Gap on his last cavalry raid into the state. Federal cavalry under Colonel John Mason Brown, Colonel Wickliffe Cooper and others attacked Morgan at Cynthiana, Mount Sterling and Augusta. At Mount Sterling, Morgan dismounted his men to burn enemy supplies and scour the countryside for horses. Morgan left his dismounted element, and his maneuvering with his mounted force succeeded in confusing Union commanders. Colonel Brown, commanding the 2nd Brigade, gained sufficient intelligence to convince his commander, Major General Stephen G. Burbridge, to change direction and descend on Mount Sterling to attack Morgan's men. In this attack, Colonel Brown's soldiers smashed through the outposts and into the unsuspecting Confederate camp. This attack decimated Morgan's men, killing or capturing about 314 officers and men.

Overall, during his raid into Kentucky, General Morgan lost over half of his men and finally was driven into east Tennessee, where he was killed at Greeneville on September 4. Colonel Brown's command of the 10th and 45th, together with his leadership in the engagements that drove notorious Colonel John Hunt Morgan's Confederate cavalry from Kentucky, earned him a reputation as an exceptional soldier. One official report stated, "There was no more gallant and efficient officer than Col. John Mason Brown . . . [who is] young, ardent, intelligent, and peculiarly acquainted with Kentucky."[48]

Leaving service in December 1864, Brown resumed his law practice at Frankfort. There he married Mary O. Preston, eldest daughter of Confederate brigadier general William Preston, and raised a family. Later moving to Louisville, he became one of the leading citizens, standing at the head of the bar and business enterprises and becoming a founder of the Filson Historical Society. Upper Missouri adventurer and Civil War leader Colonel John Mason Brown practiced law until his death on January 29, 1890, and is interred in Cave Hill Cemetery, Louisville.

Chapter 8

From Boy Warrior to Frontier Scout in War and Peace

The Service of Charles K. Bucknum

Young Charles Bucknum served in the Union army on the Minnesota frontier during the Civil War before performing valuable service as a government scout during Montana's Indian Wars and later achieving fame in frontier Wyoming.

Few obituaries capture a life as well as that of Private Charles K. Bucknum: "Civil War veteran, government scout, business man, rancher, stock man and capitalist, in every walk of life, and in every calling he chose to follow, he was not only a success, but an example of greatness and nobility of character."[49]

He was born on October 12, 1847, to Caleb B. and Evelina L. Bucknum, who moved from Indiana to McCartysville, California, in 1853. Two years later, Caleb died, and Evelina Bucknum moved with her son to Minnesota to live with a sister. Evelina remarried, and family history tells that young Charles did not get on well with his stepfather.[50]

Falsifying his age, fifteen-year-old Charles K. Bucknum enlisted and mustered in to newly raised Company F in Hatch's Independent Battalion, Minnesota Cavalry, at Fort Snelling on September 1, 1864. Companies E and F were assigned to frontier duty under Lieutenant Colonel Charles Powell Adams, who had relieved an ailing Major Hatch.[51]

Major Edwin A.C. Hatch, a former agent to the Sioux, without military experience, organized Hatch's Independent Battalion of Cavalry in the summer of 1863 for the express purpose of protecting settlers from incidents with native Indians. The battalion originally was independent of the regular

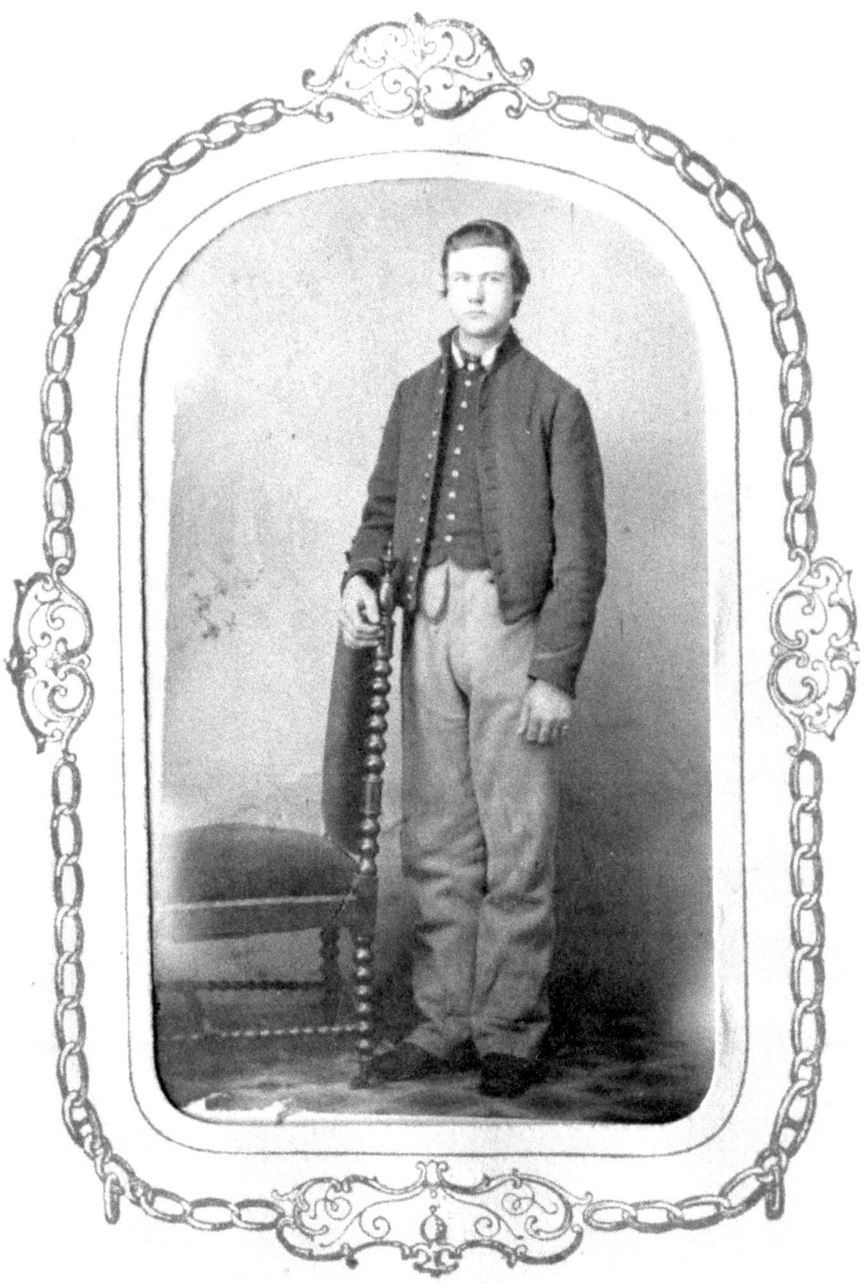

Fifteen-year-old Private Charles K. Bucknum, Union soldier, served in the Minnesota Cavalry. *Overholser Historical Research Center.*

army command in Minnesota but eventually was placed under Brigadier General Henry Hastings Sibley. Posted at Pembina in northern Minnesota, the battalion guarded against possible incursions by Santee Sioux who had fled across the British North American (Canadian) border after their 1862 uprising. Hatch's battalion aggressively patrolled the border yet fought but a single battle on December 15, 1863.[52]

Though hardly an elite strike force, Hatch's battalion, in whole or in part, performed a useful defensive and patrolling mission in northern Minnesota for the rest of the war. In doing so, the battalion saved the government from having to detach valuable combat forces from Civil War battlefields.

Companies E and F remained on the Minnesota frontier during 1865, part of a force of 1,400 men retained for the protection against "Indian depredations." Some of the posts were occupied as late as the spring of 1866, although by then the troops on garrison duty were gradually mustered out. Hatch's battalion was the last to be released. By then, Bucknum had been promoted to corporal and served two and a half years until discharge at Fort Snelling on April 26, 1866.

Two years later, Charles Bucknum started west as a wagon boss for Wilder, Marrion and Company. Freighting led him to Fort Benton during the summer of 1868, where he met a detachment from the 13th Infantry Regiment at Camp Cooke. The next year, an infantry company was stationed at newly formed Military Post Fort Benton. Bucknum met and befriended post commander Major Guido Ilges and other army leaders. By the early 1870s, Bucknum was hired as a government guide and scout, in large part because of his proficiency in many Indian languages, as well as in sign talk.[53]

Bucknum married Ioliti of the Gros Ventre about 1875, and they had two children. Ioliti died about 1882, and the children returned to the Gros Ventre Nation to live with an aunt. They later attended Carlisle Indian School in Pennsylvania, likely with their father's support.

As a scout, Bucknum's frontier experience and mastery of Indian languages made him of great value during the Montana Indian Wars of the mid-1870s. His experiences and hairsbreadth escapes from the Indians were many and varied. Time and again he was captured and threatened with death, but his quick thinking and linguistic ability always led to release from their custody.

During the Indian Wars, Bucknum's service as guide and scout reached legendary proportions under Generals John Gibbon, John R. Brooke and Thomas H. Ruger and Colonel Nelson Miles. Scout Bucknum often accompanied Major Ilges on visits to Fort Belknap and Indian camps throughout northern Montana. The pages of northern Montana's only newspaper in the 1870s, the *Benton Record*, are filled with reports of Scout Bucknum's activities during the Nez Perce War and during the years that Sitting Bull and his Sioux were in exile in Canada.

At the time of Chief Joseph's capture, Bucknum was a scout for Colonel Miles, as well as a courier between Major Ilges and Miles, and he had letters of commendation for his efforts and his "valuable services rendered" from both Miles and Ilges.

Typical of the reports carried in the *Benton Record* were the following:

> *I dispatched two of my volunteers, Charles Bucknum and William Gantes, as couriers to General Miles, paying them for their dangerous service the sum of $300; that these two couriers delivered my letter of information as to the whereabouts of the Nez Perces on September 26th to General Miles, who was then operating on the eastern slope of the Little Rockies, and that they conducted as guides for Gen'l Miles and his command to Snake creek, where the final capture took place after five days' severe fighting. From: Maj. Guido Ilges.*[54]

> *Mr. C. Bucknum, who has just returned from Gen. Miles' command, informs us that the Gen. intends to make the mouth of the Musselshell river, instead of Fort Buford, his base of supplies, and with the whole of the 7th regiment of cavalry, will remain at that point during the winter, or, if authority is given him, will camp near the* [Canadian] *boundary line and corral all the Sioux that cross to this side.*[55]

> *Charley Bucknum, the citizen scout sent by the district commander to investigate reports concerning the Sioux invasion, returned on Monday afternoon with information that fully confirms all the reports recently published in this paper.*[56]

In 1932, the *Great Falls Tribune* interviewed Mrs. Julia Payne Crane, daughter of early Montana pioneer and longtime Fort Benton resident Rufus Payne. At that time, she showed her collection of photographs of ox and mule teams, steamboats, Montana's earliest trading centers and business houses. Mrs. Crane stated that her brother-in-law Charles Bucknum, at the time in 1868 a government scout at Fort Benton, took many of the photographs in her collection.[57]

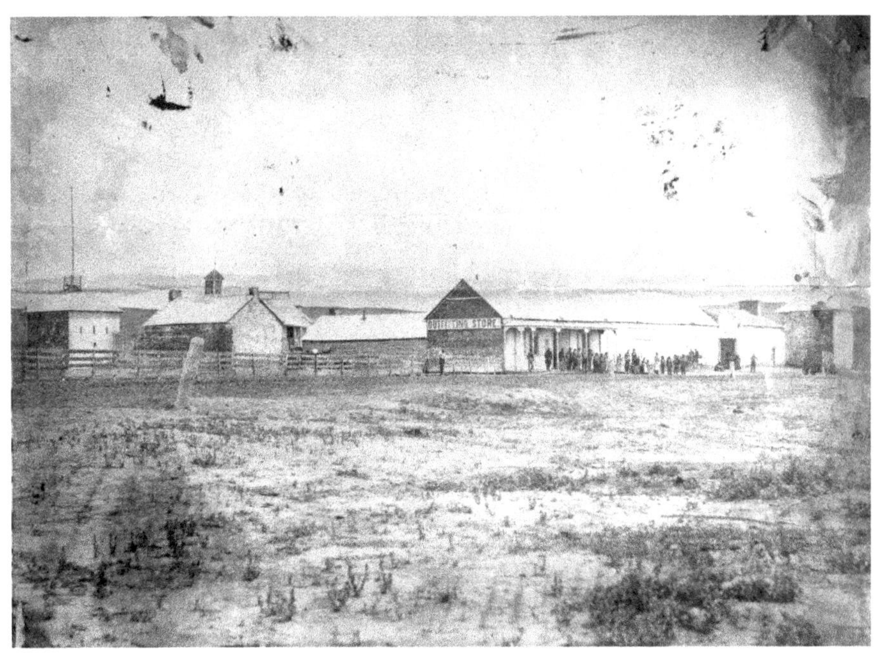

A rare photo of the North West Fur Company Trading Post at Fort Benton taken in 1868 by Scout Charles K. Bucknum. *Overholser Historical Research Center.*

On occasion, Bucknum joined Choteau County sheriff John J. Healy in excursions into Piegan Blackfeet camps seeking return of stolen horses.[58] Scout Bucknum continued on active service with the U.S. Army until 1880, when his foot was crushed while helping move a government safe into a quartermaster's tent at Fort Assinniboine. The compound fracture of his ankle changed his life. He left government service and began freighting from Fort Benton to Helena and the Judith Basin.

Leaving Fort Benton upon the death of his Gros Ventre wife in the 1880s, Bucknum began long-haul freighting. He bought road-building equipment and became a contractor for construction work in the Black Hills and Nebraska. Blazing his own path, his Montana-Nebraska freight trail was adopted as the most practical route for a railroad through Wyoming. In 1887, he joined the freighting services of Fremont, Elkhorn and Missouri, soon reorganized as the Chicago and Northwestern Railroad. When this railroad began construction into the new town of Casper, Wyoming, Bucknum freighted the railroad ties and led the construction gang.

Upon completion of the railroad, Bucknum settled in Casper, where he married Ethyl Ardell Williams, who died after the birth of a daughter.

Becoming active in Republican Party politics, he was elected mayor of Casper and later elected Natrona County commissioner, serving as chairman. From 1904 to 1908, he served as state representative in the Wyoming legislature.

Bucknum married for a third time, to Mrs. Ida May Payne Rowe, in the 1890s, the daughter of an old friend from his Benton days and fellow Freemason Rufus Payne. Bucknum entered the sheep business, building one of the largest ranches north of Casper in Natrona County.

Charles Bucknum suffered increasingly from a bronchial condition, leading him to purchase an orange grove near Pomona, California, on a historic Spanish land grant. He also bought a home in Los Angeles and passed away there on November 21, 1915. Corporal Charles K. Bucknum, government scout, freighter, politician and entrepreneur, rests today in Highland Cemetery, Casper, Wyoming.[59]

Chapter 9

Civil War Soldier and Proprietor of Fort Benton's Crown Jewel

Stephen S. Spitzley

Stephen S. Spitzley and his Michigan regiment barely survived the Civil War. Although his health never recovered fully, Spitzley became the first proprietor of the Grand Union Hotel, built in the last days of the steamboat boom in Fort Benton and, at the time, considered the finest hotel between Minnesota and the West Coast.

Born in Mayen in the Prussian Rhine district of Germany, Stephen S. Spitzley came to America with his parents at the age of nine on the passenger ship *Luconia*, arriving in New York Harbor in October 1848. The family moved west and settled on a farm in Houghton County, Upper Michigan.[60]

In the second year of the Civil War, Stephen Spitzley enlisted on August 18, 1862, in Houghton County as corporal and was assigned to a unit incorporated into the 27th Michigan Infantry when that regiment was mustered into service on April 10, 1863. The 27th Michigan, under command of Colonel Dorus M. Fox, started from Ypsilanti for Kentucky on April 12, 1863, with an enrollment of 865 officers and men. It occupied several towns in Kentucky after its arrival before fighting in its first engagement on June 2 at Jamestown. Later in June the 27th Michigan was assigned to the 3rd Brigade, First Division, Ninth Corps, and sent to Vicksburg, Mississippi, to support Major General Ulysses S. Grant's army during the Siege of Vicksburg, from June 22 to July 4, 1863.[61]

The 27th joined in a blocking maneuver near Jackson, Mississippi, in the rear of Vicksburg, when General Joseph E. Johnston attempted to come to the relief of Lieutenant General John C. Pemberton, then besieged in Vicksburg. After the fall of Vicksburg on July 4, the 27th was sent with the Ninth Corps across the mountains to take part in the East Tennessee campaign. After a long, arduous march over almost impassable roads, it reached Lenoir Station, Tennessee, and was attacked by Lieutenant General James Longstreet's forces, then advancing on Knoxville. The Union lines were gradually withdrawn toward Knoxville, but it became necessary to halt at Campbell Station to ensure the safety of the trains. Here, the Confederates fiercely attacked the Union forces, and the 27th Michigan sustained heavy casualties.[62]

Union forces rallied behind their defenses at Knoxville and in Fort Saunders, where the enemy charged them repeatedly and suffered heavy losses in an attempt to seize Union earthworks. Despite heavy casualties of their own sustained in the defense of Knoxville, the 27th Michigan pursued General Longstreet as he passed into northeastern Tennessee. The 27th Michigan suffered severe hardships during this campaign since it was poorly supplied with rations, tents, blankets and clothing, and the men's shoes were worn out by constant marching in deep mud or on frozen ground.

General Grant withdrew the Ninth Corps, including the 27th, to send it east to join the Army of the Potomac. The 27th returned to Knoxville and then marched some two hundred miles across the Cumberland Mountains to Nicholasville, Kentucky. The Ninth Corps was then placed on rail cars and sent to Annapolis, Maryland. At this point, two companies of sharpshooters joined the regiment and were designated the First and Second Companies of Sharpshooters. These sharpshooters' Spencer magazine rifles, the newest and most destructive infantry weapon then known, were hailed with delight by the 27th, for they were the only Spencer rifles in Ninth Corps.

The 27th quickly petitioned to arm the whole regiment with Spencers to make them all "Sharpshooters." To their surprise, their requisition was filled rapidly, and the coveted Spencers graced the shoulders of all the men in the regiment. These seven-shot, manually operated lever-action repeating rifles had a sustainable rate of fire in excess of twenty rounds per minute compared to standard muzzle-loaders with a rate of two to three rounds per minute. For the rest of the war, their greatest challenge was to develop effective tactics to take advantage of the much higher rate of fire.

The Spencer rifles proved a double-edged sword. With these rifles, the 27th Michigan simply dominated advanced picket or firing lines against Confederate muzzle-loaders. Yet because they were so well armed and so effective, the 27th found themselves in advanced positions on the firing lines for extended periods. This brought the men to complaints like: "Damn old Spencer and all his inventive stuff; wish they were out here weeks at a time without relief."

The 27th Michigan, now composed of twelve companies, 864 strong, joined the Army of the Potomac on April 29, 1864, at Warrenton, Virginia, assigned to the First Brigade, Third Division, Ninth Corps. The regiment crossed the Rapidan River with the Ninth Corps on May 6 and was immediately engaged in a terrific struggle at the bloody Battle of the Wilderness, suffering 10 percent casualties.

The 27th had scarcely emerged from the Wilderness before it was engaged in another bloody encounter at Spotsylvania, where its losses were 27 killed, 148 wounded and 12 missing. During the month of May, the 27th was constantly marching and fighting, sustaining frightful losses, and on June 3, it fought the Battle of Bethesda Church, suffering 76 more casualties. From Cold Harbor, the 27th crossed the James River and on June 17 and 18 charged the enemy's works before Petersburg, meeting with severe loss from the fire of both musketry and artillery. During the months of June and July, the regiment was constantly under fire, and on July 30, it took part in the disastrous charge at the "Crater," when a mine was exploded immediately in its front. The 27th was in the advance in this charge and suffered severely from Confederate crossfire, again meeting with heavy loss. Sometime during the action at Petersburg, Sergeant Stephen Spitzley suffered a severe wound in his right leg.

During the Siege of Petersburg, the 27th held advanced positions and took part in the repeated attempts to break the enemy's line at Weldon Railroad, Peebles' Farm, Poplar Grove Church and South Side Railroad, while also helping to repel the Confederates when they charged Union lines. The regiment participated in the desperate charge to capture the key point Fort Mahone in the Rebel line and succeeded in placing its colors on the eastern wing, capturing three pieces of artillery and more than 150 prisoners.

When the Confederates finally evacuated Petersburg and Richmond, the 27th followed the retreating army until April 18, 1865, nine days after the formal surrender of General Lee at Appomattox.

On May 23, the battle-hardened 27th Michigan Infantry Regiment proudly marched in the Grand Review of the Army of the Potomac. At 9:00 a.m. on a bright sunny day, a signal gun fired a single shot, and Major General George Meade, the victor of Gettysburg, led an estimated eighty thousand men of the Army of the Potomac down the streets of Washington from Capitol Hill down Pennsylvania Avenue past crowds that numbered in the

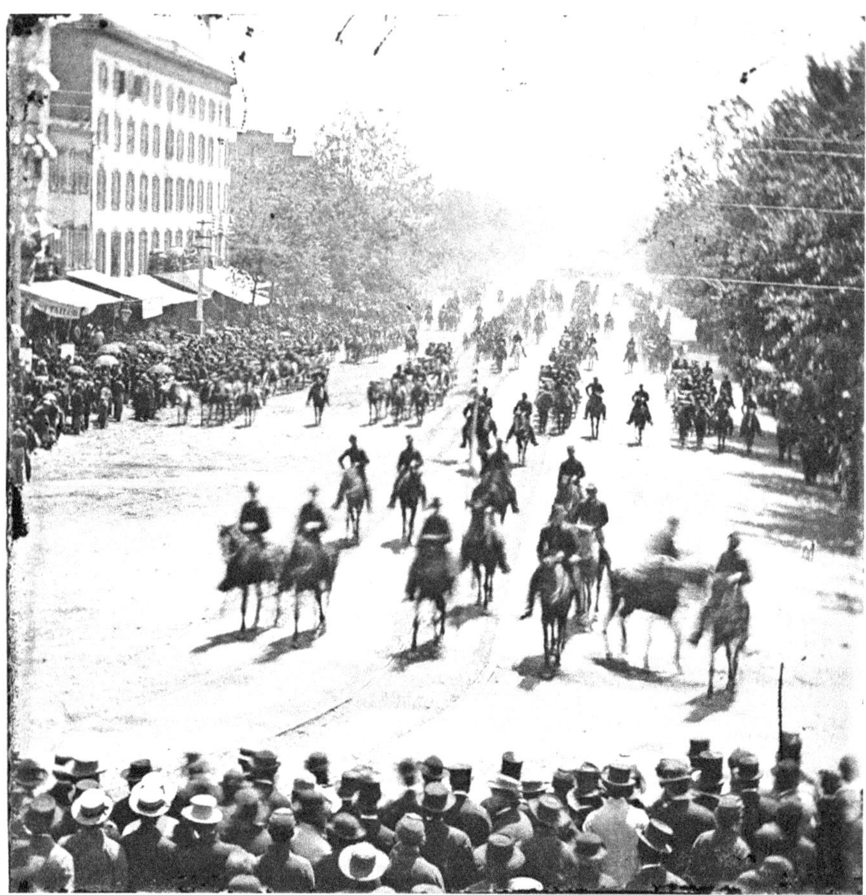

Grand Review of the Army of the Potomac, May 23, 1865, in Washington, D.C. *Library of Congress.*

thousands. The infantry marched with twelve men abreast across the street, followed by divisional and corps artillery, then an array of cavalry regiments that stretched for another seven miles. The mood was one of rejoicing and celebration, and the crowds and soldiers frequently engaged in singing patriotic songs as the procession of victorious soldiers snaked its way toward the reviewing stand in front of the White House, where President Andrew Johnson, General-in-Chief Ulysses S. Grant, senior military leaders, the cabinet and leading government officials awaited.

For three long years, Stephen Sptizley fought bravely for the Union. He suffered a severe wound in his right leg, and on May 1, 1865, he was promoted to full sergeant before being mustered out of service at Delaney House, Washington, D.C.

The 27th Michigan was one of the "Three Hundred Fighting Regiments" of the Union army, receiving special mention by the War Department and Congress in 1866 for regiments showing casualty lists of over 30 percent of total enrollment. The impact on the 27th Michigan Infantry through the course of the Civil War was staggering. Of its total enrollment of 1,897 men, the 27th Michigan suffered 1,202, or 63 percent killed, died of wounds or disease or missing in action.

With the end of the Civil War and his discharge, Stephen Spitzley returned to Michigan. Two years later, Stephen, his sister Elizabeth and her husband, Conrad Schultz, embarked a steamboat at St. Louis bound for Montana Territory. The small 140-foot steamer *Zephyr* arrived at the Marias River late in the season on September 7, 1867, unable to proceed on to the Fort Benton levee. There the boat discharged Stephen, the Schultz family and nine other passengers.[63]

Spitzley worked for the North West Fur Company from 1867 to 1869, until the dissolution of the company. He then moved on to Helena, where his sister Elizabeth and her husband had settled. Spitzley drove a stagecoach for Wells Fargo & Co. before taking charge in March 1869 of Wells Fargo's station at Birdtail Rock on Montana's Benton Road. In the fall of 1869, Wells Fargo sold its stage line to Salisbury and Gilmer.

In July 1876, Sergeant Sptizley received an invalid pension for wounds suffered while serving with the 27th Michigan Infantry. Spitzley lived for many more years, yet he never married, and news reports on several occasions emphasized his ailing health, likely from the toll taken by the war. For the next several decades, Spitzley seemed consumed by wanderlust and poor health as he moved around central Montana.

In the fall of 1880, Spitzley settled at Fort Maginnis, then under construction in central Montana near today's Lewistown. Two years later, in September 1880, as the Great Union Hotel in Fort Benton neared completion, Spitzley leased the new hotel and became its first proprietor.

When it opened on November 2, 1882, the Grand Union was widely regarded as the finest hotel between the Minnesota Twin Cities and the Pacific Coast. Completed at the height of the steamboat era on the Upper Missouri, the Grand Union welcomed weary travelers to spend a few nights in its luxury before they set out for Helena, Virginia City and points west. The architectural character of the Grand Union was special, with bricks carefully fitted into bold decorations. Its extensive corbelling, wrought-iron balconies and ornate chimneys were an impressive sight. Furnished with Victorian appointments, the dining room's silver service, white linen and Bavarian china served the rich and famous. An elegant ladies' parlor on the second floor, with a private stairway to the dining room, saved ladies from exposure to the rowdy crowd in the saloon and poker rooms. The ornate lobby desk and broad black walnut staircase highlighted the fine carpentry work throughout. No wonder that the opening ball for the Grand Union was the grandest affair of its kind ever witnessed in Benton, and most probably in the territory.

In February 1883, Michael C. Travers arrived in Fort Benton and joined Spitzley in management of the Grand Union. Seven months later, Spitzley's health was failing, and he retired from the business, succeeded by John Hunsburger. The firm of Hunsberger & Travers continued for several years.

From 1884, Steve Spitzley operated the Rock Creek stage station on the Benton Road between Dearborn Crossing and Wolf Creek. After a trip back to his home in Michigan in early 1886, Stephen Spitzley settled in the new town of Great Falls, then beginning to show signs of growth as James J. Hill's Manitoba railroad built westward. With Henry Ringwald in December 1886, Spitzley opened the Cascade Restaurant and hotel on First Avenue

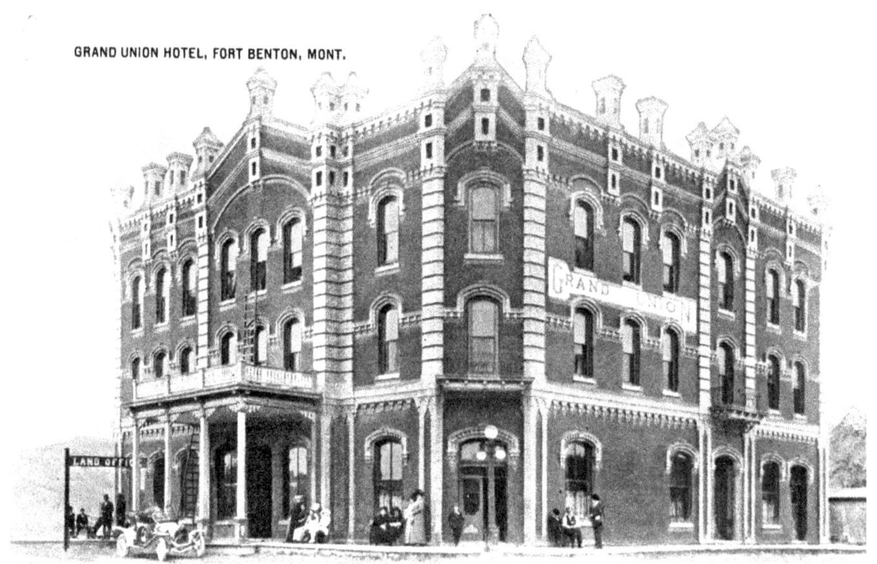

Built in 1882 with Victorian Renaissance architecture at the height of the steamboat era, the Grand Union, under management of Stephen Spitzley, welcomed weary travelers to spend a few nights in its luxury before they set out on the dusty roads leading from Fort Benton. *Author's collection.*

South between Third and Fourth Streets, featuring fine meals. In less than a year, the Cascade Restaurant failed financially, and Spitzley moved on to establish a halfway station on the new Montana Central rail line at Craig, between Helena and Great Falls.

In preparation for Memorial Day in Great Falls in 1889, Spitzley met with other veterans, members of Grand Army of the Republic (GAR) Sheridan Post No. 18. Later that year, wandering Spitzley located a ranch in the Bear's Paw Mountains in what the *Great Falls Tribune* called "the Detroit settlement, as there are so many old Detroit citizens bunched together on the head of Eagle creek."[64]

The old soldier was back in Great Falls in 1900, recorded in the census in the household of prominent Great Falls businessman H.O. Chowen and Mrs. Chowen, a niece of Spitzley. For the next two decades, he continued to board with the Chowens until 1923, when his health failed seriously. He returned to Michigan to make his home with relatives in Detroit, where he remained until January 1925, when he went to Chicago to visit a niece. Sergeant Stephen Spitzley, who saw as much combat action in the Civil War as any man, died in Chicago, Illinois, on March 9, 1925.

Chapter 10

When Myth Becomes a Reality

Milk River Pioneer William Bent

Confederate veteran William Bent fought with the 2nd Battalion Arkansas Mounted Infantry in the Civil War before finding peace and opportunity on the Upper Missouri River in Montana Territory. Settling with the Nakota Assiniboine Indians, Bill Bent became a key advisor on the Fort Belknap Reservation and a scout during the Nez Perce War. Legend poses the mystery of William Bent—was he, or was he not, the son of Colonel William Bent of Bent's Fort fame?

"When myth becomes reality" might well be the title of this saga of William Bent, Confederate soldier, Montana scout and pioneer rancher. His family legend portrays him as a son of the famed Colonel William Bent, founder of Bent's Fort. Unfortunately for this legend, Colonel Bent had no son named William.[65]

William Bent of Harlem, Montana, led a life worthy of legends even if he could not claim those of Colonel William Bent. Montana's William Bent was born on May 11, 1846, in St. Louis, Missouri, the son of William and Sarah Sullivan Bent. After attending private school in St. Louis, young William joined the Confederate army in the spring of 1863, enlisting in the 2nd Arkansas Battalion of Mounted Infantry.

On May 14, 1863, the 2nd Arkansas joined the Confederate troops of General Joseph E. Johnston engaged in the Battle of Jackson, Mississippi, as Major General Ulysses Grant moved to seize the city, cut Johnston's supply lines and disrupt Confederate troops from disrupting the ongoing Siege

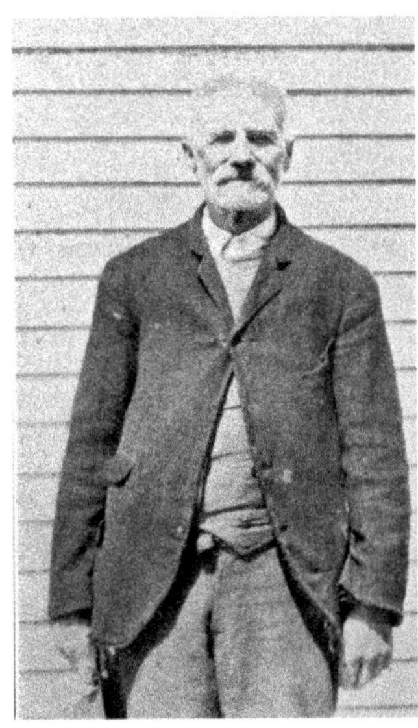

William Bent, Civil War and Nez Perce War veteran, in his later years. *From* In the Land of Chinook.

of Vicksburg. After Vicksburg's surrender to the Union on July 4, the 2nd Arkansas, with remnants of General Johnston's army, attempted once again to defend Jackson from Union attack. After a ten-day siege and strong Union probes, Johnston ordered withdrawal on July 16, ending any Confederate threat to Vicksburg by then under Union control.[66]

During the Battle of Chickamauga, Georgia, on September 19–20, 1863, the 2nd Arkansas served with General Braxton Bragg's Army of Tennessee. This bloody battle ended with the most significant Union defeat in the western theater during the Civil War and resulted in the second-highest number of casualties, next to Gettysburg. During this battle, Private William Bent was wounded severely and incapacitated for an extended period.

Bent returned to service in 1864 and remained with his battalion until the end of the war. The 2nd Arkansas participated in nine major engagements during the Atlanta Campaign from May to September 1864 as General Johnston's Army of Tennessee attempted to stem the invasion of northwestern Georgia and Atlanta by Major General William T. Sherman. The fall of Atlanta on September 2 set the stage for Sherman's March to the Sea from Atlanta to the Carolinas.

With the defeat of Confederate forces at Atlanta, the 2nd Arkansas and the Army of Tennessee, now under Lieutenant General John Bell Hood, participated in the Franklin-Nashville Campaign. In a series of five battles, Hood's army suffered repeated defeats, and on December 15–16, his depleted army was routed in the Battle of Nashville and retreated to Tupelo, Mississippi.

After the Battle of Nashville, the 2nd Arkansas of Reynolds's Brigade marched through a series of skirmishes to Tupelo, where they went into a brief winter camp on January 19, 1865. They departed Tupelo on January 30 and marched and traveled by rail to Selma, Alabama. From Selma, the battalion boarded a steamboat to proceed to Montgomery and then by rail to Columbus, Georgia. From there they marched to Mayfield, Georgia, and once more boarded trains to Augusta. They then marched to Newberry,

South Carolina, and on March 19 joined General Johnston's army to fight its last major engagement at the Battle of Bentonville, North Carolina, on March 19–21.

After suffering defeat at Bentonville, the 2nd Arkansas marched to Smithfield, North Carolina, where the depleted Arkansas brigade consolidated into a single understrength regiment, the 1st Arkansas Consolidated Mounted Rifles, on April 9, 1865. The 2nd Arkansas formed Companies C and D in the new regiment. The new 1st Arkansas Consolidated surrendered with the rest of General Johnston's Army of Tennessee at Greensboro, North Carolina, on April 26.

The men of the 1st Arkansas were paroled five days later at Jamestown, North Carolina, and offered free rail transportation to locations near their homes by the remnants of the southern railway companies. Most of the men, including presumably William Bent, traveled by rail. Adding to their misery, a large number of Arkansas men were killed or injured in a railroad accident at Flat Creek Bridge, Tennessee, on May 25, 1865.

William Bent's war was over, and after moving on to St. Louis, he considered going to Mexico with other Confederates to join Emperor Maximilian but instead drifted north. He moved on to Atchison, Kansas, and remained there a short while before proceeding westward into the Platte country. There, he fell in with a Spaniard called Sago, and the two wandered until at last they reached the wonders that became Yellowstone National Park and from there to Virginia City, Montana Territory, in June 1866. Spending only a few months there, Bill Bent moved on to Dry Gulch near booming Last Chance Gulch (Helena), and for a short time he worked as compositor on the first issues of Helena's first newspaper, the *Radiator*, printed on a hand press.[67]

In the spring of 1867, Bent joined the Montana Volunteer Militia being raised by acting governor Thomas Francis Meagher to respond to incidents on both the Bozeman Trail and the Benton to Helena Road. Bent's militia served in Helena but was soon disbanded. Many years later, after his death, William's widow was granted an Indian Wars pension for this militia service.

From Helena, Bent drifted into the Musselshell River country. During the summer of 1867, he rode for the Northern Overland Pony Express between Forts Abercrombie (near today's Fargo), on the Red River, and Helena. Bent rode with partner Henry Macdonald on the segment from Fort Hawley on the Missouri River to Diamond City in Confederate Gulch. Fort Hawley, a trading post of the North West Fur Company, located about twenty miles above the mouth of the Musselshell, was a mail station on the express circuit. The Pony Express started tri-weekly service beginning July 1, and Bent had several harrowing experiences with his companion Macdonald on that dangerous circuit. That Pony Express enterprise failed by March 30, 1868, after just nine months, and Fort Hawley closed shortly after because of incidents with native Indians.

In 1868, Bent came to Fort Benton and in August was hired out to help construct a new trading post, Fort Browning, for James Hubbell and Alpheux F. Hawley and an Indian agency, the Milk River Agency, at the "Great Bend" of the Milk River, about ninety miles upstream from the Missouri River, near today's Dodson.[68]

When work on the agency was completed, the men engaged were discharged. Bent joined William A. Hamilton and five other companions on a gold-prospecting expedition to the Little Rocky Mountains. They built a camp on Dry Beaver Creek at the east end of the mountains, where they found gold but not in paying quantities. Giving up prospecting as winter set in, they started wolf hunting and trapping for furs, with considerable success.

During 1869, Bent served as an Indian interpreter for the government along with Alexander Culbertson, the famed founder of Fort Benton. The following year, Bent worked at the Medicine Lodge trading post on the lower end of the Great Bend of the Milk River. Upon the arrival of trader James Stuart at Fort Browning on January 6, 1871, Bent began working for him. During the winter of 1871, Bent hunted buffalo and trapped on streams south of the Little Rockies and Bear's Paw Mountains.

In 1873, Bent moved to old Fort Belknap, on the south side of the Milk River (opposite today's Chinook), where he began a long career working for the Indian Service as an interpreter. That same year, he was married at the agency to Bettie (last name not known), a Nakota Assiniboine woman, and they had eight children—George, Louis, Mary, Lucy, Nellie, Emma, Ida and Florence. After the death of his first wife, Bent married another Assiniboine woman, Elizabeth "Lizzie" Canoe, on April 4, 1891, and they had six more children, including Elsie, Ruth and another Louis. The marriage license between William Bent and Lizzie Canoe confirmed that William, a white man, was the son of William Bent and Sarah Sullivan—not the mixed-race son of Colonel William Bent and one of his native Indian wives.[69]

In 1876, the Nez Perces sent a delegation with horses to trade and present as gifts to the Assiniboine. According to Bent, the Nez Perces stated that they expected to have trouble with the whites in the country where they lived in Idaho Territory. One year later, in late September 1877, the Nez Perces had moved from their traditional homeland, with the U.S. Army in pursuit, and were approaching the Missouri River with their clear destination the Province of Canada. In early October, with Brigadier General O.O. Howard and Colonel Nelson Miles in pursuit, Major Guido Ilges of the 7th Infantry Regiment, commanding the Fort Benton Military Post, sent couriers to Fort Belknap to direct Bill Bent to keep the Assiniboine from joining the fleeing Nez Perces. In 1917, Bent related his story to historian Al J. Noyes:

> *I at once called the Indians together in council and told them that the people who were here the summer before* [the Nez Perces] *with all the horses and presents were fighting the soldiers and that the soldiers were after them and coming this way and the best thing they could do would be not to have anything to do with them as the soldiers would punish all they found in arms.*[70]

Just an hour later, five Nez Perces arrived in the vicinity. The Assiniboine heeded Bent's advice, refused to offer assistance to the Nez Perces and remained in camp. Two days later, sounds of battle were heard in the distance in the direction of Snake Creek north of the Bear's Paw. To keep the Assiniboine in camp, Bent told them it would be better for him to go to scout the situation. Bill Bent related his actions:

> *So I started and kept going toward the sound and got south of the West Fork of Snake creek and it became so dark that all I could see was the flashes of the guns once in a while. I got up to where I could see the pickets in one place and laid down and waited till morning. As soon as it was light enough I went to one of the men on picket and explained who I was and he told me to go in. I could see the whole thing, the pits of the Indians, and the breastworks of the soldiers, and away back were the tents. I went over and reported to* [Colonel] *Miles. . . .*
>
> *In my report I told him what the Assiniboine were doing and the orders I had from the War Department through* [Major Ilges]. *He told me to go back and keep them in hand and see that they did not get in the fight. . . .*
>
> *After going back and telling the Assiniboine what Miles had said I returned to the battlefield. I think it was the fourth day of the fight that Miles, Sweeny, Arthur Chapman, an interpreter from Idaho, Captain John, a Nez Perce, and myself went down to have a talk with the Indians. John was sent down into the pit to talk with the Nez Perces while we laid down peeping over a hill. He rode a pinto horse with a hospital sheet tied to a pole. He would stop and wave the flag and halloo at them and at last he was allowed to approach near enough to carry on a conversation. You could*

see them throwing out the dirt, as they were occupying all their spare time fortifying. After a little some of the Indians came out and John went out of sight for a few minutes and then appeared again with six or seven of them. They all had their guns with them, and Miles said to Chapman: "You tell those fellows not to use any treachery because there are hundreds of men looking through their sights ready to shoot." They shook their heads and came on. Of course we did not know who they were.

We started towards Miles' tent but a lot of officers began to crowd around, the Indians stopped and Miles said to Arthur: "What's the matter with them?" Chapman replied that they did not like the officers to be so handy so Miles ordered them back as they were confusing the Indians.

We all went over to Miles' tent and he got some camp stools for the Indians, but not enough as some had to sit on the ground. They sat there a while and then he said that they had better have a smoke but for the Indians to furnish the tobacco as then they would be sure it was all right.

After a while Miles began to talk. He said that it pained him to do what he was doing but it was his duty. They did not make any reply. Captain Baird and another officer were taking down everything that was being said in writing. When Miles was talking he was addressing a very fine tall Indian who was sitting on a stool not far away. When Chapman was doing his interpreting he was looking and talking to an Indian sitting on the ground. The Indian to whom Miles was talking would hardly say anything but the Indian sitting on the ground would smile. A little while after I noticed an old gray-haired officer come in and stand way back, he only had one arm and the coat sleeve was pinned across his breast. As soon as the Indians saw him they seemed to be awful angry, their eyes blazed. This was [Brigadier General Oliver O.] *Howard.*

Miles once more addressed the Indian sitting on the stool and asked him if he hadn't had enough of this by now. But the Indian did not reply. Miles turned to Chapman and looked for an answer. Chapman had noticed that Miles had addressed all his talk to the particular Indian who would not reply and as Miles looked at him he said (pointing to the one on the ground). "Why don't you ask him?" Miles said: "Who is he?" "That's the leader, Chief Joseph."

Miles was surprised but he got up and handed his stool to the Chief and from that time all his remarks were made to the proper person. Joseph said that White Bird did not want to surrender and that he would take one more night so as to give him a chance to think it over. During that night White Bird escaped with his two wives and went over the line.

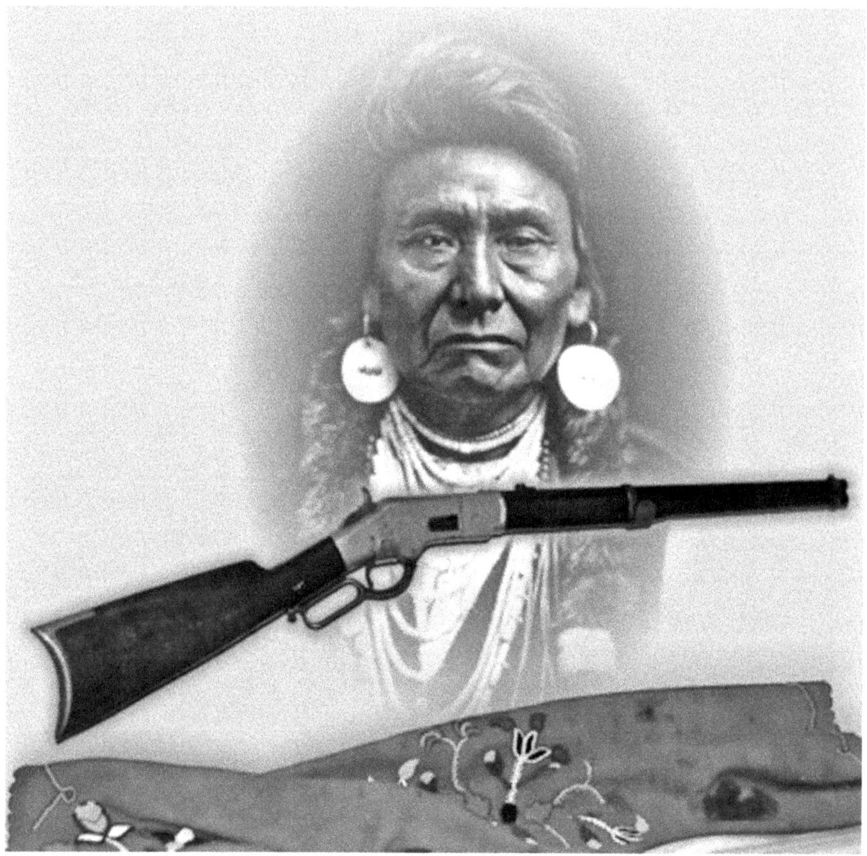

Chief Joseph symbolically surrendered this Winchester 44 Henry Model 1866 carbine to Colonel Nelson Miles, ending the flight of the Nez Perces in 1877. This rifle, belonging to the River & Plains Society, is displayed in the Upper Missouri Breaks National Monument Interpretive Center in Fort Benton. *Photo by Sharalee Smith.*

The next day, the last day of the fight, Miles said [to Bill Bent]*: "I want you to go down to the river and tell the Indians down there not to kill any more Nez Perces." The Assinniboine killed about seven Nez Perces.*

The day that Joseph surrendered he said he thought the [Missouri] *river was the line and that the Indians would be friendly but as they were enemies he would give up. He handed his gun, muzzle first, to Howard but Howard said: "No, that man, pointing to Miles, is the one who won it." He then turned and handed his gun, butt first, to Miles. I have always thought that if Howard had reached for that gun he would have been shot.*[71]

When Bent left the battlefield to go to the reservation to tell the Assiniboine what Miles had said, he was captured by some of the escaping Nez Perces. His captors claimed that Bent was a soldier since he had been on the battlefield and was riding a government horse. Bent replied, "I am not a soldier but belonged on the river and that my children were the offspring of an Indian mother." Eventually, Bent convinced his captors that he was from the Assiniboine camp, and he was released.

William Bent played a key role in counseling and convincing the Assiniboine Indians not to aid the Nez Perces. The failure of the Nez Perces to win over Indian allies to their cause as they moved through Montana Territory was a devastating blow. The actions of roving bands of Assiniboine to seek out and kill escaping Nez Perces must have been a great disappointment to Chief Joseph. The role of the Assiniboine aiding the U.S. Army was rewarded later in 1879 when a new military post on Beaver Creek near today's Havre was given the name Fort Assinniboine.

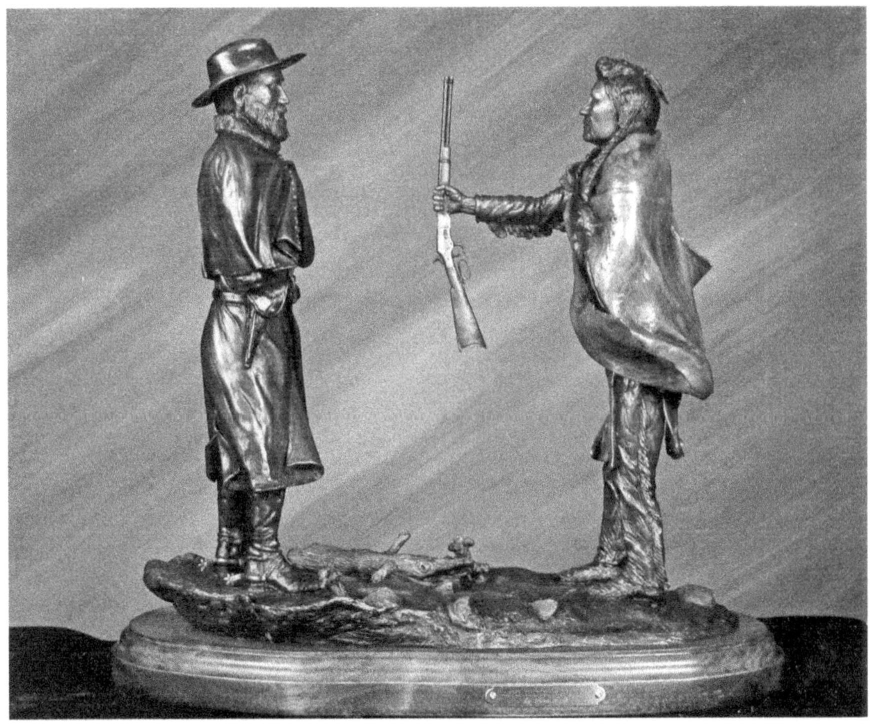

A bronze of the Nez Perce surrender by Don Beck. *Overholser Historical Research Center.*

Bill Bent continued work at Fort Belknap as interpreter until 1890, under successive Indian agents Alonzo S. Reed, C.S. Clark, W. Bird, Captain D.W. Buck, William H. Fanton, Captain Williams, Major W.L. Lincoln, Major Edwin C. Fields, Major Andrew O. Simmons and Lieutenant Macanny. When Fields was named to relieve Major Lincoln, the *Helena Weekly Herald* declared, "In the great majority of cases our Indian Agencies are among the 'fat takes' awarded to ex-confederates throughout the Northwest."[72]

As interpreter and an intermarried ally of the Assiniboine, Bent played an important role in commissions negotiating relinquishment of Assiniboine lands. His influence, together with that of Major W.L. Lincoln, was a factor in negotiations that gained the right of way for construction of the St. Paul, Minneapolis and Manitoba (later Great Northern) Railroad through the Milk River Valley. From 1890 to 1893, Bent worked as interpreter at the new Fort Belknap agency, located southeast of today's Harlem. The following year, he served as government farmer at the agency and thereafter as government butcher for two years.

In the fall of 1896, Bent located a four-hundred-acre cattle and horse ranch at the mouth of Snake Creek, five miles southwest of Harlem. Unlike most former Confederates who came to Montana, William Bent became an active member of the Republican Party.

William Bent lived the rest of his days on his ranch, working, reading and swapping old-time tales with visitors like artist Charles M. Russell. On November 15, 1919, William Bent died suddenly at his home of heart failure. The old Confederate soldier and Montana pioneer was interred on his ranch beside the graves of two of his daughters.

Chapter 11

From Drummer Boy to Ace Photographer

Dan Dutro on the Upper Missouri

Daniel V. Dutro was too young to go to war when the Civil War started, but he joined as a drummer boy in 1865. Although he served but one year, he suffered the effects for the rest of his life. His health caused him to turn from mining in Montana Territory to photography. As a result, Dan Dutro gained fame as one of Montana's greatest photographers.

Born on the Miami River at Taylorsville, Highland County, Ohio, on September 17, 1848, Dan Dutro moved with his parents to Bloomington, Illinois, when a child and lived there until he was fifteen years old. His father died just before the outbreak of the Civil War, and young Dan offered his services to the Union, but his widowed mother would not give her consent for his enlistment.[73]

During the war, the Dutro family moved to Pleasant Hill, Missouri, and at age sixteen, Dan Dutro, "animated with a flame of patriotism," determined to become a soldier despite his mother's continued opposition. He went to Springfield, Illinois, to enlist on January 25, 1865, in Company B, 150th Illinois Infantry. He was made drummer boy of his company. After serving through the end of the war and beyond, he was stricken with pneumonia, thought to be fatal, and sent home in a boxcar to die. Surprising all, he recovered so quickly that he was able to rejoin his regiment in Missouri.[74]

The 150th Illinois was assigned to Reconstruction duty as a sort of vigilance committee to wage war against the activities of Confederate guerrillas in Missouri in the postwar years. These bandits included remnants of the Bill

Anderson and Quantrill raiders, with men like Jesse and Frank James turning from war to crime. In company with his fellow soldiers, Dan Dutro helped break up a coterie of outlaws, personally capturing one of the gang, and rendered effective service in pacifying war-torn Missouri. He was mustered out on January 16, 1866, at Atlanta, Georgia.[75]

Two years later, in 1868, Dan Dutro migrated to Montana Territory and began his long residence there. He made the long trip by the steamboat *Andrew Ackley*, leaving St. Louis, Missouri, on April 14 and arriving at Fort Benton on June 17. He then continued on to Helena to find work. His first employment was as a hod carrier. At that time, he was so slender that it seemed impossible that he could carry the heavy load, and his fellow workmen watched him to see that no harm came to him as he tried to make good. As they expected, his strength proved unequal to the task, and they caught him as he fell from the ladder. The contractor, appreciating the grit of the lad, changed his job to that of stonecutting.[76]

By the time he had learned his new trade, he became expert in mineralogy, and he added knowledge of mechanics and stone decorating to his other tradecraft. Once more he overworked and his health broke down, confining him to his bed for two years. When he was able to get out and about, he realized that he must keep out of doors, so he began prospecting in the Neihart district of the Little Belt Mountains. As one of the earliest prospectors in that silver-rich area, Dutro discovered the Benton group of silver mines and a number of others that developed into the best silver producers in the region.

Again his health broke down, and he was forced to seek work at lower elevations. Retaining partial interest in the mines, he moved in 1881 to Fort Benton, where he returned to stonecutting. During this building boom, he provided stone for foundations of several new brick buildings in Fort Benton. By 1883, his health forced him to give that up, and he turned to photography.

In November 1883, Dutro bought the photographic studio and stock of S. Duffin and developed into an artist and practical photographer, gaining fame during the final years of the steamboat trade as Fort Benton boomed and construction flourished before the arrival of the railroads. Dutro's photographic record of the people, places and buildings of Fort Benton and central Montana is remarkable. He photographed the Blackfeet, Cree and Gros Ventre at a time when their lives were evolving after the end of the bison. He photographed a wide span of Fort Benton history, the river, the deteriorating trading post, the historic buildings, the street scenes and the advances in transportation as steamboats were replaced by railroads.

He captured many images of the countryside, the ranches and mines. He took many studio portraits of men, women and children and, importantly, the ethnic Chinese. After the defeat of the Metis and Louis Riel on the Red River in 1885, Dan Dutro photographed Riel's military commander, Gabriel Dumont, and others of the Metis and Cree communities in exile from Canada. He captured important aspects of the history of the Missouri River, the changes in transportation and the evolution of open-range ranching. Dan Dutro's photographs are exceptionally important historically and prized by many families in the area.

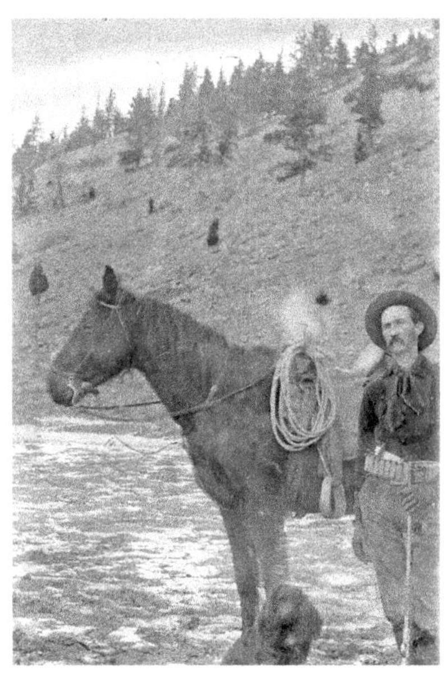

Dan Dutro prospecting and mining in the mountains near Helena, Montana. *Overholser Historical Research Center.*

Some of Dutro's photographic techniques show both innovation and humor. When he photographed the Fort Benton School at recess one day in 1885, he had the children form in front of the building. After this session, he pronounced, "It is as hard to keep them quiet as a lot of calves in a corral." He devised a "novel invention for catching the happiest expression possible, and for taking the pictures of children it cannot be beaten. It is called the 'compressed air automatic countenance catcher.'" The mind wonders what that was all about![77]

Among the many Dutro photographs in the Overholser Historical Research Center collection are two "hanging" photos taken of convicted murderers before their executions. The hangings were public events, and the photos posed the doomed men with various law enforcement and legal community officials.

Dutro's photographic record of the Fort Benton adobe trading post during the 1880s and '90s provides a valuable record of this decaying historic landmark and proved vital in the recent reconstruction of Old Fort Benton. In May 1886, in the second year of the fledgling Great Falls Townsite, Dutro visited to take photos of the falls of the Missouri and the new town. The next year, he was back for more as the growth of "the future great" began to accelerate. When the St. Paul, Minneapolis and Manitoba Railroad arrived at Fort Benton, Dutro was there to photograph the driving of the silver spike. He visited the Dan Blevins ranch on Highwood Creek to take photos of his well-known racehorses. Holiday treats during this period featured collections of Dutro's famed photographic sketches of northern Montana.

In 1894, the Chinese community of Fort Benton and other towns in the area were required to comply with provisions of a new law, and Dutro was there to photograph them. Twenty-seven Chinese were photographed in Fort Benton, a dozen at Fort Assinniboine and twenty at Havre. The next year, Dutro was back in Havre to photograph the "Wildest West" show aggregation. While there, he also captured Cree Indians just ready to commence their famous sun dance.

By the mid-1890s, Dutro's reputation as an exceptional photographer attracted the interest of a young man who was destined to greatness. In early 1896, Roland Reed came to Fort Benton to apprentice at the Dutro Studio. Dutro and Reed formed a partnership with photographic studios in Fort Benton and Havre in late 1896.[78] In 1897, Reed went north to photograph the Alaska gold rush. He then rose to national prominence during a long career photographing Native Americans, especially the Blackfeet Indians. Many of his photographs were published in association with the Great Northern Railroad.

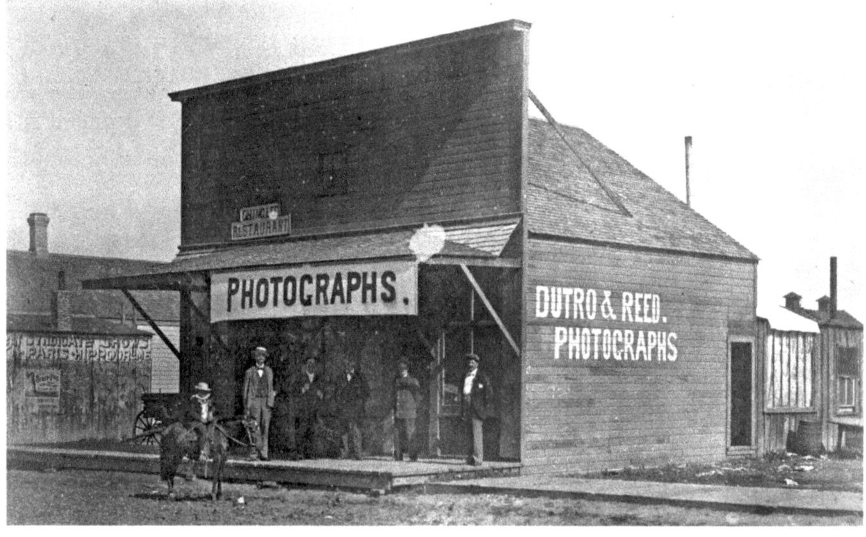

Dan Dutro & Roland Reed's Photographic Studio in Fort Benton about 1896. This studio was located on the site of today's Chouteau County Free Public Library. *Overholser Historical Research Center.*

In one of Fort Benton's greatest preservation disasters, the priceless collection of Dan Dutro's glass plate negatives, stored for many years in the Benton Record building, were destroyed when the third story of the Record building was razed in August 1929 to develop Fraternity Hall.

During his Helena years, Daniel Dutro married Caroline McBurney, a daughter of George McBurney, who came from Farmington, New York, where Mrs. Dutro was born on October 17, 1849. The 1880 census recorded the Dutro family living in Helena with four children: Alice, age eight; Flora, age five; George, age four; and David, age two.

While living in Fort Benton, Dutro was active in the community. In January 1882, Dutro, as a "patron" of the Fort Benton Public Schools, publicly supported the school board in its stand to allow African American children to attend the Benton schools when a faction tried to impose segregation. Dutro served as president of the Fort Benton Library Association and was a founding member of G.K. Warren Post No. 20, GAR, in Fort Benton.

Around 1900, Dutro's father-in-law, George McBurney, builder of the McBurney House, the first hotel in Deer Lodge County, lost his eyesight, and Dan Dutro ended his photographic career to devote himself to the care of his father-in-law until his death. Dutro then resumed mining in the Helena area and operated a mine at the mouth of Nelson Gulch, where he built a small stamp mill and foundry. Later, he discovered the Arrow Head mine of rich ore. Until his death, Dutro continued to operate his mill and take an active interest in mining affairs. Considering the state of his health, Dan Dutro was a remarkable man, and his achievements stand out as a practical demonstration of what a man can accomplish if he only possesses sufficient ambition, no matter what his physical disabilities may be.

Civil War veteran drummer boy Daniel D. Dutro died on May 8, 1918, at Logan, a railroad town in Gallatin County near Three Forks. He rests today in Forestvale Cemetery, Helena.

Chapter 12

From Army Scout to Teddy's Tennis Cabinet

Boldly Strode "Yellowstone" Kelly

Today, Major Luther Sage "Yellowstone" Kelly overlooks the city of Billings from his Rimrocks grave. During his lifetime, Kelly marched boldly through life, a teenage Civil War soldier, Montana Indian Wars scout, Alaskan expedition guide, Philippines Insurrection war hero and valued member of President Teddy Roosevelt's "tennis cabinet." Kelly left his mark from the plains and valleys of Montana to the jungles of the Philippines and the deserts of Arizona.

On March 28, 1865, at just fifteen years of age, Luther Kelly, born in July 1849 in Geneva, central New York, enlisted in Company G of the 10th U.S. Infantry Regiment. In the first of many legends, young Kelly claimed he placed a note in his shoe with the number "eighteen" written on it so that he could honestly swear that he was "over eighteen." As a soldier in the regular army, Private Kelly's term of service was three years.[79]

With the Civil War in its final months, the 10th Infantry was assigned to Richmond and then marched on to Washington, D.C., where Private Kelly served as a guard during the great victory Grand Review down Pennsylvania Avenue. In November 1865, the 10th Infantry deployed to Fort Snelling, Minnesota, for the winter, relieving a volunteer regiment. The following spring, Private Kelly's company moved on to forts in the Dakotas, where he became a company hunter providing fresh game. Kelly's enlistment ended in April 1868, and he was discharged at Fort Ransom, Dakota Territory.

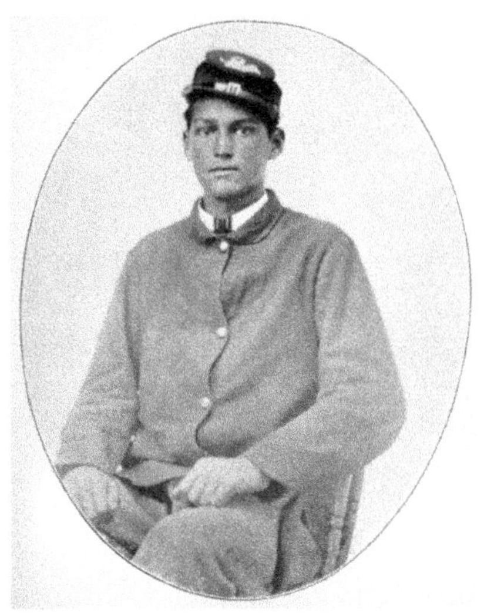

Private Luther Kelly of Company G, U.S. 10th Infantry. *Overholser Historical Research Center.*

Over the next decade, Kelly embarked on a series of adventures and established himself as one of the greatest hunters, trappers and Indian scouts in the American West. Exploring the vast reaches of the Upper Missouri and Yellowstone Rivers, he served as dispatch rider and scout. He gained fame under senior officers Major George A. Forsyth on his Yellowstone River expedition and Colonel Nelson A. Miles during the Sioux, Cheyenne and Nez Perce campaigns.

While these achievements would take many years and harrowing adventures, a sampling of Luther Kelly's actions reveal why he gained fame. Once Kelly was honorably discharged from the army in the spring of 1868, he secured a pony and rode down the Red River to Fort Garry, the Hudson Bay Company post in Manitoba in the new Dominion of Canada. On his return trip, as he started across country for the Missouri River, Kelly fell in with a party of Metis on a buffalo hunt. It was on this trip that he found the "real frontier" opening up to him in firsthand experiences.

Crossing the Assiniboine River with his Metis companions, Kelly later wrote:

> *With my blue coat and red sash, I felt more like a free lance of the prairie, especially while with those . . . buffalo hunters, who made the prairie their home a good part of the year. The* [Red River] *carts were made wholly of wood, and not a single nail or belt entered into their construction. The rims of the high wheels were covered with strips of raw bull's hide, laced on while green, making very effective tires, hard and durable as iron, and so light that the carts would float while the ponies swam across the streams.*[80]

While traveling south and west across the international boundary line into Dakota Territory, Kelly experienced some of the memorable events of his early career in the West. One adventure was an encounter with Sitting Bull, then a prominent medicine man among the Sioux. Kelly wrote of his meeting with Sitting Bull:

> *It was on Mouse river that I first came in contact with Sitting Bull and his war party. As we were going into camp one day a party of horsemen suddenly came into view, and approaching rapidly, dismounted and went through our party shaking hands right and left, using both hands in the process, which struck me as singular in an Indian.*
>
> *In our party were a man and woman of the Santee Sioux. Of course they told Sitting Bull that I was an American and the warriors gathered around me where I stood with my rifle in hand. The old man with whom I messed had assured me that though we might meet hostile Indians I would come to no harm as long as I stayed with the* [Metis] *party, so I looked them calmly in the eye while they thronged around me, regarding me with baleful eyes, hate and vindictiveness pervading every feature of their villainous faces. Without a word they abruptly left me, and mounting their horses, soon passed out of sight.*
>
> *Sitting Bull appeared to be about thirty years of age. He had a round, pleasant face, and wore a headscarf of dirty white cloth, while most of his followers affected black headgear. I suspected that the stiff leather cases tied to some of the saddles contained war bonnets, as I saw feathers sticking out of the pouches. They assume their war regalia when on the warpath, though they usually strip to the breechclout when going into action. They were armed with rifles and trade shotguns in addition to the usual bow and quiver of arrows. They reported killing a white man a short time before near the mouth of the Yellowstone.*[81]

Spending many weeks in company with the Metis, Kelly helped them on their hunts, ever alert to gain knowledge of the ways of these plains people. Finally, he left the Metis and joined Mandan and Arikara Indians, with whom he traveled to Fort Berthold, then the Indian agency for those tribes as well as the Gros Ventres.

Remaining at Fort Berthold for only a short period, Kelly moved westward alone into the heart of Sioux Indian country toward Fort Buford. Kelly was welcomed at the military post located opposite the confluence of the Yellowstone with the Missouri River by the corps of trappers, traders, troopers and other residents. He found the post trader unwilling to believe his age of seventeen since he appeared more like fourteen.

At the time Kelly arrived in the area, the Sioux Nation was celebrating its success in driving whites from the territory adjacent to Fort Phil Kearney, Wyoming Territory. The country around Fort Buford was crowded with Sioux who were conducting active guerrilla warfare on trappers and traders

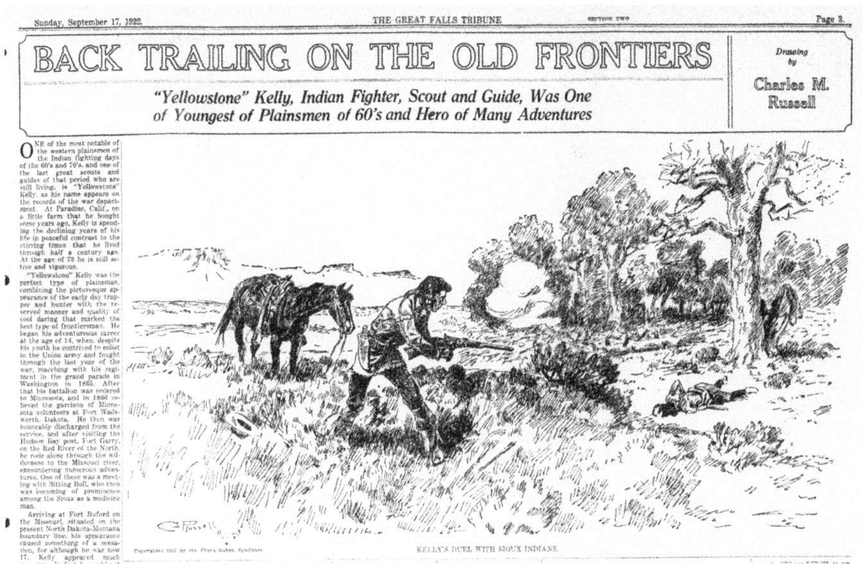

Sunday, September 17, 1922. THE GREAT FALLS TRIBUNE SECTION TWO Page 3.

BACK TRAILING ON THE OLD FRONTIERS

Drawing by Charles M. Russell

"Yellowstone" Kelly, Indian Fighter, Scout and Guide, Was One of Youngest of Plainsmen of 60's and Hero of Many Adventures

ONE of the most notable of the western plainsmen of the Indian fighting days of the 60's and 70's, and one of the last great scouts and guides of that period who are still living, is "Yellowstone" Kelly, as his name appears on the records of the war department. At Paradise, Calif., on a little farm that he bought some years ago, Kelly is spending the declining years of his life in peaceful contrast to the stirring times that he lived through half a century ago. At the age of 73 he is still active and vigorous.

"Yellowstone" Kelly was the perfect type of plainsman, combining the picturesque appearance of the early day trapper and hunter with the reserved manner and quality of cool daring that marked the best type of frontiersman. He began his adventureous career at the age of 14, when, despite his youth he contrived to enlist in the Union army and fought through the last year of the war, marching with his regiment in the grand parade in Washington in 1865. After that his battalion was ordered to Minnesota, and in 1866 relieved the garrison of Minnesota volunteers at Fort Wadsworth, Dakota. He then was honorably discharged from the service, and after visiting the Hudson Bay post, Fort Garry, on the Red River of the North, he rode alone through the wilderness to the Missouri river, encountering numerous adventures. One of these was a meeting with Sitting Bull, who then was becoming of prominence among the Sioux as a medicine man.

Arriving at Fort Buford on the Missouri, situated on the present North Dakota-Montana boundary line, his appearance caused something of a sensation, for although he was now 17, Kelly appeared much

KELLY'S DUEL WITH SIOUX INDIANS.

Charles M. Russell's sketch of *Kelly's Duel with Sioux Indians*. *Great Falls Tribune*, September 17, 1922.

along the Missouri River. The situation had become so grave that the trail from Fort Buford to Fort Stevenson, the next army post downriver, required a cavalry escort for the mail carriers.

Shortly after Kelly's arrival, incoming mail riders were overdue and assumed lost. Important mail at Fort Buford had to go out despite the fact that no cavalry escort could be spared. Despite his youth, Kelly stepped forward, offering to carry the mail alone. His offer was ridiculed and rejected. Undaunted, Kelly announced he was leaving regardless, so the Buford commander relented and provided a pony, and Kelly started out with a mail sack at dusk on a winter's evening.

Crossing the Missouri River on the ice, Kelly reached a camp of friendly Mandans at midnight. Moments later, he rode on, and in two days he dismounted at the gate of Durfee & Peck's trading post, two hundred miles below Fort Buford. The next evening, he was back in the saddle again, and by the following morning, he was inside the stockade at Fort Stevenson, where he delivered the mail and dispatches to Colonel Philip Regis de Trobriand. Just two hours later, Kelly started out on his return to Buford. Fifty miles above Fort Berthold, Kelly camped with the famous Arikara chief Bloody Knife, who welcomed the young mail rider. Farther along the trail, Kelly came face to face with two mounted Sioux warriors. In Kelly's own words:

On seeing me they at once dismounted and apparently sat down beside a large cottonwood tree that stood near the trail. This did not strike me as unusual, as Indians often get down to smoke and chat when meeting friends on the road. Nevertheless, I drew my gun out of its case and checked the speed of my horse. When I had approached within about twenty or thirty yards they suddenly rose and fired at me, one with a shotgun and the other armed with a bow and arrow.

At the same instant I dropped from my nag and fired quickly at the Indian who was running to the brush for cover. He never got a chance to empty the remaining barrel of his gun, for as he ran I fired at him without taking sight as far as I know, and he dropped. I had no idea that I had hit him, for it was a common ruse for an Indian to drop at the shot, and the brush concealed him. The uncertainty that he might pop up at any moment in my rear was a very disturbing factor during my engagement with his companion.

At the outset when the Indian fired at me my horse plunged, but I was already on the ground. I felt that he was hit, and later perceived that he had joined the other two horses. Now ensued a duel with the remaining Indian, who had quickly taken station behind the big cottonwood tree. I do not mind confessing that this duel had little charm for me. My opponent did not appear to have a gun, but from his vantage point behind the tree he would shoot an arrow at me whenever the opportunity presented itself. I had the bluff behind me, while for a background the Indian had the forest. Neither of us could retreat without presenting a mark for the other to shoot at, but I kept backing away step by step.

I think it must have been while I was dismounting that an arrow was sped which grazed the skin above my right knee, for it occasioned but a slight, dull pain, which at first I scarcely noticed. The warrior had a fancy for exhausting my ammunition, for he would stick out his robe in the most enticing manner on both sides of the tree, and the moment my bullet shivered the bark, like a flash he would discharge an arrow. But his every action, which I closely watched, gave me the cue as to the proper moment or movement to dodge the arrow so that presently, as I backed away, my course led me to where arrows were sticking in the ground on each side of my trail. This was kept up for some time.

Once as I held the carbine poised ready to take aim, he watched me out of his snake-like eyes, and I had a good look at his malignant, treacherous face. He had a piece of wolf skin wrapped around his head and his body was hidden beneath his fine silky robe. Whenever I took aim he retired within himself, as it were, behind the tree. I was cool enough, my chief anxiety being in regard to the situation of the other Indian, who had disappeared at the shot; also the possibility that these might be the advance of a war party.

"Who are you?" I demanded once during an interval.

"Ogallala me," he replied, but to further questioning he made no answer.

I fell to studying the movements of his robe as he stuck it out to attract my fire and finally I managed to break his arrow arm by a well directed shot. He rushed toward me in fury and despair, attempting, meanwhile, to place an arrow in the string of his bow, but I dropped him in his tracks. During the encounter my horse had joined the Indian ponies, and the three animals were working around the hill out of sight. In the hope of detaining my mount, I fired at one of the Indian ponies before they were lost to sight. I was not disturbed at the thought of being set afoot so much, for I was young and lusty, and could make nearly as good time on foot as I could mounted, but the horse belonged to the government and I was accountable for him.

The Indian lay sprawled at my feet, dead. I surveyed the situation and listened for sounds, for I was obsessed with the fear that there was a war party close by. I knew that not far up the river was a camp of friendly Indians with whom I had stayed on my way down. I longed for company. At last I turned and made for the stockade camp of [an old hunter] *Red Mike as fast as I could travel, looking back every moment expecting to see a bunch of mounted Indians in pursuit.*[82]

On reaching Red Mike's stockade, Kelly cared for his wounded knee and prepared to continue his ride. With the old man, Kelly returned to the scene of his fight with the Sioux. Kelly rode on to Fort Buford, accomplishing the remainder of the journey without further incident, finding upon his arrival that the news of his combat had preceded him carried by Indian runners. His fame was established, as he had single-handedly killed two Sioux warriors, and his standing at Fort Buford had changed dramatically. The Indians around the post named Kelly the "Little-Man-With-a Strong-Heart."

Kelly's restless spirit took him into new territory, and he moved on to the wilds of the Yellowstone River Valley. Here he spent many months hunting and trapping and becoming familiar with every mile of the valley. He then moved on to the Missouri River.

In 1873, Major George A. "Sandy" Forsyth, an aide to General Philip Sheridan, was ordered to take military command of the Missouri River steamboat *Key West* and explore the Yellowstone River as far as the mouth of the Powder River. Up to that time, no steamboat had ever ascended the

Yellowstone to that point, and the main objective of the expedition was to determine whether the river was navigable that far.

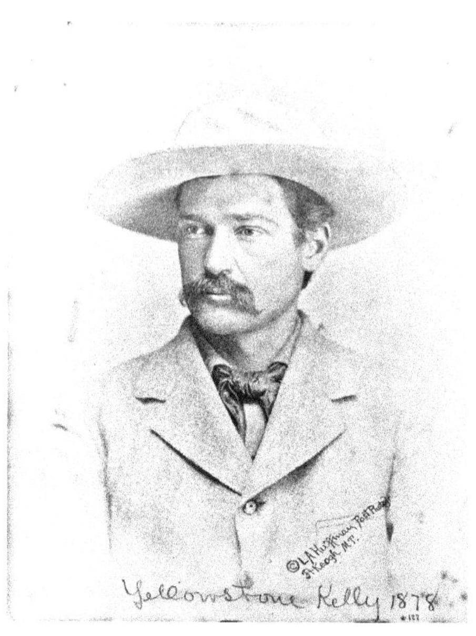

Yellowstone Kelly, legendary government scout. *Author's collection.*

Major Forsyth prepared for his expedition, but he could find no guide competent to lead through this uncharted country. Captain Grant Marsh, the master and pilot of the *Key West*, said that he knew just one man who was thoroughly familiar with the Yellowstone valley, and that was Yellowstone Kelly. The captain advised that they would find Kelly shortly on one of the river bottoms of the Missouri River above Fort Buford where he was known to be trapping and cutting wood. The following day, his log cabin was sighted. As the *Key West* tied up, Captain Marsh and Major Forsyth went ashore to talk with Kelly.

Captain Marsh later described their meeting with Yellowstone Kelly, who was dressed in a suit of fringed buckskin, with his feet encased in beaded moccasins. His face, darkly tanned by the sun and weather, was smooth-shaven except for a slender moustache. His features were lean and hard, with the muscular gauntness of a hunting animal that carries not an ounce of extra flesh. A mass of thick hair, straight and black, was swept back from his forehead and hanging below his shoulders. Across his arm he carried a long, breech-loading Springfield rifle, on the butt of which was carved the name he had bestowed upon this trusty guardian of his lonely life: "Old Sweetness." The rifle's barrel from muzzle to stock was covered with the skin of a great bull snake shrunk on so tightly that it resembled varnishing. This was the appearance that impressed Major Forsyth, and this was the guide he chose to pilot the expedition. This, too, was the man who became a keen friend of the military leader throughout the years that followed.[83]

Kelly's services that summer proved invaluable to Major Forsyth, who admitted frankly that the important work of mapping the region for military purposes could not have been accomplished had it not been for the knowledge of his guide concerning the Yellowstone basin.

Kelly had many other exciting adventures that were passed from mouth to mouth along the borderland, and far and wide he was known by the name of "Yellowstone" Kelly. In 1877, Colonel Nelson Miles chose Kelly as scout during his campaigns in southeastern Montana and early that year during the Wolf Mountain Campaign. The knowledge Kelly was able to provide to army leaders in the 1870s proved of great value during the campaigns against the Sioux. As a scout, he served successively General Alfred Terry, Lieutenant Colonel George A. Custer and Colonel Nelson Miles.

Over the decades, Kelly roamed widely through the West, and in 1898, he joined Captain Edmund Forbes Glenn as guide on an Alaskan expedition. With the outbreak of the Spanish-American War, Kelly accepted a commission as captain in the 7th Volunteer "Immunes" Infantry. The following year, he joined Company A of the 40th Volunteers for duty in the Philippines. He led troops in combat in southern Luzon and commanded a military post in Mindanao before leaving the army to serve as treasurer for a large Philippine province. In Surigao in 1903, he conducted a heroic defense of the town against insurgents, saving teachers and many civilian lives.

Returning from the Philippines, Kelly's heroism was recognized when he received orders from the Interior Department to proceed in late 1903 to the troubled San Carlos Indian Agency, in southwestern Arizona, to assume charge of the sprawling agency for the Apache Indians. San Carlos had a bad reputation and was known as "God's 40 acres of hell"; many felt that "the heat was terrible. The insects were terrible. The water was terrible."

As he neared the end of his term of office in 1909, President Theodore Roosevelt convened his famous "tennis cabinet" for a farewell luncheon at the White House. Among the thirty-one members who had been closely associated with him were advisors and companions such as Deadwood sheriff Captain Seth Bullock, Chief of the Forest Service Gifford Pinchot and Captain Luther S. Kelly. Teddy Roosevelt had first met Yellowstone Kelly on the Little Missouri in his years of roughing it in the West.

As the grand affair of food, spirits and conviviality drew to a close, the president addressed his friends with brief remarks:

> *Gentlemen, you are here nominally as members . . . of the "tennis cabinet"—that is, as men with whom at tennis or hunting, or riding, or walking, or boxing, I have played, with whom I have been on the roundup, or in the mountains, or on the ranch country. But really, as you know, you are not here for that reason at all; you are here because you are the men,*

> *and because you represent the men, with whom I have worked while I have been president.*[84]

After five challenging years at San Carlos and half a century of government service, Kelly moved on to more adventures mining gold in Nevada before finally settling down on a small fruit farm near Paradise, California, where he died on December 17, 1928. The old frontiersman transcended the typical adventurous pioneer. His duration of service and his insightful observations and ability to record them in his memoirs set him apart. With his words "I feel my body will rest better in Montana," Yellowstone Kelly was buried with full military honors on Kelly Mountain on the high Rimrocks overlooking the Yellowstone River, just north of Billings.[85]

Part III
Cradled in Dixie:

On a Highway from Slavery to Opportunity

Chapter 13

On Being a Black American in Territorial Fort Benton

A Modest Beginning

York came first—the first recorded African American to travel to the Upper Missouri. He came as a slave, the "property" of Captain William Clark, yet he participated actively as the Lewis and Clark Corps of Discovery blazed the trail to the West. York symbolically forecast the future—when white Americans came west, so, too, traveled black Americans, moving into the ancient lands of Native Americans. In successive waves, fur traders, adventurers, Indian traders, gold seekers, boatmen, freighters, laborers, whiskey traders, miners, merchants, tradesmen, soldiers, service personnel, wives, domestics, soiled doves, ranchers and farmers came to the Upper Missouri. Most were white men and women, but there were always blacks present, sometimes as slaves but more often as free men and women.

Histories of the Upper Missouri focus on the path-breaking activities of white pioneers on the frontier or the Native American nations long present in the region. Until recent years, the lives and activities of black pioneers in this historic area have been little researched and largely ignored. Symptomatic of this neglect of black history is the fact that Fort Benton's premier journalistic historian, Joel F. Overholser, published almost nothing on early black history despite the emphasis of his *Fort Benton River Press* on history during his four decades as editor.

By the mid-1870s, the darkness of repression was descending on "the States," as the United States was known on the Upper Missouri. The post–Civil War Reconstruction "revolution" was giving way to a "counter-revolution" in the border states and the South. The return of thousands of Confederates and secessionists from their wartime exile on the Upper Missouri and the other western territories, the withdrawal of the occupying federal military, the birth of the Ku Klux Klan, the resumption of white dominance as the seceding states were welcomed back into the Union and the wavering of northern resolve to enforce equal rights in the South in the face of massive southern resistance left newly freed slaves and freedmen with a disheartening balance of modest economic acceptance with increasingly restrictive political and social rights—from slavery to freedom to repression, all in a single generation.

Many blacks accepted their fate in the South, but some migrated northward or westward. Black pioneers came west for many of the same reasons as whites, seeking adventure and social and economic opportunities with the added incentive to escape the repression descending on the South. By the early 1860s, at least four free black men worked for the American Fur Company at its Upper Missouri Outfit post at Fort Benton. In the mid-1860s, the town of Fort Benton began to develop at the head of navigation on the Missouri River to become the hub for steamboat traffic and overland freighting into new territory of Montana and the southern British possessions that would become Canada. Increasing numbers of blacks began to arrive on the Upper Missouri on steamboats, often as crewmen, sometimes as passengers. Others came overland on emerging transportation routes.[86]

By 1870, Fort Benton's black community had at least twenty-five residents, and the growth of both the town and its black community was accelerating. A decade later, some seventy-six blacks resided in Fort Benton, and both the newly formed Choteau County and Fort Benton showed the highest percentage of blacks of any county or city in Montana Territory. While Montana's black population was never large, a close look at Fort Benton during the decade of its earliest period of "civilization" from 1875 to 1885 reveals a robust black community with surprises and fascinating stories.

The story is much more than a statistical game. During the early 1880s, Fort Benton showed positive signs of opportunity and acceptance for its black residents despite an ever-present element of intolerance and racism. At least six blacks owned their own businesses, and in two cases, blacks and whites co-owned businesses. Among the black businesses, some were located in prime real estate on Front Street facing the steamboat levee. Black-owned residences were spread around the town, not confined to one area, and some blacks built their own homes. Black families were being formed, and after a sharp struggle over segregation in 1882, black students were admitted to Fort Benton schools. Blacks were acquiring property, with several black male and female entrepreneurs on the county property tax lists with substantial accumulation of property.

So why were black Americans "accepted" in early Fort Benton? While there were many reasons, perhaps two were primary. Fort Benton in the late 1870s and early 1880s was booming. New businesses were essential to serve the steamboating and overland freighting industries. New hotels, restaurants, barbershops and other services were in demand. Blacks were moving up the Missouri River, ready to take those service industry jobs. In Fort Benton, they had opportunity. Perhaps equally important, the fur trading post of Fort Benton had a long tradition of mixed race and nationality with general acceptance of fur trader intermarriage with Native American women. Many of the early fur traders were of French or Canadian descent, yet most early residents had come upriver from St. Louis, and Fort Benton became known as an extension of this gateway to the West.

Complicating the environment throughout Montana Territory, created in 1864 during the Civil War, was the rush into Montana's gold-mining camps led by thousands of Southern and border state secessionists and Confederates. The Upper Missouri became the exile of choice for many men and families avoiding or evading the violence of their war-torn homes. Other Southerners came to honor paroles banishing them to the "western territories" or because their Confederate units were losing the war in the western theater of Missouri and Tennessee—bringing an element of truth to the early saying that "the left wing of Price's Army" came to early Montana Territory.[87]

Early Fort Benton featured a multiracial "melting pot," and perhaps without oversimplification, early Fort Benton society formed a hierarchy with whites at the top followed roughly in order of apparent acceptance by mixed-race white-blacks, black Americans, mixed-race white-Indian children, Chinese and at the bottom native male Indians. Among the whites, too, there was a diverse mix of the old resident fur traders and a new influx from the border states and immigrant Irish, many having served in Union army Irish brigades. In fact, a strong Irish Fenian element soon emerged, gaining power through Democratic Party dominance. An important final element in early Fort Benton was the presence of a U.S. Army infantry company from a regiment stationed nearby in Fort Shaw. From 1869 to 1881, army officers—some with wives—and soldiers were present and a major influence in security and social affairs.

The many native wives of white men formed a special category, numerous and accepted until numbers of white women began to arrive from the 1880s until the end of the nineteenth century. Many families in Fort Benton in the 1860s and 1870s involved interracial marriages of native Indians and whites and at least four white and black marriages. Among the 523 residents of

Fort Benton in 1878 were 34 native wives with 93 mixed-race white-native children, as well as 31 white-native adults. At that time, about 34 percent of Fort Benton's population was nonwhite or mixed race.[88]

Population of Fort Benton, 1878

White	
Males, over twelve years of age	247
Males, under twelve years of age	22
Females, over twelve years of age	50
Females, under twelve years of age	24
Black	
Males, over twelve years of age	6
Males, under twelve years of age	3
Females, over twelve years of age	9
Females, under twelve years of age	2
Indian	
Males, over twelve years of age	0
Males, under twelve years of age	0
Females, over twelve years of age	34
Females, under twelve years of age	0
Mixed	
Males, over twelve years of age	8
Males, under twelve years of age	45
Females, over twelve years of age	23
Females, under twelve years of age	48
Chinese	
Females	0
Males	2
Total	523

So, what can we learn from black history in early Fort Benton, Montana? Black Americans shared with whites the challenges and violence of living in a rugged frontier environment. Blackfeet Indians killed young black carpenter James Berry in the Ophir massacre of 1865. Edmund Bradley, another black carpenter with Donnelly's Mounted Civilian Volunteers, fought and died in action at Cow Creek Canyon in 1877 during the Nez Perce War. Bradley was given a military hero's funeral and burial at Fort Benton. Other blacks shared the opportunities for business and homeownership. Through hard work, black Mattie Bell Bost acquired her own laundry. She married adventurous white John K. Castner, and the two "founded" the coal town of Belt. Young black Alex Martin parleyed his culinary talent into a position as head chef on the opening of the Grand Union Hotel, a lavish jewel constructed in the height of the steamboat trade. Martin and eight other blacks held nine of the eleven jobs on the staff of the Grand Union.

Two black women, sisters Maria and Mary Adams, brought fascinating experiences from their work in the household and even in the field on campaigns with Lieutenant Colonel George Armstrong Custer. Several blacks gained special respect among all races in their community. "Old Aunt Leah" was eulogized upon her death as Fort Benton's "angel of mercy" for her care for paupers and the infirm.

As the steamboat era waned, many of Fort Benton's blacks moved on to other communities in Montana, and some became pillars in their new communities, including Edward Simms in Great Falls and Duke Dutriueille in Helena and Belt.

The story of black Americans in early Fort Benton is the story of many lives and events. Among the free blacks and newly freed slaves from the border states and the South who made their way up the Missouri River to frontier Montana Territory in the years after the Civil War were five young African American women—Mary and Maria Adams, Mattie Castner, Millie Ringgold and Adeline Hoffman—all seeking freedom and opportunity on the Upper Missouri. Intertwined lives are those of Duke Dutriueille and John K. Castner. These are their stories.

The title of this section, "Cradled in Dixie," honors the freed blacks and former slaves who came to the Upper Missouri to find peace and opportunity. It also commemorates an unsuccessful attempt to present the fascinating lives of Mattie Castner and Maria Adams Dutriueille in book form during the 1950s. A planned book titled "Cradled in Dixie" fell victim to racial prejudice in Montana at that time. Author Florence B. Franklin proposed to present sketches of life in early day Belt and

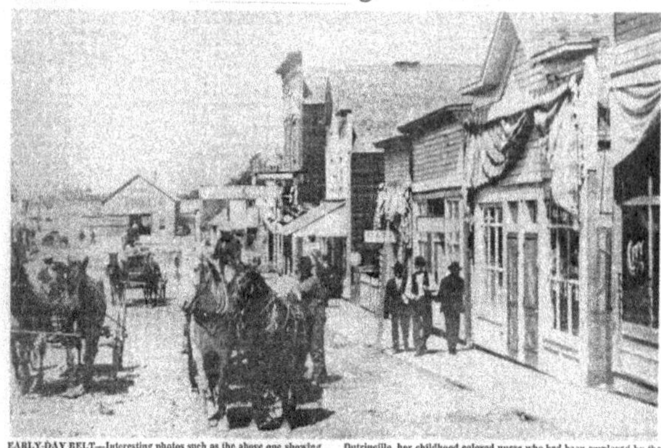

Book Throws New Light on Custer's Life

EARLY-DAY BELT—Interesting photos such as the above one showing Belt at the turn of the century, have been obtained by Mrs. Florence B. Franklin, who lives in the Donovan Park area south of Great Falls, to illustrate her book, "Cradled in Dixie," which contains new sidelights about General George A. Custer and the famous Battle of the Little Big Horn in which Custer and his cavalrymen were killed by the Indians June 25, 1876—80 years ago tomorrow. Mrs. Franklin obtained considerable information about Custer and his wife from Maria Adams Dutriueille, her childhood colored nurse who had been employed by the Custers. For instance, Mrs. Dutriueille reported that Mrs. Custer was clairvoyant and knew her husband was killed before being notified of his death. Much of "Cradled in Dixie," revolves around Mrs. Dutriueille, to whom the book is dedicated, and Mattie Bell Castner, another colored woman. Mrs. Castner and her husband, John K. Castner, opened the first hotel and eating place in Belt and he became wealthy in the coal and fuel business. A Belt park was named after the Castners.

Left: Announcing a new book *Cradled in Dixie* in the *Great Falls Tribune Parade*, June 24, 1956.

Below: Great Falls librarian Alma Jacobs "AJ" explained why *Cradled in Dixie* would never be published. *Great Falls Public Library Vertical Files.*

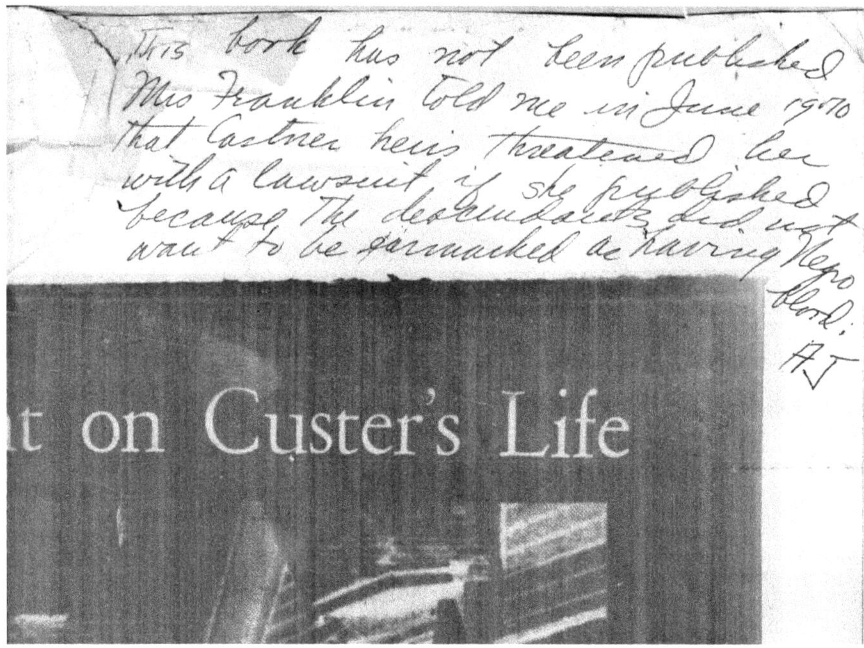

This book has not been published
Mrs Franklin told me in June 1970
that Castner heirs threatened her
with a lawsuit if she published
because the descendants did not
want to be earmarked as having Negro
blood.
AJ

t on Custer's Life

Fort Benton, as well as outlining the lives of Maria Adams Dutriueille and Mattie Bell Castner, both of whom she had known as a child in Belt. The mystery of why "Cradled in Dixie" was never published was answered when this author discovered an article on the proposed book in the vertical files of the Great Falls Public Library. Written on the article in the handwriting of legendary African American librarian Alma Jacobs was the following explanation:

> *This book has not been published. Mrs. Franklin told me in June 1970 that Castner heirs threatened her with a lawsuit if she published because the descendants did not want to be earmarked as having Negro blood. AJ* [The initials "AJ" for Alma Jacobs in her handwriting.][89]

Chapter 14

Black Steamboatmen on the Upper Missouri

From Slaves to Free Men and Women

We don't know the first black American to come up the Missouri River to Fort Benton by steamboat, though he no doubt came not as a passenger but rather as a crewman. We do know that many blacks worked on steamboats on the Upper Missouri, while others came as passengers. Some remained to become Montana pioneers.

Black Americans, both slave and free, had long served on riverboats in the antebellum years. Steamboat owners employed their slaves as roustabouts, or "roosters," along with immigrant Irish and Germans, other foreign-born people and young Americans. Free blacks served also as stewards, cooks, cabin boys and chambermaids.

With black emancipation and the end of the Civil War, the composition of steamboat crews underwent change. For freed blacks, working on the river offered jobs and some opportunity for advancement and relocation. Mixed-race crews became common on the western rivers, including the Missouri.

The 1880 U.S. census provides some insight into crew racial composition on the Upper Missouri. Collected in Fort Benton in early June, this census shows that two steamboats were moored at the levee with their crews recorded in the census records. The steamboat *Key West*, under Captain Frank Maratta, brought about 270 passengers to Fort Benton from Bismarck, including 200 North West Mounted Police. Among the crew of 41 were 17 Scandinavians and 3 blacks. The black Americans were Kate Murphy, age twenty from Kentucky, working as a laundress; Frank

Thomas, age twenty-four from Virginia, a rooster; and David Homes, age thirty-three from New York, a rooster.

The second steamboat, the *Nellie Peck*, under Captain Martin Coulson, was manned by a crew of thirty-nine with eleven foreign-born immigrants and four blacks. The black Americans were Lucy Chapman, age thirty from Missouri, a servant; Bush Glenn, age eighteen from Kentucky, a waiter; Henry Randoff, age twenty from Tennessee, a cook; and George Stockwell, age twenty-five from Virginia, a waiter.[90]

A reminder of the dangers of travel on the Upper Missouri comes from the experience of Wesley McClellan, a young black deckhand, age about twenty from Nashville, who fell off the deck of the steamer *Helena* en route to Fort Benton in June 1882 and was presumed drowned.[91]

The best details we have of the experiences of a black crewman who remained on the Upper Missouri for many years comes from remarkable Edward D. Simms. Ed Simms was just nineteen years old when he made his first trip by steamboat to Fort Benton in 1873. Simms had been born into the slave society of Arkansas in 1853 and, after emancipation, worked for a time in Texas. On the steamer, he worked as assistant steward on that first trip, and in his words, "The people and the country looked good to me from the first, and I determined to live here." Simms continued his account:

> *After a time I got employment on another boat, the* Red Cloud, *on which I worked from 1878 to 1880. It was owned by Howard Conrad and later by the firm of Conrad & Baker. I quit the boat on August 15, 1880, and went to work for Joseph A. Baker and after that I worked for Charles Price, both of them living in Fort Benton. I served them as cook and general handy man about the home. One of the colored people in Fort Benton then was Henrietta Johnson, now living in this city* [Great Falls].[92]

In the period from 1878 to 1880 that Simms was on board, the *Red Cloud* made a total of thirteen trips to Fort Benton. Each year, the *Red Cloud* began the season at St. Louis, making the long trip up to the Upper Missouri with an average of 110 passengers and 300 tons of cargo. Subsequent trips each year from Bismarck, Dakota Territory, to Fort Benton averaged about 80 passengers and 250 tons of cargo.[93]

Ed Simms continued his story about his early life in Fort Benton: "I worked in the dining room of the Choteau house at Fort Benton for Jere Sullivan, and then I went to Fort Shaw to work for Mr. [Joseph H.]

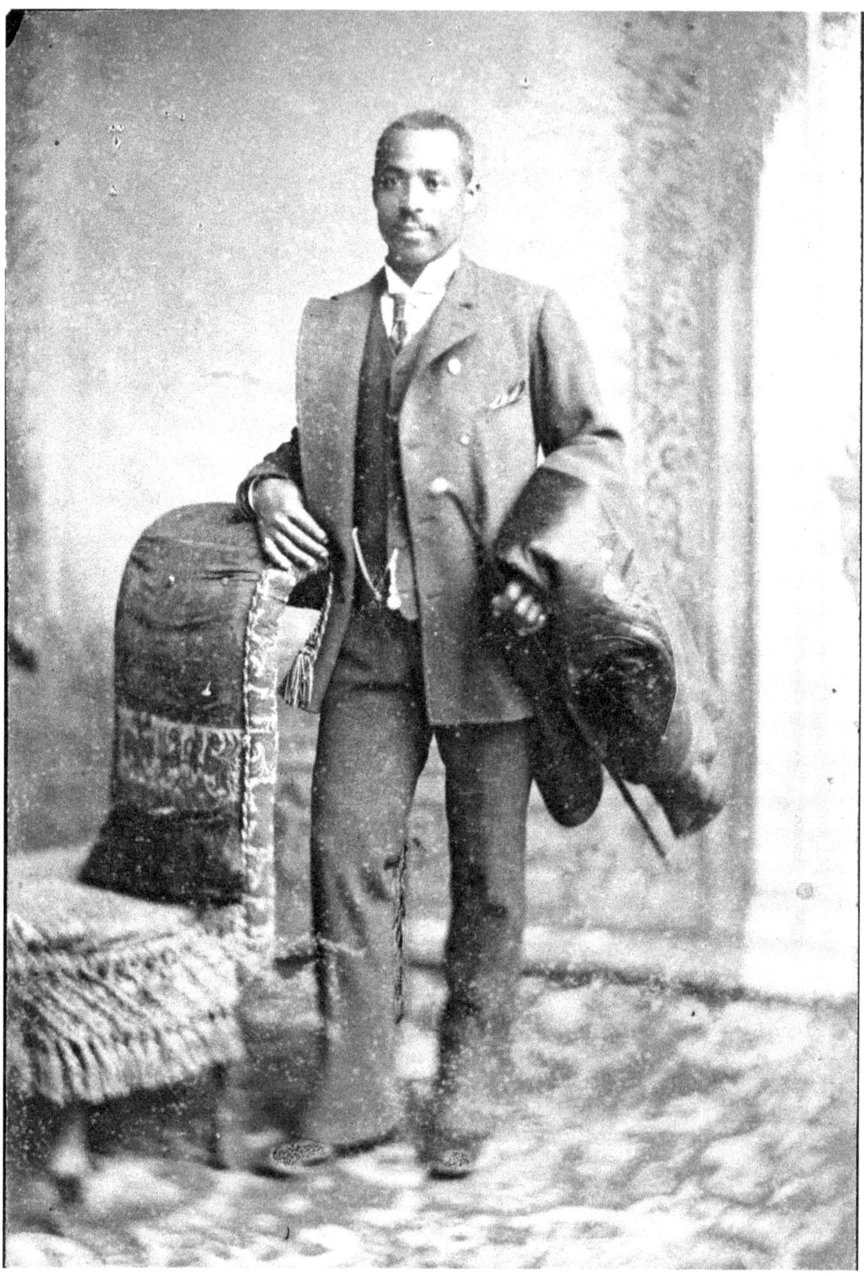

Edward Simms rose from slavery to a career on the western rivers before settling in frontier Montana. *Author's collection.*

ED SIMMS TELLS HOW BLIND MAN FOLLOWS BALL GAME

His Eyesight Gone, He Is One of Great Great Falls' Most Enthusiastic Fans. Played the Game Himself Back in Texas When a Young Man.

EDWARD D. SIMMS

Right: The *Great Falls Tribune* of December 17, 1911, featured an extensive biographic sketch of Edward Simms, including his love of baseball, even during his declining years. *Author's collection.*

Below: The steamboat *Red Cloud* made many trips to the Upper Missouri with Ed Simms and other black crewmen. *Overholser Historical Research Center.*

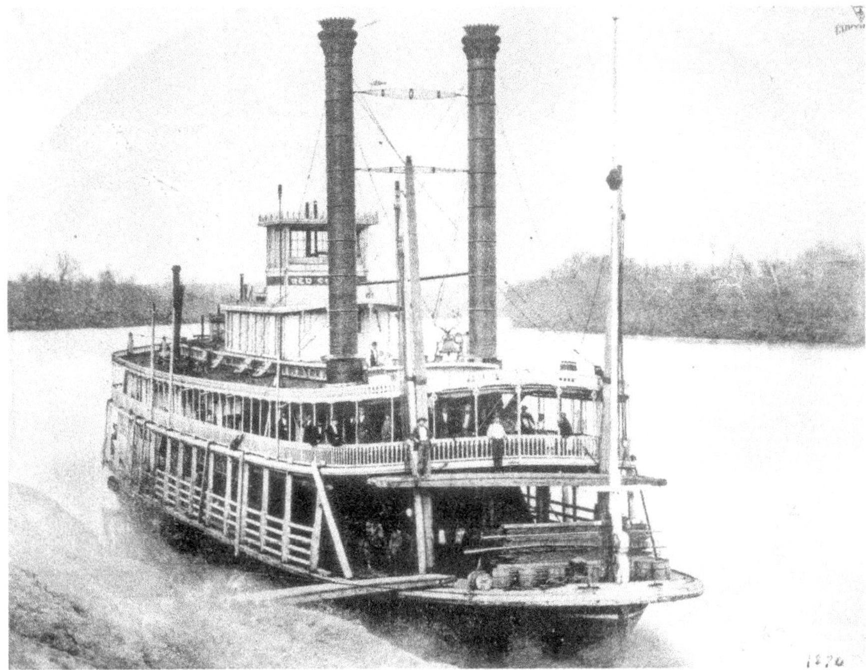

McKnight [the post trader at Fort Shaw]. That was 1882, and I stayed there till 1886, when I came to Great Falls."[94]

Ed Simms became the first black resident of Great Falls, and in the summer of 1886, he returned to St. Louis, likely by steamboat and train, to marry Elizabeth Miller. Their daughter Gertrude, born in Great Falls in 1887, was the first black child born in the growing town. Simms worked as chef at the Cascade Hotel and later as steward for the exclusive Rainbow

Club. Ed and Elizabeth Simms became social, religious and civic leaders in the black community of Great Falls.[95]

Despite the expense and adventure into the unknown on the northern frontier, black passengers came by steamboat up the Missouri River. The first known black passenger came to Fort Benton on the steamboat *Emilie* in June 1862, either as the slave or servant of William Hurlbert at the beginning of the gold rush. In the 1870s, adventurous Mattie Bell Bost, who was born a slave in North Carolina and freed by the Emancipation Proclamation, brought two white children to Fort Benton to join their mother. She achieved remarkable success on the Upper Missouri.

By 1878, Fort Benton had begun an impressive building boom, and the word spread downriver that there were jobs and good times at the head of navigation. In that year, Henry and Henrietta Johnson came up the Missouri by steamboat. The Adams sisters, Mary and Maria, mixed-race young ladies who had just ended an exciting experience working at Fort Abraham Lincoln for General George and Mrs. Elizabeth Custer, came on the steamboat *Nellie Peck*.

We can learn from the steamboat adventures on the Upper Missouri of black Americans, whether crew and passengers, as they joined Native Americans and white adventurers in the challenges and opportunities that frontier Montana offered for all.

Chapter 15

From Slavery to Campaigning with Colonel Custer

The Exceptional Lives of Mary and Maria Adams

Maria and Mary Adams stepped off the gangplank onto the levee at Fort Benton in the spring of 1878. The Adams sisters had already led lives of adventure before coming to the Upper Missouri on the steamboat *Nellie Peck*, and more would come in frontier Montana Territory.

Maria Adams was born on May 15, 1852, in Lexington, Fayette County, Kentucky, likely to a free black family. Soon after her birth, the family moved to Owensboro, Kentucky, where she was reared. After the Civil War, at age fifteen, Maria was hired as a cook for the Baker Boyd family for ten dollars a month and her room and board. Major Boyd, formerly a Confederate soldier in the 7th Kentucky Mounted Infantry during the war, served as Kentucky commonwealth attorney.[96]

About 1872, Maria traveled by packet steamer, probably the *War Eagle*, on the Ohio River from Owensboro to Louisville, a distance of about 156 miles, for a six-dollar fare. There she made her home working for the family of the Reverend and Mrs. William H. Clagett, pastor of the Fifth Presbyterian Church.

Maria's older sister Mary Adams was born in 1849 in Lexington and moved with the family to Owensboro in the mid-1850s. After the Civil War, Mary Adams moved on to Louisville, Kentucky, before the 1870 census and is recorded as an African American, age twenty-two, born in Kentucky, serving in the household of white coal dealer James N. and Virginia Kellogg and their four children.[97]

The following year, in April 1871, Lieutenant Colonel George Armstrong Custer and his U.S. 7th Cavalry arrived in Kentucky for Reconstruction duty with regimental headquarters in Elizabethtown. Elizabeth "Libbie" Custer, Colonel Custer's wife, had experienced a tempestuous relationship with the family's longtime black cook and head of household, Eliza Brown. In the fall of 1869, the conflict finally erupted to the breaking point, and Libbie fired Eliza and hired Mary Adams. Mary quickly drew praise from both Libbie and her husband. Libbie recorded in her diary, "My very economical cook is black woman named Mary Adams, I think we shall manage to 'eat up' considerably less of the pay than we did while Eliza cooked for us & entertained her visitors." Libbie added that unlike Eliza Brown, "Mary's temper has never failed her. . . . She is so much better than Eliza."[98]

In June 1873, the 7th Cavalry was ordered to Dakota Territory to provide protection for the Northern Pacific Railroad while it surveyed a route along the Yellowstone River. The overall expedition was under the command of Colonel David S. Stanley. Colonel Custer brought along his cook, Mary Adams, who rode along in an ambulance and cooked on a cast-iron stove, drawing the ire of Colonel Stanley. In letters Custer wrote back to Libbie, he raved about Mary, who had a fine meal waiting at the campsite each evening, relating that Mary "is a great favorite with all and never complains although she had some rough experience already." In turn, Mary asked that Colonel Custer "tell Miss Libbie I like it better out here than I thought I would." Custer added, "She is a great favorite, never complains, and takes things humorously. All are kind to her."[99]

In November 1873, the Custers reunited at their new post, Fort Abraham Lincoln, across the Missouri River from Bismarck, Dakota Territory. Arriving at their newly constructed quarters, Libbie wrote, "Our friends had lighted it all, and built fires in the fireplaces . . . and Mary had a grand supper ready." Libbie later recorded in her diary: "I have no housekeeping cares for she [Mary] manages the other servants and attends even to the refreshments we offer on Friday nights for our reception hops. It is no light social care to be wife of the Commanding Officer of so large a Post, and I find my time fully taken up with entertaining."

Two years later, Mary Adams sent for her sister Maria to work as a housemaid for the Custers. Maria joined Colonel Custer at St. Paul, and they arrived at Fort Abraham Lincoln in the spring of 1875. In addition, younger sister Karlene Adams and a cousin, Nancy Mucks, eventually served the Custers. Maria spent the next year in the Custer household, and she later described life with colorful Colonel and Libbie Custer at Fort Abraham Lincoln. Editor Edith Rolfe Maxwell, Herbert and Martha Rolfe's daughter, included Maria's story in the Works Progress Administration book *Great Falls Yesterday*:

> *Fort Lincoln housed about 600 people. A small town within its constant guard, where the cavalry lived with the infantry numbering around 200 located one mile away. On one side of the main street were the officers' homes and on the other, the soldiers' barracks. There were few children. The average home was about four or five rooms. They were painted gray and white.*
>
> *After his first quarters burned* [in February 1874] *the General's new home had fourteen rooms including a billiard hall, reception room, and double parlor, all of the furnishings were beautiful, especially her table appointments. A solid silver tea pot and creamer, and sugar bowl, salt and pepper shakers in the shape of an egg on tiny gold feet, silver soup tureens and vegetable dishes; everything was silver except the Haviland china plates which were white with three pin stripes of pink and green; one set was decorated with bands of red.*
>
> *The Custers entertained twice a month for the officers and their wives. The music was furnished by the cavalry's brass band and a string quartet. Waltzes at the balls were the favorite with lancers, polkas, the gallop and square dances.*
>
> *. . . Tom Higgins, one of the outstanding characters of the fort was a huge six-foot Irishman who was in charge of the General's forty gray foxhounds. The hounds often went hunting alone and sometimes returned with a hind leg of a deer or elk. The soldiers did not hunt often as it was dangerous to wander too far from the fort on account of the treacherous Indians.*
>
> *One morning during the summer of 1876 the fort was quiet as the mounted cavalry troops marched for Big Horn. . . .*
>
> *Mrs. Custer, who possessed a wonderful disposition loved to paint animals and portraits for her own amusement. She was also an excellent horsewoman and on the fateful day rode with the General and his escort until dusk. As she took leave of him she said; "I'm kissing you for the last time." This made the General very blue and despondent for the campaign. When she received the news of his death she was not surprised because her presentiment had come true—but* [she] *fainted. Not one of Custer's cavalry returned and with heavy hearts furniture was crated and packed and the houses at Fort Lincoln were closed. After 30 days' preparation all remaining left on transportation fees furnished by the government.*[100]

With the death of Colonel Custer on June 26, 1876, and the closing of quarters at Fort Abraham Lincoln one month later, the Adams sisters accompanied six Little Big Horn widows to the home of Colonel and Mrs. J.W. Raymond in Bismarck. The widows left Bismarck on July 30 by steamboat down the Missouri River, while the Adams sisters remained at the Raymond home for some time before moving down the Yellowstone River to the new army post Fort Keogh with the promise of jobs. Captain Lyman Smith, a storekeeper, hired Mary for $100 a month, while Maria began working for Lieutenant H.K. Bailey, U.S. 5th Infantry Regiment, for $50.

Mary and Maria's time at Fort Keogh likely began in the fall of 1876 and ended about a year later. They returned to Bismarck in October 1877, and three months later, on January 16, 1878, General Nelson A. Miles interviewed Mary as part of the army's investigation into the Battle of the Little Bighorn. The notarized affidavit acquired from Mary Adams by General Miles at Bismarck later became a key piece of evidence in the debate about what orders Colonel Custer had received as he and his 7th Cavalry rode into history.

Over the decades that followed the death of Colonel Custer and the men of the 7th Cavalry, debate raged about whether Custer had disobeyed orders given to him by his commander, Brigadier General Alfred H. Terry. In 1896, General Nelson Miles announced that he had an affidavit that recorded the last conversation between General Terry and Colonel Custer in Custer's tent at the mouth of the Rosebud River on the night of June 21–22, 1876. The testimony recorded that General Terry ordered Custer to "Use your own judgment, and do what you think best if you strike the [Indian] trail. And, whatever you do, Custer, hold on to your wounded."[101]

At the time, General Miles did not reveal that the affidavit came from Custer's cook, Mary Adams. When that became known, it was given little credence since several senior army officers claimed that Colonel Custer's "colored" cook had remained at Fort Abraham Lincoln and had not been on the expedition. In fact, Mary Adams had accompanied Custer as his cook in June 1876 and had been present in Custer's tent the night of that fateful last meeting. General Miles obtained the affidavit testimony from Mary Adams in Bismarck in January 1878. In recent years, research by historian John S. Manion has proven conclusively that two "M." Adamses, Mary and Maria, worked for the Custers and that Mary was present at the meeting. Her testimony has provided crucial evidence confirming that Custer did not disobey orders and had a free hand going into his tragic last campaign. The confusion over whether a black servant named M. Adams remained with Mrs. Libbie Custer when her husband departed for the campaign was clarified by discovery that Maria Adams had remained behind while Mary had, indeed, accompanied the expedition.[102]

In the winter of 1878, while staying in Bismarck, Mary and Maria Adams heard of boom days and good wages at Fort Benton, the head of navigation on the Missouri River, and the sisters decided to try their fortunes when spring came in the famous frontier town. They paid their fifty-dollar fares and boarded the steamboat *Nellie Peck*, departing Bismarck on July 1 with six other passengers bound for Fort Benton.[103]

Notice to Creditors.

In the Probate Court, of the County of Choteau, Territory of Montana.

In the matter of the estate of Mary Adams, deceased:

Notice is hereby given by the undersigned, administratrix of the estate of Mary Adams, deceased, to the creditors of and all persons having claims against the said deceased, to exhibit them with necessary vouchers, within four (4) months after the first publication of this notice, to the said administratrix, at her residence on Main street, in the town of Fort Benton, County of Choteau, Montana Territory.

MARIA ADAMS, Admx.

Dated at FORT BENTON, May 13th, 1879.

An ad for Maria Adams, administrator of the estate of her sister Mary Adams. *Benton Record Weekly*, May 16, 1879.

After arriving at Fort Benton on July 11, Mary was hired by Joseph S. Hill, bookkeeper at I.G. Baker's store at Fort Benton. Shortly after, Mary moved to Fort Shaw to work in the household of Dr. Charles R. Greenleaf, 3rd Infantry Regiment and post surgeon, and his wife. Mary cooked for the family and helped Mrs. Greenleaf care for their four children while the latter led an active social life in the Fort Shaw community. Early in 1879, Mary became ill and moved back to Fort Benton to be near her sister and live in a house on property she and Maria owned. Mary passed away at the age of thirty on March 22, 1879, and was buried in the old Fort Benton cemetery.[104]

The June 1880 U.S. census recorded that Maria Adams, a mixed-race twenty-eight-year-old woman born in Kentucky who could read and write, was living in Fort Benton and working as a laundress. She lived in the household of Indian trader Oliver Pichette and old-time fur trader Charles Mercier Rondin. The previous year, Maria paid taxes on a sizeable $400 worth of assessed property consisting of three town lots, $200 in "moneys and credits" and $25 in watches and jewelry—some $15,000 in 2015. By 1880, thrifty Maria's taxable property had increased again by one-third.[105]

Fate and ability would hold an interesting future for young Maria Adams.

Chapter 16

Barber to the Presidents Joins Maria Adams in Frontier Montana

Duke and Maria Dutrieueille

During the Civil War, Duke Dutriueille served as personal servant to several senior Union officers, including Major General "Fighting Joe" Hooker. Duke took great pride in relating the story that in his lifetime he had the honor of shaving three presidents of the United States—Presidents Buchanan, Lincoln and Grant. Duke had a pleasing personality and was well read and conversant on many subjects, with a wealth of anecdotes gleaned from his adventurous career. He gained a reputation for unswerving honesty and held the respect of many friends, black and white. On the Upper Missouri, Duke and Maria Adams would meet.

On September 3, 1880, Maria Adams married Duke Dutriueille in Helena, Montana. After the wedding, Mr. and Mr. Dutriueille resided for a few months in Marysville, a mining camp in the mountains near Helena. Maria and Duke had met in Fort Benton, where Duke and has partner operated Dutrieuille & Rosier Barbers and Perfumers next to the Wetzel Block and advertised that "Sharp Razors, Clean Towels, Artistic Work are our Specialties."[106]

Duke Dutrieuille was a remarkable mixed-race African American, and during more than four decades in Montana, he knew and became known to thousands. John Lambert "Duke" Dutrieuille was born on board a ship in Philadelphia Harbor on March 22, 1837. The son of a Frenchman with family lore claiming historic ties to the French court and a native woman of Santo Domingo, his early boyhood was spent in Philadelphia, where he received a fair education. At age sixteen, he enlisted in the U.S. Navy as a cabin boy on a man-of-war. After his service ended, he returned to Philadelphia to serve an apprenticeship as a barber, and on March 15, 1857, he received a diploma.

Duke came up the Missouri River to Fort Benton in the late 1860s, roaming from mining camp to camp, always in demand with his talents as a barber. After shaving the citizens in Virginia City, Butte, Helena and Marysville, Duke settled down in Fort Benton in 1878 to operate Duke's Place Barber Shop on Front Street. There he became a social and political leader in the small African American community and no doubt met Mary and Maria Adams shortly after their arrival. His property in 1879 was assessed at $485 value, consisting of two city lots, and the value of his merchandise was $35.[107]

Duke and Maria Dutriueille moved on from Marysville to Fort Benton in the late winter of 1881. Maria remembered that trip to Fort Benton and the winter of 1880–81 as "dreadfully cold," not ending for several more months. Maria later related their trip by stage to Fort Benton, as well as a brief account of life in frontier Fort Benton in 1881:

> *The fare was $20. The stage drawn by six horses carried 18 passengers. The trip from Helena took 24 hours. Every 20 miles approximately horses were changed and 10 minutes was allowed for eating. At this time there was no fear of Indian attacks and those eating stops were ranches along the road that served as stations. Sun River was the leading town, there being no Great Falls at this time.*
>
> [Arriving in Fort Benton] *snow was so deep that coal could not be freighted from Belt. . . . Families were suffering from cold and it was finally decided to burn the jail which was built of logs. All fences were also used for fuel. It is said of those years that they had nine months of winter and three months of spring. In the spring it would rain for six weeks at a time. Water was sold in barrel lots for $1. It was so muddy it would have to be cleared by putting stale bread or whites of eggs into it.*
>
> *. . . A very common thing for cowboys to do when in town would be to ride into the saloon and demand drinks, and if not served at once would start shooting at the roof and making everyone duck under tables. After having their fun they would go on to the next place. A cowboy once demanded that the barber take his chair out into the street and cut his hair, which the barber was glad to do rather than have his place shot up. In those days a person learned to do things even though they were not to his liking.*

In Fort Benton Joe Baker and T.C. Powers [Power] *ran the leading general stores from which everything could be obtained. Living was high and the only use for a dime was to buy a spool of thread. Women wore high felt boots in winter and moccasins in summer. Foodstuffs were shipped by boat and hunting and farmers supplied the rest. In the line of food, dried apples, peaches, onions, eggs at $1.50 a dozen, flour, sugar $100 per hundred pounds and butter $1 per pound. All canned fruit sold for 50c a can. No oranges or bananas and when finally brought up by the boat were $1.50 and $2 a dozen. Plums cost 25c for two.*

On return trips the boats were loaded with furs and buffalo hides—these were beaver, mink and fox furs, brought from [Fort] *"Whoop-up" on bull trains. On account of low water the boats could not come to Fort Benton and came as far as Cow Island where they unloaded the goods once a month and then it was freighted to Helena by ten-mule teams owned by Broadwater called the "Diamond R Train."*[108]

In the early 1880s, Fort Benton was booming, with steamboat traffic at its zenith and construction of new brick buildings underway replacing many smaller wood-frame businesses of the 1860s. Duke and Maria were leaders in the social life of the small African American community, and Duke participated in local politics once the local Republican Party began to emerge from the shadows of Irish and southern Democratic domination during the 1870s.

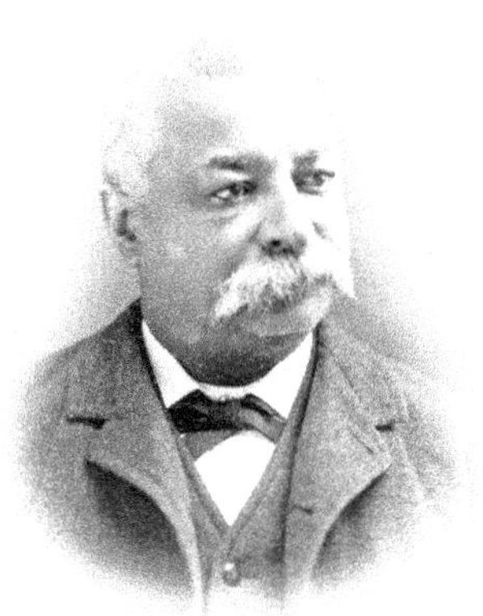

Duke Dutriueille, a leader in Helena's black community. Photo by R.H. Beckwith. *Author's collection.*

After the steamboating season ended in the summer of 1884, it became clear that railroads soon would drive steamboats out of business in Montana Territory. Prospects for the head of navigation on the Missouri River were beginning to fade, so the Dutriueilles decided that their future economic and social opportunities were in the rapidly growing black community in Helena. There, Duke purchased the International Barber Shop, soon renamed Duke's Barber Shop, and announced that fact to the people of Helena in a characteristic "open letter" to the *Helena Independent*. For seventeen years, the Dutriueilles resided in Helena, where both were active in the St. James African Methodist Episcopal (AME) Church and the social affairs of the black community.[109]

Duke played a leading role in politics in the black community, largely supporting the Republican Party and often attending county and state party conventions as Montana moved from territory into statehood in 1889. In 1892, he broke with the Grand Old Party to support the Democratic nominee for governor, Timothy E. Collins. The Democratic newspaper *Independent* featured the importance of Duke's letter and a growing trend in the black community to leave the party of Lincoln. In his fiery letter, Duke made his reasons clear—Collins, while living in Fort Benton and a member of the school board, stood staunchly with the black community when racists in the community tried to establish segregated schools.[110] In addition, Duke castigated the GOP for taking the black vote for granted:

> *When a white man changes his political faith he is never questioned, nor is his right to do so ever challenged. But let the negro dare to speak one word in favor of the democratic party . . . he is at once waited upon by some of the leading lights of the G.O.P. and shown the enormity of his proposed crime. "What on earth do you mean? Do you not know that*

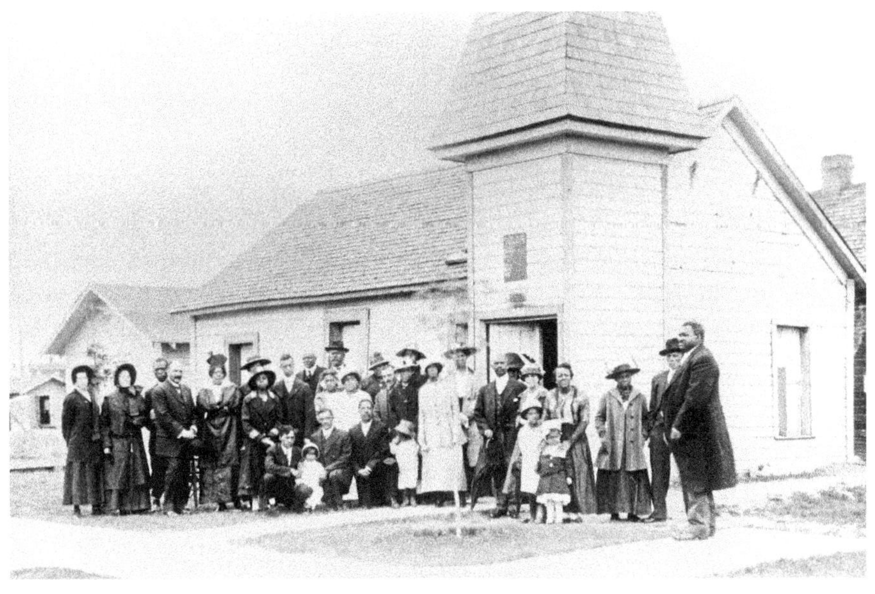

Maria Adams Dutriueille, *fifth from the left*, with the congregation of the Union Bethel African Methodist Episcopal Church in Great Falls in 1916. *Author's collection.*

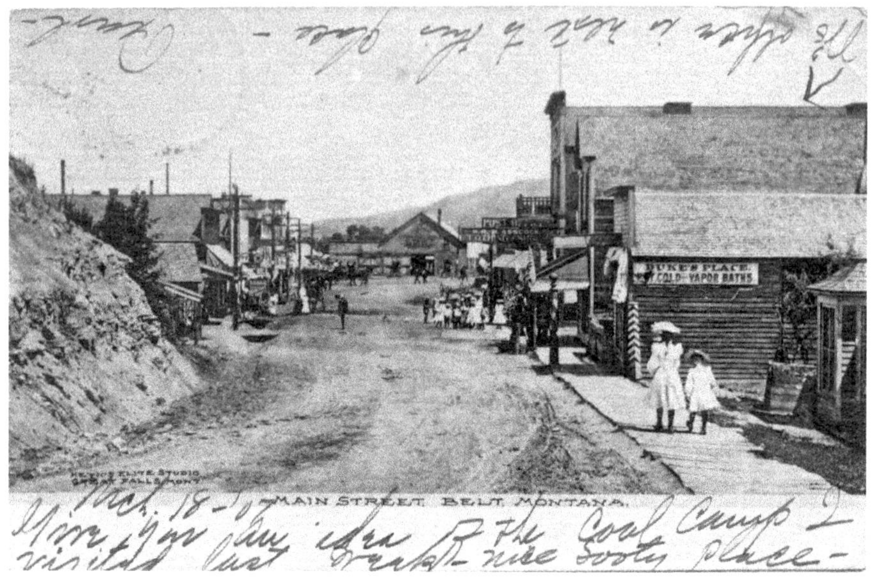

Above: Duke's Place Barber Shop in Belt, Montana. *Author's collection.*

Left: Barber for the presidents Duke Dutriueille. *Great Falls Tribune*, January 19, 1911.

BARBER FOR PRESIDENTS

"Duke" Dutrienille of Belt Dead—Gen. Hooker's Personal Aid in Civil War.

John Lambert Dutrieuille, of Belt, better known as the "Duke," whose proud record included that of having shaved three presidents, Buchanan, Lincoln and Grant, and whose experience in life ranged from the vicissitudes of a cabin boy on a man-of-war, sailing through the Carribean sea, to the trials of the early settler of Montana, is at rest.

The "Duke" died last Monday and his funeral was held yesterday morning in the Catholic church with interment at Belt.

"Duke" Dutrieuille was born in Philadelphia, March 22, 1837 and lived there till he was 16 years of age, when he enlisted as a cabin boy on a man-of-war. After his service ended in this he returned to Philadelphia and served an apprenticeship as a barber and on March 15, 1857, he was given a diploma by B. G. Gaines, under whom he had worked.

The "Duke" served in the Civil war as aid to General Hooker and after the war he came to Montana, where he had since lived. He had shaved citizens of Butte, Helena, and Virginia City before coming to Belt, having had a shop in all these places at different times.

> *we fought for you, for your liberty?" Well, now, what does that liberty mean? It means the right to vote . . . the republican ticket at state, county or municipal elections, and at general elections particularly. It means that we rescued you from slavery of the body to put you into a slavery of the mind and a slavery of the soul. You are to vote for the republican party, no matter how venal, how corrupt they may be. Vote under the lash and after the election be ignored entirely until the next election season.* [Signed Duke Dutriueille, Helena, September 24, 1892.][111]

During visits to Helena to consult a doctor, Mrs. Mattie Castner stayed at the Dutriueille home and became close friends with Maria Adams Dutriueille. The Castner hometown of Belt in Cascade County began to thrive in the 1890s as the demand for coal grew to support the copper mining and refining industries in Great Falls and Butte. In 1899, the Dutriueilles moved to the booming coal mining town of Belt, allowing Maria to be close to her friend Mattie Castner. Duke opened his signature barbershop Duke's Place on Castner Street.

Duke Dutriueille died on January 16, 1911, in Belt, and the *Great Falls Tribune* paid tribute with a headline "Barber for Presidents," while the *Belt Valley Times* reported that Duke "probably had the widest acquaintances of any colored man in Montana." Two years later, Maria moved with children Frank and Marie to the substantial black community on the lower Southside in Great Falls and became a stalwart in the Union Bethel AME Church. When Maria Adams Dutriueille died in Great Falls at age eighty-six on May 1, 1939, the *Great Falls Tribune* paid tribute with an obituary titled "Woman Who Served Custer at Fort Lincoln Dies Here. Mrs. Maria Dutriueille, 87, One of Few Negro Woman to Come to Montana by River Steamer, Saw Seventh Cavalry Ride Westward."[112]

Chapter 17

The True Story of the Mother and Father of Belt, Montana

Mattie Bell Bost and John K. Castner

In 1989, Mattie Castner was named to the Gallery of Outstanding Montanans in the state capitol in Helena. The first Montana African American so honored, her plaque paid tribute to this remarkable pioneer on the Upper Missouri: "Montana lost more than a leading citizen with Mattie's death; it lost the sense of community spirit that 'the Mother of Belt' personified. Mattie Castner's career in Montana epitomizes the 'pioneer spirit' on which the state has been built in the twentieth century."[113]

Mattie Bell Bost was born a slave on the plantation of Reuben Setzer near Newton, Catawba County, North Carolina, on April 10, 1849. She remained in bondage on the Setzer plantation until Union soldiers freed her under the Emancipation Proclamation. Mattie then worked in domestic service in Newton as a child's nurse until 1870, when she sought greater opportunity, moving on to St. Louis. There she worked as a hotel maid until lured by reports of golden opportunities on the Upper Missouri.[114]

According to Mattie's biography in *Great Falls Yesterday*, in the spring of 1876, she came up the Missouri on the steamboat *Nellie Peck*, departing St. Louis on April 8 and arriving at Fort Benton on June 9 after "a long tiresome trip." The story tells that Mattie brought two "Sire" children to their mother, who was already at Fort Benton. Mrs. Sire and Mattie had become friends at St. Louis, and the children had been left in Mattie's care.

"Mattie Bell" did arrive at Fort Benton with "two children," name not given, but not on the steamboat *Nellie Peck* and not in 1876. The *Benton*

Record reported that Mattie Bell arrived in Fort Benton with 2 children on the steamboat *Red Cloud* on the evening of May 11, 1879. This steamer was crowded with 150 passengers, including 23 children. While it seems clear that the 1879 trip up the Missouri brought Mattie and the "Sire" children to Fort Benton, it is likely that Mattie had come up from St. Louis as early as 1876 but not with the Sire children. Unclaimed letters to "Mattie Bell" were reported in 1876 and 1878 in Fort Benton and Helena Post Offices, respectively. Thus, the family legend that Mattie arrived at Fort Benton in 1876 may be true—the *Nellie Peck* arrived on June 9 that year.[115]

The identity of the "Sire" family is also a puzzle. The U.S. federal census of 1880 in Montana recorded just one "Sire" family, that of Louis Sire in Gallatin County, yet this family was white–Native American, with their children born in Oregon and Montana Territory. Analysis of the 1880 Montana territorial census leads this author to believe that the family most likely to be the "Sires" was the Edward and Nancy Siria family of Indiana. The Sirias were living in 1880 in Glendale, Beaverhead County, Montana, with four children, three of whom were born in Kansas and the youngest, age three, born in Montana.[116]

At Fort Benton, Mattie obtained work for John Hunsberger at the Overland Hotel, where she took charge of the laundry at a salary of $100 per month. John Hunsberger, a veteran of the 16th Ohio Infantry Regiment in the Civil War, was married to mixed white–Piegan Blackfeet Cecilia Armell, the daughter of a prominent fur trader. By 1880, Mattie owned and operated her own laundry in Fort Benton.

In 1879 in Helena, in an uncommon mixed-race marriage, Mattie Bell Bost married John K. Castner, a freighter and coal mine operator. This was a marriage of two hardworking entrepreneurs. John Castner, a white man, was born on September 22, 1844; raised in Pennsylvania coal country; and educated in public schools and at a business college in Pittsburgh. With no Civil War service, in the spring of 1867, Castner boarded the newly constructed steamboat *Nora* at Pittsburgh bound for the Upper Missouri River via St. Louis. The *Nora*, "loaded with freight and passengers," snagged and sank below Decatur in Pratt's Cut-off, north of Omaha, on May 28, 1867. *Silver Lake No. 4* loaded the 130 passengers off the sunken steamer and proceeded up the Missouri to the new army post Camp Cooke, at the mouth of the Judith River eighty-seven miles below Fort Benton. *Nora*'s freight was lost, including a quartz mill. At Camp Cooke, the steamer *Guidon* loaded the *Nora* passengers and proceeded to Fort Benton, arriving on June 20 with about 187 passengers.[117]

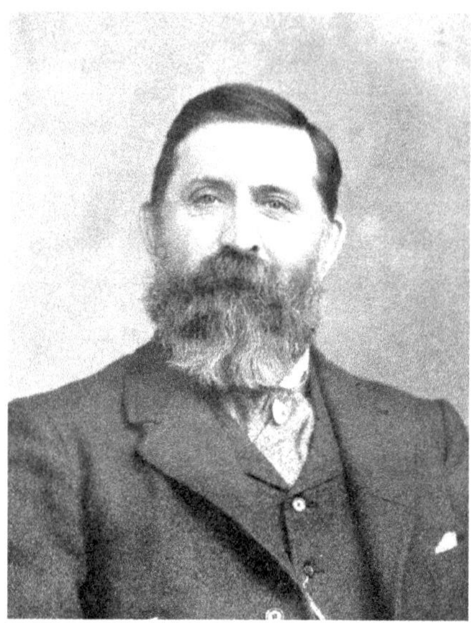

John K. Castner, pioneer coal miner and the "father" of Belt, Montana. *Author's collection.*

John Castner quickly mastered "whacking bulls," moving from wagon master to operating a freight line with three good ten-mule teams hauling freight from Cow Island and other destinations to Fort Benton. He began ranching and exploring the region, visiting the site of the great falls of the Missouri in 1869 and examining mineral resources in the Belt Valley in 1870, where he recognized substantial quality coal formations. He continued freighting until 1877, when he began to develop the coal deposits, mining and hauling coal to Fort Benton while acquiring extensive mining claims and platting a townsite, originally known as Pittsburg Landing. Castner's first load of coal to Fort Benton was a trial load with visiting geologist and explorer Professor Raphael Pumpelly, who pronounced it to be the "best coal showing in the country." Castner coal quickly came into demand at Fort Benton for both residents and steamboats with the price per ton: four dollars at the mine and twelve dollars for the cost of freighting. John Castner formed a business relationship with merchant trader T.C. Power, and Castner became the "Coal King from Little Pittsburg," employing six men at the mines and more for freighting for the three-day trip in good weather and as long as two weeks in bad. One Fort Benton observer noted "that the road from Benton to Castner's is fairly lined with teams hauling coal."[118]

After Mattie's marriage to John Castner, the couple moved to Little Pittsburg, where together they built the first log cabin. John hewed the logs while Mattie helped cover the cabin with brush, and both worked to daub it with mud and buffalo chips, chink the cracks and line it with unbleached muslin that was kalsomined. This was the beginning of what was to become the Castner Hotel and the start of the town that became Belt.

The Castner cabin quickly became a stopping place for travelers on the road to the Barker silver mines in the Little Belt Mountains and, after the town of Great Falls formed in 1884, a station on the Great Falls–Lewistown stagecoach line. As travel through the region increased, the Castners added log additions to the original cabin until the complex assumed the picturesque appearance of a southern plantation.

Mattie operated the hotel and restaurant, while John's interest and attention lay in his growing mining properties. Eventually, John Castner also owned two thousand acres of farmland acquired through pre-emption claims.

In 1894, Castner and Thomas C. Power sold Castner Coal and Coke Company to the growing giant Anaconda Copper Mining Company. John turned to real estate and insurance, public service and politics while Belt grew into a multiethnic mining community of 2,500 residents from Finland, Italy, Wales, England, Norway, Canada and the Midwest.

Both John and Mattie Castner were entrepreneurs, handling their businesses with skill while building exceptional reputations in the growing community. As the Castner Hotel expanded, Mattie added staff and operated a first-class establishment. Her multiracial staff included black, white and at least one Chinese cook. In addition, she successfully managed a substantial 640-acre ranch in the Highwood Mountains stocked with horses and cattle, some years shipping about one hundred cattle in railcars off to Chicago markets.

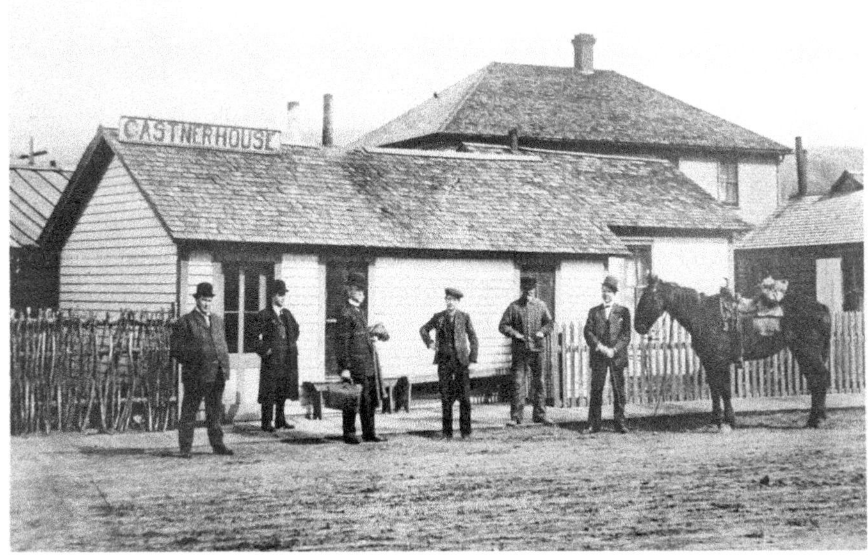

Passengers waiting for the stage at the Castner House in Belt, Montana. Mattie Castner's hotel resembled a southern plantation with so many buildings that an unidentified traveler called it "a Chinese puzzle." *Author's collection.*

Although most of Mattie's time was spent in managing the Castner Hotel, she also cared for a baby boy, named Albert, left by a young woman with the Castners about 1880. This would be the Castners' only child, and although Albert was never legally adopted, Mattie was a loving mother to him. Each spring, Mattie would put in a large garden, and as she supervised her workers, passing residents would hear old-time sweet lullabies in the air.

Using the fresh vegetables, including Montana's first sweet potatoes, to complement the diverse menu of wild game in the hotel, Mattie grew more than she needed for the hotel. In the early summer, Mattie hauled vegetables to Fort Benton three times a week, a distance of forty miles one way. She would load the vegetables after sundown and drive all night to arrive there by sunrise. Prices for fresh vegetables were high in the booming riverport, and Mattie received one dollar a bunch for carrots and the same for a head of cabbage. On these trips, she would take baby Albert with her. Once Maria Dutriueille was accompanying her friend to Fort Benton when Indians stopped them and took all the vegetables and one of the horses. Mattie rode the other horse back to Belt and returned with another horse to take Maria and the baby back home.[119]

With Mattie's expert management, the fame of the Castner Hotel grew widely over time. In 1903, a Butte newspaper gave a rave notice:

> [The Castner Hotel was not] *only a stage station,* [but also] *an eating house that was popular among travelers. In the old days, before the Neihart branch of the Montana Central* [Railroad] *was built,* [by] *passing Belt, Castner's hotel did a rushing business with travelers on the stages running to Fergus county and to Neihart and Barker.*
>
> *As the four or six horse stage rolled into Belt there was scurrying around in the Castner hotel to provide plates and food sufficient for the passengers. In about half an hour the bell, or rather the triangle, sounded and everybody filed into the dining room. All were seated at a long table and the food was served steaming hot from large plates. It was one of the most home like meals to be had in a meeting house and no one ever went away from Castner's kicking.*
>
> *Even that perennial kicker, the drummer, forgot his troubles and admitted that Mrs. Castner's chicken, her mealy potatoes, her succulent corn as well as her fine pie and coffee could not be beaten. The development of the coal mines and the growth of Belt have somewhat robbed Castner's of its old time glory, but the place still stands and still feeds many people every day.*[120]

In the fall of 1886, Mrs. Castner made her first trip back to Newton, North Carolina, to find family members. Reflecting on the complexity of reconstituting her slave family of five siblings, she found only a sister in Taylorsville and a brother in Charleston, North Carolina. Her mother and father and other members of the family had been sold to other masters, and no record could be found. After returning to Belt, Mattie sent for her sister and brother-in-law, Mr. and Mrs. Byers. Mr. Byers was active in revival meetings held by Reverend Wesley Van Orsdel, the famed Methodist minister, that were held from a covered wagon, while Mrs. Byers suffered from ill health. In 1889, Mr. and Mrs. Byers returned to North Carolina because of the failing health of Mrs. Byers.

Mattie Castner made a second trip to North Carolina in 1897, bringing back her great-niece and namesake, Mattie Bell Byers. Young Mattie Bell made her home with Mrs. Castner and attended school, completing the eighth grade. In 1900, Mattie Bell married John L. Novotny, of Austrian descent, and the Novotny family moved into nearby Great Falls.

Albert Castner married Annie Segla in 1907, and the wedding dinner was held at the Castner Hotel dining room. Mattie Castner continued to operate both the Castner House hotel and her Highwood ranch until about 1913, when she retired as hotelkeeper. Over the years, Mattie visited friends in Great Falls and attended the Union Bethel AME Church on occasion.[121]

John and Mattie Castner became major benefactors of the Belt community, donating land for schools and churches. Mattie's attention and reputation were centered on the hotel and ranch, while John's business enterprise benefited the community in many ways. He paid special attention to development of the Belt school system, serving as president of the board of education and even donating an extensive library to the high school. He served as justice of the peace and as a director of the North Montana Fair Association. He was an enthusiastic Republican and a leader in the Cascade County Republican Party. When Belt was incorporated in 1907, John Castner was the unanimous choice of the citizens for the office of mayor, a post he held for three years.

On December 29, 1915, John K. Castner died at the Castner House after his health had been failing for several months. His funeral was held in the Belt school auditorium, packed with more than five hundred who listened to the sermon of Brother Van, followed by burial in Highland Cemetery in Great Falls. The *Belt Valley Times* paid tribute to the "Father of Belt":

> *What can we say as to the lovable personality of our friend, John K. Castner, who passed to the great beyond yesterday morning that is not already known to every reader of this paper. We do not think he had an enemy in the world. . . . He had nothing but charity and kindness for all. In the full strength of his mind in later years, his whole energy was devoted to the betterment of conditions in his home city. The clear vision of the future which marks the character of the sturdy pioneer, was retained by him until death's call, and the loss will be keenly felt in many ways in Belt.*
>
> *Mr. Castner did not live in vain. While his success is not reassured by monetary standards, he has left lasting monuments to his worth as a citizen, a neighbor and a friend. His personality will be enshrined in the hearts of all as that of a broad-minded, considerate, sincere and kindly gentleman.*[122]

John Castner's estate was valued at $20,000, and Mattie received $17,800—more than $400,000 in today's dollars. Although retired from the hotel, she continued to make her home in Belt and operate the ranch until 1918, when she sold it for $17,000. She maintained a fine garden and held extensive land, including one tract a mile long parallel to the Great Northern Railroad.

On April 3, 1920, Mattie Bell Bost Castner, a daughter of the slaveholding South but a respected businesswoman in frontier Montana, passed away. In the words of her granddaughter Ethel Castner Kennedy, "Mattie commanded the respect of the people of Belt because of her generosity, industry and integrity, and probably, to some extent, because she was the wife of John K. Castner, the highly regarded founder of Belt." Regrettably, no photograph has ever been found of Mattie Castner.

Mattie Castner's funeral was held in the Belt High School. She had won the love and respect of the Belt community, and in her memory, the high school students were dismissed from classes so they could attend the funeral, "one of the largest ever held in Belt. A second funeral was held at the chapel of W.H. George in Great Falls with both the Belt Methodist minister Rev. Alvin Taylor and the Union Bethel AME minister Rev. A.W. Johnson officiating with interment in Highland Cemetery, next to the body of her husband."[123]

"'The Mother of Belt' Is Dead," the *Great Falls Tribune* proclaimed, yet this was not the end of her remarkable story. Mattie Castner had long planned the distribution of her wealth among family, friends and charities. Her more than $32,000 estate (approaching $750,000 in today's dollars) left money to relatives in Montana, North Carolina and

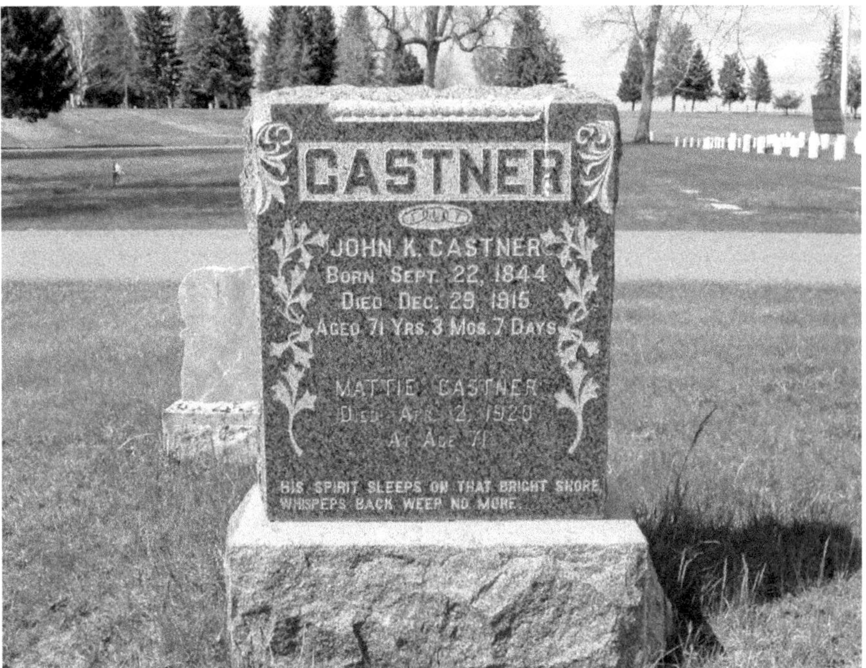

John K. and Mattie Bell Bost Castner are buried in Highland Cemetery, Great Falls, Montana. *Author's photo.*

Pennsylvania and to friends like Maria Adams Dutriueille; a small yellow house in Belt and ground, including a rhubarb patch, and $500 to a friend in Highwood; her piano and $100 to a Belt friend; twenty-six acres of land in Taylorsville, North Carolina, subject to life occupancy of her brother-in-law; $10,000 to the Freedman's Aid Society of Cincinnati; money and life interest in the Castner residence in Belt to a friend; monthly payments to brother-in-law Allen Watts of Taylorsville, North Carolina, sufficient for his welfare during his life and funds for his burial at the time of his death; to Casper Fisher, the privilege of a room in Castner residence "as long as he behaves himself and remains in his right mind"; and to her lawyer, J.W. Freeman, her two-thirds interest in eighty acres of land. The residue of the estate, about $5,000, went to charity, to be distributed to the poor and the sick through the Union Bethel AME Church of Great Falls and the Methodist Church of Belt, through the trustees of these churches. An annual report was to be filed by them with the District Court showing the names and addresses of persons benefited and the amount received by each, and the reports were to be read before the congregations of the churches named until the fund was exhausted. Additional distributions included an adjacent lot to the Catholic Church of Belt, $1,500 to the Methodist Church of Belt and $1,000 to the Union Bethel AME Church.[124]

Long after their passing, the good work and legacy of John K. and Mattie Bell Bost Castner lived on.

Chapter 18

From Slave to Stampeder . . . "de Gulch Am a Booming"

Millie Ringgold Keeps the Faith

Millie Ringgold was a rugged individualist in a rough country. She emerged from slavery to migrate up the Missouri River with the family of a senior army officer. After serving the family, Millie settled in frontier Fort Benton and opened a boardinghouse. When gold was struck in Yogo Gulch in a remote region of the Little Belt Mountains, she stampeded with others from Fort Benton. There, in soon-to-be ghost town Yogo City, Millie Ringgold spent the rest of her life.

Millie was born a slave in 1845 near Chestertown in Kent County on the Eastern Shore of Maryland. The 1850 Maryland Census Slave Schedule reveals Millie's most likely owner was seventy-three-year-old Samuel Ringgold, who owned eight slaves, including a five-year-old female. At that time, Ringgold families owned a total of just fifty-four slaves in Maryland. The Ringgolds were among the earliest settlers of Maryland and had been Loyalists during the American Revolution, and in subsequent generations, the family maintained a conspicuous position among the landed gentry of the state.

A decade later, the 1860 Maryland Slave Schedule indicates the ownership of fourteen-year-old Millie had passed to J. Ringgold of Chestertown, his only slave. Millie may have remained with her master until Maryland finally abolished slavery on November 1, 1864. Slavery's legacy was so imbedded in Maryland that the state refused to ratify the Fifteenth Amendment, giving African Americans voting rights, until March 28, 1973, even though federal law had long since passed them by.[125]

After gaining her freedom, like many other newly freed blacks during the Civil War, Millie Ringgold moved into Washington, D.C., and in 1870, she was living in Ward 2 in the capital, a twenty-five-year-old laundress born in Maryland who could read and write. There she was living with two other black laundresses, both born in Virginia.[126]

About 1872, the family of Nelson B. Sweitzer engaged Millie Ringgold to help with their growing family. Sweitzer, then a major in the 2nd Cavalry of the post–Civil War army, had been brevetted brigadier general at the end of extended service in the Civil War. General Sweitzer began the war as aide de camp on the staff of General George B. McClellan, commander of the Army of the Potomac. Colonel Sweitzer served under Major General Philip H. Sheridan in the Shenandoah Campaign and then assumed command of the 16th New York Cavalry. On the assassination of President Lincoln, Colonel Sweitzer and his regiment were ordered to Washington, D.C., to patrol southern Maryland and Virginia in the hunt for Lincoln's assassins. A detachment from his command, under Lieutenant Colonel Everton Conger, captured and killed assassin John Wilkes Booth in the greatest manhunt in American history.[127]

In the spring of 1873, General Sweitzer was assigned command of Fort Ellis, near Bozeman in Montana Territory. The general proceeded by coach from Corinne, Utah, to Helena, arriving on March 18, and then on to Fort Ellis to assume command of the post. His wife, Helena; their daughter Mary; and Millie Ringgold came up the Missouri River by steamboat to Fort Benton later in the spring and reunited the family at Fort Ellis by the early summer of 1873.[128]

At this time, settlers were arriving along the Yellowstone River and in Gallatin Valley with the growing importance of this promising section, amid concerns of the increasing threat from the Lakota Sioux. The mission of Fort Ellis was to protect settlers and travelers.[129]

Social life at Fort Ellis placed many demands on the post commander and his wife—and on their cook and servant, Millie Ringgold. Shortly after they had settled into their quarters on the post, General and Mrs. Sweitzer hosted a visit by Lieutenant Colonel C.C. Gilbert, commanding the Montana Military District and Fort Shaw in the absence of Colonel John Gibbon, and his wife, as well as Major and Mrs. George A. Forsyth and army paymaster Major Robert C. Walker and his family. The *Helena Weekly Herald* offered this glimpse into what life was like at Fort Ellis in the 1870s:

It has long been the happy custom of the officers and ladies of this post to give, as often as convenient, small dinner and evening parties, which are always gotten up in good style, made to pass off pleasantly, and are heartily enjoyed by all present. . . .

And such was the crowning event of last evening on the occasion of the brilliant reception and social hop given to Gen. Gilbert and party from Fort Shaw, and Major Walker and party from Helena, by Gen. Sweitzer, commander of the post, and wife. The guests began to assemble at 9 p.m., and were received at headquarters by the gallant Gen. and his estimable lady in their most hospitable and make-you-feel-perfectly-at-home manner. Those from Bozeman were taken up in carriages sent from the post under the care of Major Thompson and Lieut. Roe, the well-known fluency and persuasiveness of whose conversational powers must have contributed largely to the pleasure of the ride, and caused some of the ladies to sigh for the shortness of the distance. The officers all appeared in full military dress, and added not a little to the brilliancy of the occasion in their new and showy uniforms while the toilets of the ladies were tasteful and elegant in the extreme, and far beyond the descriptive powers of your correspondent. I will, however, be pardoned for referring specially to the hostess, who seemed never to have looked so well as she swept from point to point amid the gay and happy throng, discharging with becoming ease and grace the agreeable but delicate duties of the occasion. General and Mrs. Sweitzer were untiring throughout in their attention to their guests, and Major Forsythe and his affable lady were, as ever upon such occasions, active in contributing to the enjoyment of the evening. And I trust it may not be regarded as improper in this connection to remark that Mrs. Gen. Gilbert, by her culture, winning manners, and great vivacity, contributed very much to the charm and felicity of the occasion.

When all had arrived, they were conducted to the quarters occupied by Lieuts. Jerome and McClernand, which were attractively draped with national flags and ornamented with portraits of the leading General of the army, side arms, etc., when the enlivening strains of music by the Fort Ellis string band were struck up and the merry dance began, lasting till 4 o'clock a.m. At 12 o'clock a most choice and bountiful supper was served at the General's headquarters to about fifty persons, which, suffice it to say was composed of everything suitable to the hour that an officer's commissary and the markets of the country could supply. . . .

This was without doubt the most elegant and recherché *affair of the kind ever gotten up in this part of the Territory, and Gen. and Mrs. Sweitzer*

> *will long be gratefully remembered by those present for their goodness of heart and youthfulness of disposition displayed in its conception and execution.*
>
> *The parties referred to left for the* [Yellowstone] *National Park today.*[130]

It takes little imagination to comprehend who bore the brunt of the work of house cleaning, cooking, serving and cleaning up for the extravagant social events and parties at Fort Ellis in frontier Montana—Millie Ringgold and the other army officer servants did.

During the mid-1870 years of the Montana Indian Wars, Fort Ellis played an important role. Troops from Fort Ellis, including the 2nd Cavalry, under Lieutenant Colonel Eugene M. Baker, had precipitated the infamous Marias Massacre against a camp of Piegan Blackfeet on the Marias River on a frigid winter day in January 1870. Six years later, troops from Fort Ellis joined with the 7th Infantry from Fort Shaw as the "Montana Column" under Colonel John Gibbon campaigned during the Sioux War of 1876. In addition, Fort Ellis provided military escorts for prominent expeditions into the Yellowstone region and into the newly established Yellowstone National Park.

Three weeks after the big social event at Fort Ellis, in mid-September 1873, General Sweitzer, accompanied by Lieutenant Gustavus C. Doane, made a weeklong grand tour of the new national park. General Sweitzer quickly established a reputation as an effective commanding officer, imposing reforms and discipline lacking under the previous command of Lieutenant Colonel Baker. Overall, Fort Ellis was a "showcase" army post on the Montana frontier, and the social demands on Mrs. Sweitzer and Millie were immense.[131]

General Sweitzer was relieved of command at Fort Ellis in 1876, and as the general and his family departed Montana Territory, Millie Ringgold stayed behind, perhaps accompanying Mrs. Sweitzer and the children to Fort Benton, where the Sweitzers boarded a steamboat for the long trip down the Missouri River. By 1878, Millie was living in Fort Benton, and in December of that year, she opened a new boardinghouse on Baker Street. In the spring of 1879, she received payment by the Choteau County commissioner for care of pauper wards of the county. In August, she moved her boardinghouse to prominent Front Street on the levee, advertising as Ringgold Boarding House and Restaurant, where boarding cost $6 per week, and meals cost $0.50. Millie's county tax assessment for 1879 showed that she had acquired considerable property with an assessed value of $1,395 consisting of monies and credit, watches and jewelry—worth over $33,000 today.[132]

New Boarding House.

MILLE RINGGOLD, Prop.

BAKER Street, near MAIN, FORT BENTON, M. T.

Board by the week......................................$6 00
Lodging, per week,......................................$2 50
Single Meals..50

An ad for Millie Ringgold's new boardinghouse in Fort Benton. *Benton Record Weekly*, January 24, 1879.

In mid-September 1879, word reached Fort Benton that gold had been struck in a remote canyon in the Little Belt Mountains. Despite her successful business in Fort Benton, Millie Ringgold joined the stampede of miners and adventurers hastily departing Fort Benton for the new Yogo Gulch mines. She bought a wagon and two condemned army mules, loaded up provisions and a barrel of whiskey and headed for the Little Belt Mountains. By the end of September, she had established a restaurant, saloon and small hotel at Yogo City.[133]

For a short while, times were booming at Yogo City, and Millie profited handsomely as miners flocked in. But the major bedrock find remained elusive, and the placer mining boom soon faded into "bust," with only modest amounts of gold dust gained. During the good times, everyone knew Millie and enjoyed her good cooking and well-conducted hotel. Everyone could eat at Millie's place whether they had money or not, all promising to pay when they cleaned up bedrock.

Miners and travelers remembered Millie as a short and stocky lady with shiny black hair and musical talent demonstrated as she played old southern songs on odd instruments such as handsaws, mouth harps, washboards, sticks and dishpans. Visitor Finch David of Martinsdale commented, "She could make better music on an empty five-gallon can than most people can on a piano, and her favorite tunes were 'Coming Through the Rye' and 'Coal Oil Johnnie on a Bum-Bum Solree.'" David added, "[Millie] could get up the best meal with the least grub of anyone I ever saw." As a young girl, Rose Gordon of White Sulphur Springs knew Millie. She had once seen a photograph of Millie as a young woman and described her as having "a comely young face with earnest, beautiful eyes, a far different woman from the one I remember who knew poverty, excessive outdoor work and exposure."[134]

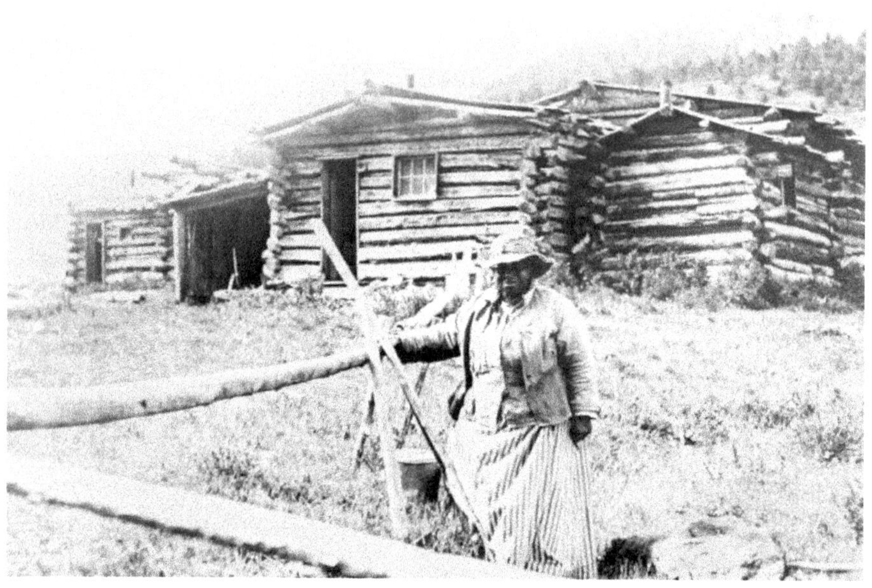

Millie Ringgold at her hotel in the gold mining camp of Yogo City. *Overholser Historical Research Center.*

In November 1880, future territorial Montana Supreme Court justice William H. Hunt visited Yogo City, reporting to the *Benton Record*:

> *All day long while I was in Hoover* [as Yogo City was first called], *it snowed and blew and stormed. The wind howled down the gulch and piled the deserted town full of high drifts. The few men about Hoover were determined to leave as soon as the snow melted. Millie Ringold is there, and proposes to remain. She told me "de gulch am a booming" and it was—with sleet and snow.*[135]

As disappointed miners began to drift away, Millie bought their claims, and she continued to tend her waning business and work her claims. She located several claims in the gulch and named them all for presidents. There were the Garfield, the George Washington and the Jefferson, among others. The George Washington paid the most, but none of the claims was worth a great deal.

In addition to working her mining claims, Millie continued to run her boardinghouse for travelers through the area. All who wrote about her raved about the immaculate house and dining room, complete with white linen and polished silver, that she kept up even though the town was all but deserted. During the 1890s, Millie made a precarious living by washing for a few prospectors, raising a small number of chickens and turkeys and occasionally cooking or nursing for ranchers. When dollars were scarce, George Washington, her cat, provided many of her meals. It would catch a rabbit and bring it to the cabin, where both Millie and her cat enjoyed it immensely. Sometimes Bedrock Jim, another Yogo character, would share in the feast by providing potatoes and an onion or a carrot to make a mulligan.

The 1900 federal census listed Millie Ringgold as prospector-owner of her claims. She had hired a black man to work for her, likely Abraham Carter, the only other black resident then in the Yogo District and one of the nine who then remained. When Millie ran out of funds to pay him, she continued to perform the manual work herself, often wearing men's overalls and reduced to living on frozen rutabagas.

Increasingly crippled by rheumatism, Millie left Yogo City in the winter of 1903 to accept county relief. But after a month in the Cascade County Poor Farm, Millie so ached to return to her home in the Little Belt Mountains that she was taken back when the weather improved.

For the last years of her life, Charles T. Gadsden, supervisor of the English Sapphire Mine, ordered the mine wagon and team to haul supplies to Millie. In December 1906, Millie was found on the floor of her cabin gravely ill. Dr. Abram Poska, of Utica, was notified, but he could do nothing more than remain with her until she died two days later. In an exceptional tribute, Charles Gadsden personally drove the English mine wagon and team, bringing out the body of Millie Ringgold for burial in the Utica Cemetery.[136]

Millie Ringgold simply never lost faith in the Yogo mines. For almost three decades, the ex-slave who joined the gold rush to Yogo Gulch clung to life and hope for the future of the camp. Cowboy artist Charles M. Russell—who became a Montanan in his early years in the Judith Basin "learning the ropes" from his mentor, Jake Hoover—paid tribute to Millie Ringgold as he painted her standing behind Hoover in his painting *A Quiet Day in Utica*. Millie had always said she would be the last "man" to leave Yogo City—and she was.

Chapter 19

Slave to Servant, a Family Tradition

The Life of Adeline Hoffman

Adeline Hoffman's unusual life story is featured as she transitioned from slave to servant serving generations of the same southern family from North Carolina to Missouri to Montana. Woven into Adeline's story is that of Union private Alfred Skaggs. Adeline lived for decades as a servant and member of the Skaggs family in Montana.

For Adeline Hoffman, the Civil War and Emancipation never happened. From slavery to freedom, Adeline served the same southern family, passing from generation to generation and locale to locale. She was born a slave in 1848 on the plantation of Daniel Rhyne in Gaston County, North Carolina. The Rhynes were a prominent family of German descent, and remarkably, at least thirty-two Rhynes served in the Confederate army from North Carolina.[137]

In the era of slavery, slave marriages were not permitted in the South. Adeline's mother was a slave belonging to Rhyne while the nearby Ford family owned her father. The North Carolina Slave Census of 1850 recorded Daniel Rhyne's slave property holdings: five adult males; two adult females, one fifty-five years old and the other thirty-five years old and likely Adeline's mother; and three children, two girls ages four and two years, the latter likely Adeline, and a male baby. While later dates recorded for Adeline's age vary, the predominant evidence is that she was born in May 1848.[138]

As a household slave, young Adeline served the Rhyne family until the death of her master in 1856. Rhyne's will allocated his slave children to his sons and daughters. Margaret "Peggy" Rhyne, wife of farmer Jacob S. Hoffman, became Adeline's new master. At that time, the Hoffman family lived on a plantation in Madison County in southeastern Missouri after having moved west several years earlier from Gaston County, North Carolina.[139]

On receiving news of Daniel Rhyne's death, Jacob Hoffman drove by wagon to the Rhyne plantation to bring Adeline and her younger brother and sister to Missouri. The two younger slave children were destined to join other Rhyne relatives living in the Midwest. Loading the slave children on his wagon, Hoffman headed west in the summer of 1856.

Later in life, Adeline recalled that trip:

> *I sure must have cried all the way back. I remember that grandpa (Jacob Hoffman) gave me candy and tried every way to make things nice for me but I just wouldn't listen. I wanted to stay with my mother. Grandpa said he almost made up his mind to turn around and take me back to her only she (the mother) had gone to join my father* [on the Ford Plantation].
>
> *When we reached the Mississippi and the ferry at Cape Girardeau I just closed my eyes and wouldn't look until we were over. I never saw the river just thought that once we were over, I would be gone from home for good.*
>
> *Grandpa promised me that I never would be whipped and that no one ever would run over me in general dealings. He always kept his promise.*[140]

As she got used to life in the Hoffman family on the Missouri plantation, Adeline lived in a sea of Hoffman children, thirteen of them. She became attached to the second youngest, a girl of four named Rose Angeline or Rosie. Amazingly, for the next eighty-three years, Adeline would work for Rosie, first as a slave and after the Civil War as a servant, becoming in some ways a member of the Hoffman family.

Then came the Civil War, ripping Missouri apart. In October 1861, Brigadier General M. Jeff Thompson led a 1,500-man secessionist Missouri State Guard force into southeastern Missouri, wreaking havoc on the Iron Mountain Bridge. Brigadier General Ulysses S. Grant commanded loyal Union forces in the District of Southeast Missouri at that time. In response to the threat of the Missouri State Guard, General Grant ordered two Union columns, one under Colonel Joseph B. Plummer with 1,500 men and another under Colonel William P. Carlin with 3,000 men in pursuit.

The Union force engaged Colonel Thompson's men in the Battle of Fredericktown on October 21, 1861. Fredericktown was the county seat of Madison County and located near the Hoffman farm. Outnumbered and outmaneuvered, the Missouri State Guard was defeated and forced to withdraw. Some Union soldiers believed that locals assisted Thompson in the engagement and that the State Guardsmen mistreated Unionist citizens in the area. This resentment led to retaliation against the town, with at least seven homes burned and other buildings damaged before Union officers regained control of their men. The victory at Fredericktown consolidated Union control of southeastern Missouri for the duration of the war.[141]

Adeline recalled that it was a hard struggle to live on the farm during the war. It was near a major highway, so troops were passing constantly. Horses, fodder, food and money all were taken from the Hoffmans during these turbulent times. She never made clear why Union troops didn't "free" her from slavery, although her loyalty to the family must have played a role—she likely simply refused to leave. Later, she remembered outlaw bands raiding and the family hiding "terror-stricken" children in the timber for days while "mounted gangsters raided" the Hoffman home. Adeline was hidden together with Rosie and the other white children.

At last the war came to an end, order was restored and farming resumed. Union forces had freed most of Missouri's 115,000 slaves during the war. Yet Adeline, although no longer a slave, remained in the Hoffman household by her choice—at this point she was alone and simply knew no other life. She apparently was treated well by the family and had formed a close bond with young Rosie Hoffman. As Adeline later related, her older sister came to take her along their road to freedom. Adeline declined, saying, "I didn't see how I could better myself with that foolishness, so I just stayed on. Grandma [Mrs. Margaret Hoffman] was needin' me, and I'd passed my promise to my folks and I didn't need what they called freedom."[142]

Life swept on in postwar Missouri. Rosie Hoffman met a young man named Alfred Ferguson Skaggs, who had lied about his age, entered the Union army at fifteen and served during the last year of the war. Private Skaggs, born on October 5, 1848, enlisted in Company F, 50th Missouri Volunteer Infantry, when that regiment was organized on September 11, 1864. His wartime experiences are an important part of the story.[143]

Private Skaggs's Company F was engaged heavily at the Battle of Pilot Knob, Missouri, on September 26–27, 1864, during Major General Sterling Price's last invasion of Missouri. As the Battle of Pilot Knob unfolded, Private Skaggs and his company with 60 men of the 50th Missouri were stationed in the ditch connecting the fort with the town of Pilot Knob along with other Missouri volunteer units and two pieces of artillery on the flank.

The Union forces with 1,000 men repulsed the attacks of Price's Army of more than 12,000 men, inflicting about 1,500 casualties, and successfully retreated with their artillery battery a distance of one hundred miles in the face of pursuing and assailing cavalry, a force five times their number.

General Price's invasion passed through southeast Missouri and onward and ultimately failed. For the rest of the war and until August 1865, the 50th Missouri Infantry remained on guard duty in southeast Missouri. For Private Alfred Skaggs, the war was over, and he returned to his home farm in Madison County.

After his discharge, Alfred Skaggs befriended young Rosie Hoffman, and when she was sixteen, he married her in September 1868. The couple set up housekeeping on a farm near the Hoffmans' with Adeline joining Rosie in the household. Soon, Jacob Hoffman needed help on his farm, and the Skaggses moved there.

The Skaggses and Hoffmans continued to farm in Missouri until 1886, when they heard about the fertile valley of the Gallatin River near Bozeman, Montana Territory. Soon all of them boarded a train and headed westward to Billings and then continued on to settle in the Gallatin Valley. Adeline lived with the Skaggs family for the rest of her life as cook, housekeeper and nurse.

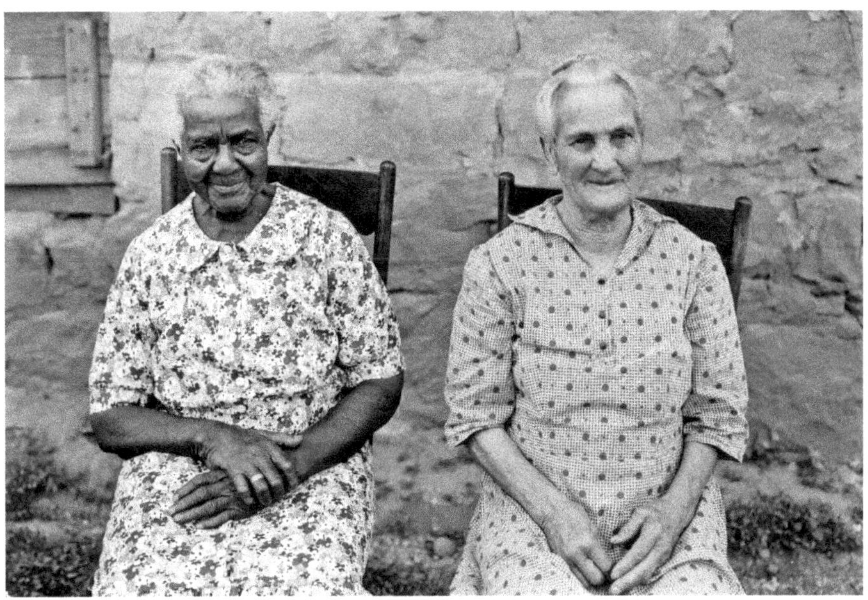

Aunt Adeline with her lifelong friend Rosie Hoffman Skaggs. *Lewistown Public Library.*

Gold was discovered in central Montana, and the town of Gilt Edge in the Judith Mountains near Lewistown boomed as the Gold Reef and Whisky Gulch diggings brought rich strikes. The Hoffman and Skaggs families moved to Gilt Edge in 1896 after a decade in the Gallatin Valley.

Adeline became the community nurse, often caring for the patients of Dr. William J. Lakey, who operated the Miners' Union Hospital in Gilt Edge. The early miners called her "Doc" or "Aunt" Addie. In addition to helping with the birth of the eight Skaggs children, Adeline was present as midwife at the birth of many of the children of the surrounding communities. By the time the ore ran out and the mines closed down, Adeline's capable hands had brought scores of children into the world in central Montana in the days when it was a week's ride to the nearest doctor. Adeline enjoyed seeing "her children," literally hundreds of them, move to all parts of the world and have their own children.

By day and night, on foot and in wagons, Adeline answered the constant appeal of those about to be born or in need of care. Snow filled the canyons or spring freshets rushed down the coulees, but Adeline kept on going. Among those whose children Adeline ushered into the world were "Teddy Blue" Abbott of "We Pointed Them North" fame and Bill Burnett, who trailed north with three Texas herds, captained the first big Montana roundup and led the vigilantes who pursued the outlaw Kid Curry.

Adeline's activities didn't stop with the children. She mothered cowpunchers and miners, gamblers and touts, and no one was turned down. "I can't remember Adeline ever saying 'no' to anyone," recalled William Skaggs. "To all the family she was the boss and still is to most of us now. When we were hurt we went to the Doc. When we were hungry we went to her and, if she had nothing on hand, she cooked something for us. Not only us but also the neighbor's kids. After payday the miners and cowhands would come to her broke and hungry after a party and be cured of hangovers. Everyone knew her and knew she would help."[144] Adeline was loved and respected by all who became acquainted with her, among them Governor Roy E. Ayers and state historical librarian John B. Ritch, once a cowpuncher.

After Gilt Edge became a ghost town, the Skaggs family moved to a ranch nearby and then, a few years later, to a ranch location near the Judith Mountain Divide where the Skaggs brothers operated the largest coal mine in the district.

"I take my time," Adeline often said. "Young folks today could learn to take theirs and be happier. I've seen just lots of them rush into marriage just to get married and then bust up. I'd say folks who are going to be

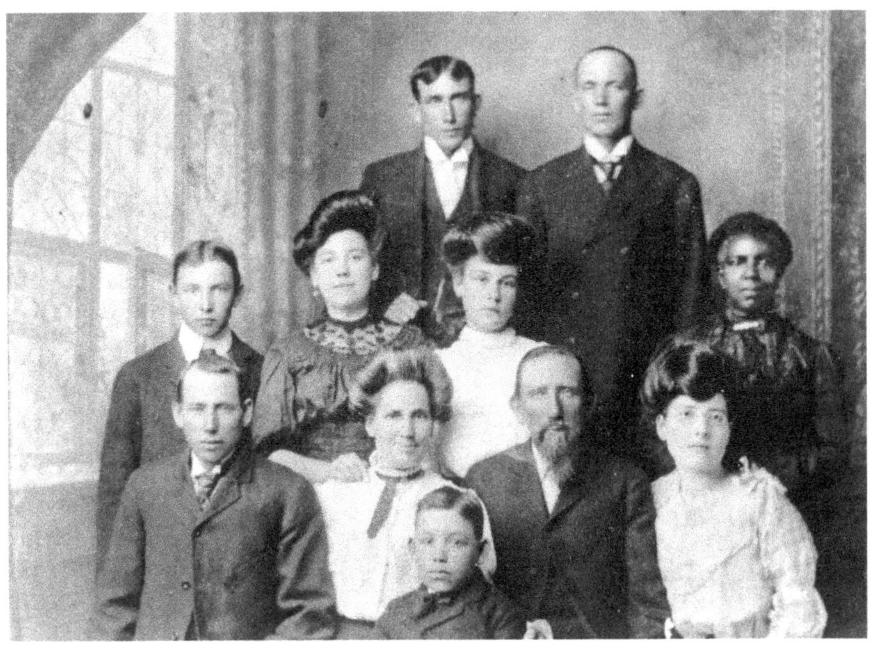

Adeline Hoffman is shown in this photo of the Skaggs family with Rosie and Alfred Skaggs seated front center. *Find A Grave.*

married ought to find out how they get along. Then there would be fewer bust-ups. Marriage is a business, not just the result of liking another person for a spell. . . . Yes sir, what folks need to know is how to take their time."[145]

The long life she lived brought Adeline her own philosophy, not so much cultured as acquired without conscious effort. She remained bright of mind with a good and accurate memory as she neared the century mark. Adeline had a quiet laugh and an eagerness for the new and interesting. She always showed an interest in life as she went on cooking, washing, working in the fields, nursing and mothering not only her own family but half the countryside as well.

Late in her life, Chadbourne M. Wallin visited "Aunt" Adeline. Of his memorable visit, he wrote:

> *I had Snooker, the 3-year-old* [son], *in my arms when I walked through the yard mud and into the big, two-story stone Skaggs ranch house in the coulee on the east slope of the Judith mountains, near Lewistown, Mont. Aunt Adeline was in the kitchen, washing dishes. She came out and I put Snooker on his feet. She saw him and said, "Whose boy are you?" Snooker,*

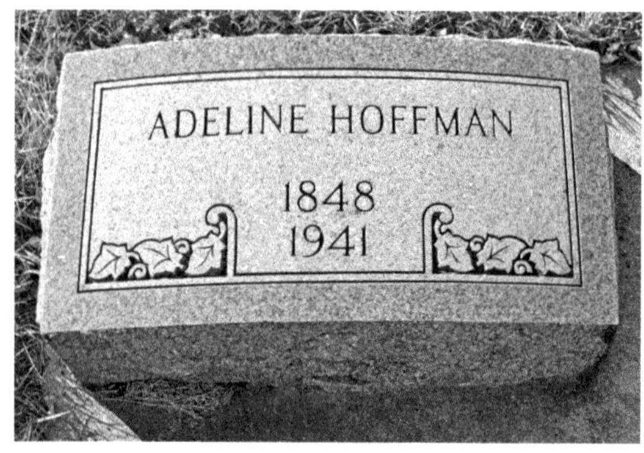

Adeline Hoffman's grave in the Skaggs family plot in Lewistown City Cemetery. *Author's photo.*

> *as usual when startled put half his right hand in his mouth tucked in his chin and looked out from lowered brows. Then they stood and beamed at each other, the span of a century between.*[146]

Adeline Hoffman lived with her Skaggs family until her death in January 1941. Her obituary read:

> *Beloved Negro Slave Laid to Rest Tuesday. Adeline Hoffman, 96, who was born in slavery on a plantation of the Old South 17 years before the start of the Civil War and who spent most of her life as a loyal and beloved member of the household of William Skaggs and his forebears tracking back over three generations, was laid to rest* [in the Skaggs family plot] *in the Lewistown city cemetery.*[147]

In tribute to Aunt Adeline, Skaggs family descendant Millie Hoves Salomon wrote these words:

> *Some People Say that Slavery Was Bad*
>
> *I'm sure we all agree*
> *It was real nice of Lincoln*
> *to set the slaves all free*
> *my great grand parents got this little girl*
> *when she was only nine*
> *they loved her like their very own*
> *her name was Adeline*
> *When they told her years later*
> *the slaves were all set free*

she cried and said, now mam & pap
I'll never leave thee
and so they kept her years and years
till they left this world behind
Then my grandfather & grandmother
kept sweet Adeline
My father told this to me
some years ago you see
he told me how she took care of him
when he was only three
and so you see there's good in all
if we could only see
I'm thankful for the story told
that my father passed to me.[148]

Nostalgic tributes aside, slavery was far more than a "peculiar institution"—it was evil. Bless her white families, who valued her as a family member, enabling Adeline Hoffman to lead a rewarding life.

PART IV
Memorable Characters and Outlaws:

Roaming the Montana Frontier

Chapter 20

From Civil War Glory to Indian Wars Disgrace

Major Guido Ilges

Many Civil War veterans later served in the Indian Wars in frontier Montana. Among these was the colorful and popular Major Guido Ilges (1835–1918), who, like many German immigrants, served in the Civil War and continued to make the army a career after the war. Major Ilges served with distinction during both the Civil War and the Montana Indian Wars, playing an important role during the Nez Perce War and commanding the Fort Benton Military Post from 1875 to 1879, only to fall victim later to bad judgment, court-martial and disgrace.[149]

Born in Ahrweiler, Coblenz, Prussia, on November 10, 1835, Guido Joseph Julius Ilges immigrated to America when he was twenty years of age. After practicing law at Vincennes, Indiana, before the Civil War, he joined the Frontier Guard as a private in April 1861. Newly elected Kansas senator and general James H. Lane raised the Frontier Guard to protect the White House in the chaotic early days of the war when Southern sympathizers in and around Washington, D.C., threatened President Abraham Lincoln and the capital.[150]

At that time, there was no Secret Service and very few Union troops stationed in Washington, so General Lane responded to the danger by raising loyal troops from Kansas and Illinois from men living near Washington. The government accepted Lane's volunteer Frontier Guard to protect the White House. On April 19, a few days after the guard was formed, the *Washington Evening Star* reported:

> *Beside the regular guard which has been stationed in the vicinity of the President's house for some time, a guard of sixty under the command of Gen. James H. Lane, of Kansas, occupied the east room and slept upon their arms last night. This company has been organized but a day or two, yet a large force is already enrolled, and the corps increasing rapidly. Late in the evening the President attempted to enter the east room, but as the sentinel at the door had received orders to admit no one without the countersign, Mr. Lincoln was forced to beat a retreat, to the no small amusement of the company. . . . This company goes on duty at the Executive Mansion every night at 8:30 o'clock and will continue to guard the White House until there is no danger of an attack upon the city.*[151]

A week later, the *Evening Star* reported that the Frontier Guard had been stationed for the past week at the Executive Mansion and on April 26 had joined the president in a body at the White House: "They formed at General Lane's headquarters, Willard's Hotel, numbering 120 men and marched thither, making a formidable appearance. They were ushered into the east room where they formed in line, and upon the entrance of the President were introduced by their commander."[152]

Private Ilges's performance of his duties with the guard attracted the personal attention of the president, who promoted Ilges to a captaincy in the regular army. On May 14, 1861, Ilges left the Frontier Guard to accept his commission as captain in the 14th U.S. Infantry Regiment, one of nine regular army units newly formed as part of the army's rapid buildup as the Civil War began. Captain Ilges served with the 14th Infantry during the first three years of the war, earning brevets to major for gallantry in the Battle of the Wilderness and to lieutenant colonel for gallant and meritorious service at Spotsylvania.[153]

Captain Guido Ilges saw action in many of the bloodiest battles of the Civil War. He was engaged in the Siege of Yorktown; Battles of Gaines' Mill, Charles City Cross-Roads, Malvern Hill, Second Bull Run, Antietam and Chancellorsville; action against the "Gray Ghost" John S. Mosby at Ewell's Chapel; Battles of Gettysburg and Rappahannock Station; operations at Mine Run; and Battles of the Wilderness (where he was wounded), Laurel Hill, Spotsylvania (when Ilges assumed command of his regiment), North Anna and Petersburg, Virginia.

The 14th U.S. Infantry Regiment compiled a distinguished record during the war. Its ranking captain, John "Paddy" O'Connell, who often led the 14th into battle, once said, "I would take the 14th to the very gates of Hell, but I want a chance to whip the Devil when I get there."[154]

Just weeks after the Battle of Second Bull Run on September 16–17, 1862, at the decisive Battle of Antietam, the 14th Infantry Regiment assigned to the Second Division under Brigadier General George Sykes was in the eye of the storm. At Antietam, Captain Ilges commanded Company E, First Battalion, 14th Infantry. Historian Brian Downey noted, "Few military organizations find themselves on the precise spot, at the precise moment, to be a trigger to war's conclusion. For Brigadier General George Sykes' 2nd (Regular) Division, Fifth Army Corps, one such golden opportunity came at Antietam." Of course, the war did not end at Antietam, but this "lost" battle for the Confederacy proved in many ways its high-water mark.

In the spring of 1863, acting on good intelligence, General George Meade ordered a trap set for Confederate major John S. Mosby and his partisan rangers at Ewell's Chapel in Prince William County. Mosby, known as "the Gray Ghost," and his rangers of the 43rd Battalion, 1st Virginia Cavalry, were noted for their lightning-quick raids behind Union lines.

On the morning of June 22, a thirty-man detachment of the 17th Pennsylvania Cavalry was exposed as bait while Company E, 14th U.S. Infantry, with one hundred men, commanded by Captain Ilges, hid in the rear of Ewell's Chapel and along a farm lane that entered the Old Carolina Road near the chapel. As Mosby and about twenty-five men passed through the Ewell Farm, they saw the Union cavalry and attacked. The trap had worked, but the concealed 14th Infantry found half their weapons failed to fire because of damp and rainy conditions and delivered such poorly directed fire as the Rebels approached that Mosby and his men quickly scattered, suffering only three wounded. While Union forces suffered just a single casualty, the trap had failed, causing General Meade to lament that they had failed the "prettiest chance . . . to dispose of Mr. Mosby."

The eight companies of the 14th U.S. Infantry arrived near Gettysburg on the morning of July 2 and took position with the rest of the First Brigade, Second Division, Fifth Corps, near Twelfth Corps on the right. They moved with the division from the right to the left of the line and at 5:00 p.m. with the brigade moved across Plum Run near Little Round Top and supported the Second Brigade in its advance to the crest of the rocky wooded hill beyond and, facing left, engaged the enemy. The 14th retired under a heavy fire on both flanks and from the rear after the Confederates had possession of the Wheatfield in the rear of the brigade and went into position on Little

Round Top. The 14th remained in the same position through July 4, when the regiment with the 12th supported the 3rd, 4th and 6th U.S. Infantry in a reconnaissance and developed a force of the Confederate infantry and artillery in front. During the Battle of Gettysburg, the 14th suffered 16 killed and 132 overall casualties. A regimental monument for the 14th Infantry stands today along Ayres Avenue on Houck's Ridge.

From May 8 to 21, 1864, Grant and Lee conducted a series of engagements, including the costly Battle of Spotsylvania Court House. The Union Fifth Corps, including Major Ilges and his 14th Infantry, was heavily engaged in battle at Spotsylvania. In this action, Ilges was cited for gallantry and meritorious service, received a battlefield promotion to brevet lieutenant colonel and assumed command of the 14th. While General Grant failed to defeat or destroy the Army of Northern Virginia, General Lee failed strategically to keep the Army of the Potomac out of central Virginia. It was during this battle on May 11 that General Grant sent his famous dispatch declaring, "I propose to fight it out on this line if it takes all summer." It took that summer and more.

Lieutenant Colonel Ilges continued to serve in combat at the engagement at North Anna River on May 24 and skirmishes leading to Petersburg in mid-June 1864. After coming under fire in some forty engagements, being twice promoted and suffering wounds, Lieutenant Colonel Guido Ilges ended active combat duty with his appointment as acting assistant inspector general, Second Division, Fifth Corps, Army of the Potomac, from June to August 1864. During the fall of 1864, he served as a member of the Inspecting Board of General Hospitals for the State of Pennsylvania from October to November. Finally, the decorated warrior Lieutenant Colonel Ilges ended the last months of the war on recruiting and mustering duty in New York from December 1864 to May 1865.

Following the surrender of the Army of Northern Virginia at Appomattox on April 9, 1865, the Union army prepared for its triumphant parade through Richmond celebrating victory. When asked where the gallant 14th should be placed in line, General George Meade, commander of the Army of the Potomac, immediately responded, "To the Right of the Line. The 14th has always been to the front in battle and deserves the place of honor." While Lieutenant Colonel Guido Ilges no longer served with the 14th, there is no doubt he was with the troops in spirit and memory as they marched through the captured Rebel capital and later at our nation's capital.

Prussian-born Guido Joseph Ilges was a natural soldier and leader and remained a captain in the 14th Infantry Regiment after the war, serving in the

Southwest during the Apache Indian Wars. Stationed in Arizona, Captain Ilges was active in scouting and operations against the hostile Apaches.

In 1867, Captain Ilges rescued a seven-year-old boy named Ernest Amelung, who had been captured by the Apaches. Ilges adopted the boy as his ward, sending him to San Francisco to live with Ilges's aunt until relatives could be located. Finally, an uncle was located near Frankfurt, Germany, and Ernest was sent to live with him. About 1882, when Amelung was twenty-two, he returned to the United States and secured work as an interpreter in the War Department. He began a long search for the man who had saved his life and finally found Ilges in 1912 in Cincinnati, Ohio.

Promoted to major on December 10, 1873, Ilges joined the 7th Infantry Regiment under Colonel John Gibbon in frontier Montana Territory. Assigned to command the Fort Benton Military Post, Major Ilges became a popular and respected figure around that lively riverport town.

On September 25, 1877, with a depleted company from the 7th Infantry and a strong mounted civilian volunteer column, Ilges fought the Nez Perce at Cow Creek Canyon, suffering light casualties. In 1883, Ilges responded to an account of the Nez Perce War with which he took exception. In a letter to the *Benton Record* of August 12, 1883, Ilges, then of the 18th Infantry, wrote:

> *In justice to one enlisted man, Private Bundy, Company B, Seventh Infantry, and thirty-seven citizen volunteers under my command, I desire to say that this* [Ilges's] *column took up its line of march from Fort Benton at noon of the 21st of September, 1877, crossing the Missouri at Fort Claggett, and reaching the opposite shore of Cow Island on the evening of September 24th, six hours after the departure of the Nez Perces from that point and having traveled about two hundred miles; that this column on the morning of the following day (September 25th) crossed the Missouri, followed the trail of the Nez Perces leading up Cow creek, overtook these Indians at noon and engaged in a battle of two hours' duration with them, during which one volunteer and several Indians were killed; that during the following night I dispatched two of my volunteers, Charles Bucknum and William Gantes, as couriers to General* [Nelson A.] *Miles, paying them for their dangerous service the sum of $300; that these two couriers delivered my letter of information as to the whereabouts of the Nez Perces on September 26th to General Miles, who was then operating on the eastern slope of the Little Rockies, and that they conducted as guides Gen'l Miles and his command to Snake creek, where the final capture took place after five days' severe fighting.*

Although these services rendered by my command have for some unaccountable reason never been publicly recognized, either officially or otherwise, I hold in my possession a private note from Gen. Miles of subsequent date, in which he acknowledges the receipt of my information and service rendered, of which he made such good use.

In justice to my independent command, I claim that the same discovered the trail of the Nez Perces, after evading the different commands in pursuit, and the exact location of their crossing of the Missouri; that it relieved the dangerous position of Fort Claggett; that it saved by its prompt advance and pursuit two steamboats (then near Cow Island) and over one hundred tons of Government freight; that harassed, fought and delayed the Nez Perces for about two days, and that it furnished the information to General Miles which rendered final success probable and even possible. Guido Ilges Lieut. Col. 18th Infantry.[155]

While Ilges exaggerated the impact of his small army and civilian force, no doubt its greatest contribution came in delaying the movement of the Nez Perces to safety and the intelligence delivered by his scouts to Colonel Nelson Miles.

National interest and newspaper coverage of Montana's Indian Wars of 1876–78 was intense. On June 2, 1878, the *New York Times* headlined "An Indian War Threatened. News from Sitting Bull—Hostile Demonstrations—A Speech from the Old Chief—Runners Dispatched to Arouse the Northern Tribes." In these and other reports, the latest exciting actions of Major Ilges and the 7th Infantry were covered.[156]

By the summer of 1878, the 3rd Infantry Regiment had relieved the 7th at Fort Shaw and Fort Benton. On October 22, Major Ilges used his Fort Benton–based 3rd Infantry Company to capture a camp of thirty-five Metis from the Red River in Canada and returned them northward across the border.

In December 1879, Major Ilges transferred to the 5th Infantry at Fort Keogh, near today's Miles City. One year later, with five companies from his new regiment, he moved through bitter winter weather from Fort Keogh to Camp Poplar on the Missouri River. On January 2, 1881, with about 300 officers and men, Major Ilges attacked a strong camp of Sioux on the north side of the Missouri River, killing 8 and forcing about 300 to surrender. One week later, some 20 additional Sioux were captured, and on January 29, 64 more were taken, without casualties to the U.S. Army except for many cases of frostbite because of the bitterly cold weather. Among the captured Sioux

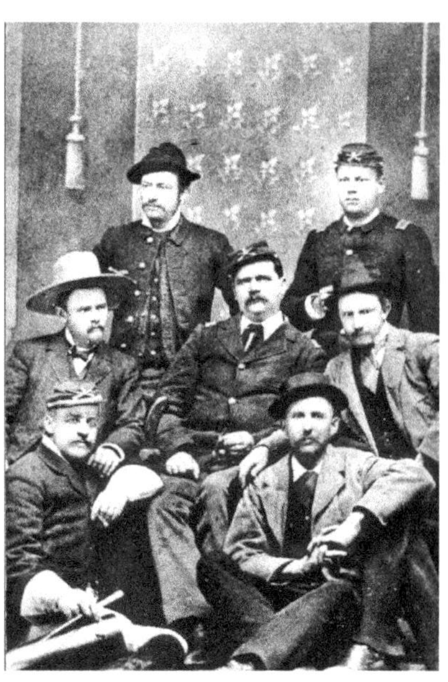

Lieutenant Colonel Guido Ilges, *seated center*, with officers in his 14th Infantry Regiment during the Indian Wars. *Overholser Historical Research Center.*

were warriors Gall and Iron Dog, who had participated in the Custer defeat on the Little Big Horn River five years earlier. Continuing to pursue the hostile Sioux, Major Ilges arrested 185 in a Yankton camp at Redwater, Montana, on February 12, 1881. One year later, on February 6, 1882, Ilges was promoted to lieutenant colonel of the 18th Infantry.

The next year, in 1883, Lieutenant Colonel Ilges found himself with financial problems and was charged with conduct unbecoming an officer and a gentleman and in violation of the 61st Article of War for depositing duplicate pay accounts. Colonel Ilges pleaded not guilty to the charges and was court-martialed. His trial was conducted in St. Paul from July 17–20. Colonel Ilges admitted his errors but denied any intent to defraud anyone. He pleaded that his twenty-two years of faithful and hard service to the country be considered.

Despite his eloquent protestation, the court found Lieutenant Colonel Ilges guilty of financial irregularities in filing for duplicate pay for two months the previous year, although no dishonesty was involved. The court recommended his dismissal from the army. President Chester A. Arthur approved the recommendation, and on October 31, 1883, Guido Ilges was cast out of the army.[157]

Ilges's friends in Fort Benton rose to his defense. The *Benton Record* of October 27 editorialized:

> *We cannot allude to the recent action of the President in approving the sentence by which Lieutenant-Colonel Ilges was dismissed from the army, without emotions of grief and indignation. . . . Col. Ilges had climbed too high upon the military ladder for a man who was without family influence. His sole claim to preferment was, that for long years he had undergone all the privations attendant upon early campaigning in this country; that he had conducted the most successful campaigns ever made*

> *against the Indians in this country; that he had furnished information which made it possible for Miles to capture Chief Joseph; that his energy was unequalled and his bravery unsurpassed; that no man in this country who ever knew him did not recognize in him the brave soldier, the courteous gentlemen, the steadfast friend.*[158]

After the crushing blow of dismissal, Ilges traveled around Montana speaking of the Apache Wars and his other experiences to enthusiastic and supportive audiences. Eventually, civilian Guido Ilges settled in Cincinnati, Ohio, and began working for German-language newspapers there. For eighteen years, Ilges worked as a journalist in Cincinnati and then another thirteen years as a weight master at a city hay market.

In March 1905, a Cincinnati reporter visited the old soldier just as he was celebrating his sixty-seventh birthday. The journalist described his visit with Guido Ilges:

> *The tall* [six feet, two inches], *commanding form of this distinguished old soldier looms up into the cupola of the little shanty when he rises from the little old desk where he keeps his accounts and at the side of which he adjusts the balance for the loads of hay and other produce and all sorts of things needing certified weighing. The bronze of many campaigns during the great Civil War and of many marches against Apache and Hunkpapa Lakota Sioux clings to his face and reminds one immediately of the Indians, against whom he marched and fought for many years.*[159]

By 1917, Ilges was crippled from war wounds, nearly blind and almost destitute. As a last resort to avoid the poorhouse, he applied for a pension based on his Civil War service, rising from private to brevet lieutenant colonel. After a lengthy delay, his pension finally was granted for thirty dollars per month. Yet Civil War hero Lieutenant Colonel Guido Ilges never cashed his first pension check—he died on January 13, 1918, a few days before it arrived.

Chapter 21

From a Civil War Prison to the Montana Legislature

Captain Samuel A. Swiggett

Bolstered by an indomitable spirit of optimism, Samuel Aaron Swiggett survived thirteen months in Confederate prisoner-of-war camps and left an impressive record of achievement in territorial Montana. Life simply could not keep this good man down.

Samuel A. Swiggett was born in Dorchester County, Maryland, on May 19, 1834, the son of William H. and Henrietta M. Hurst Swiggett. When he was thirteen years of age, his mother died, and left on his own, Samuel became a tailor's apprentice. In 1852, he moved west to Cambridge City, Indiana, and three years later on to Iowa, where he settled at Blakesburg, Wapello County. In 1856, he married Eliza H. VanCleave, daughter of Cyrus VanCleave, one of Bakesburg's co-founders. Working as a tailor and postmaster with a small general store, on August 8, 1862, Samuel Swiggett enlisted for a three-year term and was mustered in to the 36th Iowa Infantry Regiment at Camp Lincoln, Keokuk, on October 4. Active in recruiting, he was elected captain of Company B. Captain Swiggett served three years and one month in Arkansas and Tennessee, and his army experience was full of extraordinary hardship and suffering.

Much of what we know today about the 36th Iowa Infantry and Captain S.A. Swiggett comes from a small volume he published in 1895, while he was living in Montana. This book, entitled *The Bright Side of Prison Life*, makes his personal experiences and that of his regiment the keynote of the narrative. Captain Swiggett described his 36th Iowa Infantry Regiment and the important battles they fought at Helena and Little Rock, Arkansas. He wrote about the good and the bad of the war, filtered by his sunny optimism.[160]

The men of the 36th Iowa were first issued old Austrian and Belgian smoothbore muskets with "sword" bayonets, but these antiques were eventually replaced with more effective Enfield rifled muskets. Following basic training at Camp Lincoln, the regiment departed Keokuk on November 1, 1862, aboard two steamboats for St. Louis to await corps and division assignment and to continue training.

At St. Louis, the 36th Iowa went into garrison at Benton Barracks. The troops were attached to the 13th Corps, Army of Tennessee, and commenced drill by brigade and division. On December 20, 1862, they embarked a steamboat for the Federal garrison at Helena, Arkansas. On board the steamer, Captain Swiggett and his men were surrounded by "soldiers, hard tack and coffins," and he wrote, "None knew where we were going and the conflict between hope and fear was in many a breast—hope of success and glory, and distrust of the issue."

The steamboat halted at Memphis when local citizens hailed it from shore with an alarming report that Confederate brigadier general Nathan Bedford Forrest and his cavalry were nearby and were preparing an attack on the city. That night, the men of the 36th slept in Jackson Square with their arms stacked nearby. The regiment later moved to old vacated mule sheds and remained in Memphis performing guard duty until January 1, 1863, when it resumed movement to Helena, Arkansas.

At Helena, the regiment became part of the 1st Brigade, 13th Division, 13th Corps, under Major General Benjamin M. Prentiss. The regiment participated in the Yazoo Pass Expedition. This operation was designed to blow an opening through the east bank of the Mississippi River below Helena to open a channel connecting with an inland water route that would enable General Ulysses Grant to encircle the Confederate stronghold at Vicksburg from the north. Captain Swiggett noted that the 36th Iowa had a "sharp exchange" with the Rebels, and the regiment was engaged on this march for forty days. They found no unguarded route to Vicksburg, and the expedition was abandoned. The men suffered because of almost continuous exposure to the elements on this campaign, including freezing rain, wading through cold swamp water and high winds that blew down their tents. The constant cold and dampness took a heavy toll, with dozens of soldiers suffering with colds, flu and fever.

Returning to Helena, the 36th began a physically demanding daily routine of drill and fortification building in anticipation of a Confederate attack expected with the arrival of spring weather. The 36th Iowa was assigned to build breastworks and trenches in support of Battery A at Fort Curtis, on the northernmost end of the Union defenses. The Federal line ran in a semicircle around the town with the Mississippi River on the east flank.

On July 4, 1863, a Confederate army of 8,000 to 10,000 under Major General Theophilus H. Holmes attacked Helena. With devastating artillery fire and fire support from the U.S. Navy gunboat *Tyler* anchored offshore, the Union force repulsed the assault in a savage, bloody, all-day donnybrook under a burning hot sun. The Confederates nearly captured some of the Federal redoubts where the fighting devolved into gory hand-to-hand combat. The attacking Confederates suffered devastating loss of about 3,200, while victorious Union forces had some 500 killed, wounded or missing.

On July 5, the 36th Iowa joined other Union forces in celebrating Independence Day a day late by collecting and burying Rebel corpses. Vicksburg also surrendered to General Grant on July 4. These two victories ended further serious Confederate threat to Federal operations along the Mississippi River and essentially cut off regular lines of communication and supply between Rebel forces on either side of the Mississippi for the duratuon of the war. With New Orleans, Vicksburg, Helena, Memphis and St. Louis all in Federal hands, the Mississippi became the uncontested transportation corridor for the Union.

Despite these earlier successes, Captain Swiggett was headed for drastic defeat and capture along with most of his regiment. The 36th Iowa, along with other Union forces, was assigned to escort a critical Union resupply wagon train through dangerous territory in Arkansas. En route, the regiments were ambushed by Confederate brigadier general Joe Shelby's cavalry brigade. After a five-hour firefight that ended in hand-to-hand combat, some of the 36th Iowa were rounded up and disarmed. A last-ditch effort to break the Confederate lines created enough confusion and diversion for part of the regiment to bolt and attempt to warn an oncoming Ohio regiment. The commanding officer of the 77th Ohio Infantry ignored the warning and ordered his regiment forward at the double quick into the melee, and soon that regiment was also overwhelmed by the three Rebel cavalry divisions and surrendered.

By 3:00 p.m. on April 25, 1864, the 36th Iowa Infantry had ceased to exist. Captain Swiggett's Company B had suffered seventy-three killed and wounded. Captain Swiggett and thirty-five of his men were captured, and the Rebels robbed most of them of their possessions and even their clothes. The event of that fateful day that most disturbed Swiggett involved the flag, and he wrote:

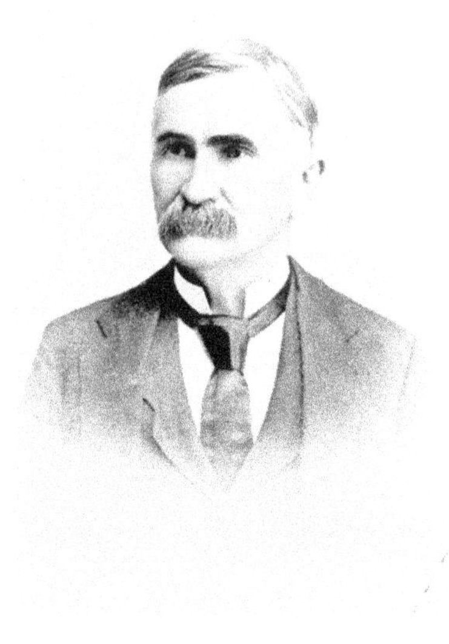

Civil War prison survivor Captain Samuel A. Swiggett. *Author's collection.*

> *We were quietly standing there, awaiting the final* [prisoner] *count, when we suddenly caught sight of an approaching body of rebels bearing a lot of captured flags, among which I recognized our own, all torn and disfigured as it was, the very scars enabling the recognition.*
>
> *We can talk lightly of a flag as being only a distinguishing mark or emblem, but its true emblematic character is not realized until some occasion arises to impress upon us what is meant by the flag of our country.*
>
> *When my gaze rested upon that shot-torn flag all the memories of its associations flashed through my mind in an instant, as well as the full realization of what its possession would mean to us and what its absence signified. Words cannot express my feelings. I looked around me for a moment, and meeting the eye of one of our men looking at me, his countenance twitching and his eyes filled with tears, I broke down completely and sobbed like a child for a few minutes.*
>
> *O ye men, who have only looked upon our country's flag as a pretty emblem! You, who only think of it as a necessary distinguishing mark among nations! And the many who never think of it as anything except a piece of bunting! Be ye once in a position where inability to possess that strip of colored fabric means privation, loss of liberty, separation from home and friends, possibly death, and you will then realize what it means to you as no language can depict!*[161]

The Union prisoners were marched over 1,700 miles and confined in thirteen jails and prisons along the way in Arkansas, Louisiana and Texas. Finally, they were imprisoned at Camp Ford, Tyler, Texas, the largest Confederate prison west of the Mississippi. Over the next year, many of the prisoners died of malnutrition and disease.[162]

Among the four to five thousand prisoners at Camp Ford, the favorite pastime was planning escapes. From tunnels to clever ruses, the prisoners tried every tactic imaginable. Tunnel escapes often proved abortive events with early discovery or construction miscalculations ending the tunnel short of its goal. In one case, some fifty prisoners escaped, though most were recaptured within a few days. It was a long way to Union lines from Tyler, Texas, through Rebel territory.

Captain Swiggett twice made his escape, once succeeding for a distance of 110 miles from the prison before he was recaptured. On his second escape, he ranged 275 miles from Camp Ford but again was recaptured. In both his escapes, black slaves defied the Confederates by giving aid and directions to Captain Swiggett and other Union escapees.

In his first escape attempt in August 1864, Captain Swiggett and five other officers of the 36th Iowa bribed the guards and made their escape. They traveled by night, remained hidden in the woods during the day and in this way succeeded in covering a distance of 110 miles, but when they reached the vicinity of Boston, Texas, they were recaptured and were marched back to Tyler. When taken, most of the men were exhausted from exposure and want of food, and the return to Tyler was made under great hardship. They were returned to the stockade at Camp Ford in late September. On December 23, Captain Swiggett, with two officers of the 120th Ohio Infantry, made a second attempt to escape, and after traveling twenty-one nights, they reached the Codo River. Again, he and the two officers who were with him were captured, this time being confined from time to time in different jails and finally landing in the stockade at Shreveport before being marched back to Camp Ford.

When they weren't planning escapes, the prisoners were speculating about parole exchanges. Captain Swiggett observed:

> *Exchanges at this time were considerably delayed by the trouble which resulted from the paroles given to the large number of prisoners at Vicksburg. These men were tired of fighting, had no desire to serve the Confederacy again, and not only refrained from again carrying arms against the United States, until regularly exchanged, but sought to avoid doing it at all by keeping out of the way of exchange.*[163]

Captain Swiggett's regiment was being exchanged in early 1865 in Shreveport at the time of his second escape attempt. Because of his two escapes, Swiggett was not allowed to gain freedom with his men. In fact, Captain Swiggett was the last Yankee prisoner to leave Camp Ford's stockade on May 22, 1865.

With his release, on board a Rebel transport boat en route to the Union fleet, Captain Swiggett talked with the Confederate prisoner exchange commissioner. In his conversation with the commissioner, Colonel Samansky, who was a Pole who had risen to colonel in the Confederate army, asked Swiggett how he had been treated as a prisoner. Swiggett replied:

> *The only complaint that I could consistently make against those having me in charge was that I had not been exchanged with my regiment. I claimed to him that I had been of more service to the Union as a prisoner than I could have been if I had remained in the service, as I had kept, on an average, two men busy watching me ever since I had been captured.*[164]

Captain Swiggett continued to describe his release:

> *At the mouth of the Red River we met some Federal boats coming up with Confederate prisoners.* [The prisoners were exchanged at that time, so Swiggett was back in Union hands.] *One notable feature of this occasion was the fact remarked by everyone that you could tell a Yankee from a rebel as far as you could see him, even without his clothes. The reason for this was that our confinement in the open air had caused us to be burned brown by the sun, even through our clothing, while the rebels were white from confinement within walls.*[165]

Captain Swiggett and the other released prisoners were taken down to New Orleans and housed there for ten days in a cotton press. From the time of his capture to his arrival in New Orleans, he had only once been able to get word through to his wife, so he promptly wrote to her. He heard later that she had learned of his condition through an earlier escaped prisoner. On the way back to Benton Barracks in St. Louis, Swiggett learned that his reconstituted 36th Iowa Infantry Regiment was at Devalls Bluff, Arkansas, on guard duty. After a great reception with his 36th Iowa and being mustered out, Swiggett proceeded home to Iowa.

Throughout his ordeal, Captain Swiggett remained positive about the future. As he observed, "My natural disposition being to see the bright side only, the hardships of which I had to tell were made to have another aspect than the usual one presented of prison life." He continued:

> *There were cases of personal ill treatment which came under my notice, but they were the great exceptions, and, as a rule, the rebels of my acquaintance did for their prisoners all that was possible with the means in their power and treated them as well as prisoners could expect to be treated.*

> *The war is over. Our foes had neither our resources nor our advantages in its prosecution, and many things that were easy for us were impossible for them. . . . Incidents by the thousand of heroic, heart-touching actions performed for humanity's sake during our war by those on one side for those on the other reflect as much credit upon rebels as upon Yankees, and I have always felt that, on the whole, our antagonists did the best they could for their prisoners.*[166]

Returning to his family in Iowa, Swiggett was elected sheriff of Wapello County, Iowa, in 1869, remaining in office until 1874. In 1887, he caught Montana mining fever and moved west to settle at Clancy, Jefferson County. He bought an interest in a quartz mine and engaged in mining. Although he'd been a resident for just one year, he attended the Jefferson County Republican convention. There were sixty-two members in the convention, only two of whom he knew; nevertheless, he was nominated on the legislative ticket. That fall, he was elected to the Sixteenth and last Territorial House of Representatives, and from January to March 1889, he served on the important committee on mines and minerals.[167]

Captain Swiggett continued mining until 1890, when he was appointed by President Benjamin Harrison as registrar of the United States Land Office in Helena. In March 1894, Republican governor John E. Rickards named Swiggett register of the newly created State Land Office. He served just two years before Democratic governor Robert B. Smith removed him because of Swiggett's opposition to free silver. In 1896, the Merchants & Miners National Bank of Philipsburg failed. Captain Swiggett was appointed receiver and within twelve months had skillfully paid all creditors one hundred cents on the dollar.

Mrs. Eliza Swiggett died in 1894, and a year later, Captain Swiggett married Mrs. Florence (Grabill) Kelly. A lifelong Republican, Swiggett cast his first vote for the first Republican presidential candidate, John C. Frémont, in 1856. Swiggett was a prominent member of the GAR. In August 1898, he was appointed United States deputy collector of customs based in Great Falls, and he remained in office until his death on July 22, 1904, in Helena. Fellow Civil War veterans Colonel Wilbur Fisk Sanders (Union) and Shirley C. Ashby (Confederate) served as honorary pallbearers. Old soldier, prison survivor and eternal optimist, Captain Samuel A. Swiggett rests today with his first wife in Ottumwa Cemetery, Wapello County, Iowa.

Chapter 22

Rising from Private to General "A Man of Iron Nerve"

Charles S. Warren

Charles S. Warren was a most remarkable man. In the words of Montana historian Tom Stout, General Charles S. Warren lived "on terms of intimacy with miner and prospector, mine operator, capitalist, statesman. . . . and perhaps no one in Montana . . . is better informed and could describe from his own experience and knowledge the real forces that have shaped and formed the political and industrial fabric of the state."[168] Over the course of his long career, Warren provided energy and leadership as Montana moved slowly from territory to state.

Charles Warren was born near historic Starved Rock State Park in Utica, LaSalle County, Illinois, on November 20, 1846, a descendant of a prominent Quaker family of Pennsylvania and a Revolutionary War family of New York. The Warrens became early farm settlers in the Illinois Valley of central Illinois.

During the Civil War, seventeen-year-old Charles Warren enlisted on May 2, 1864, and was mustered in as private in Company A, 132nd Illinois Infantry Regiment, on June 1. Organized at Camp Fry, Chicago, and commanded by Colonel Thomas J. Pickett, the 132nd was formed for just one hundred days' service. Departing on June 6 for Columbus, Kentucky, the 132nd moved on to Paducah, Kentucky, to assume guard duty there.

Earlier in the Civil War on September 6, 1861, Union forces under Brigadier General Ulysses S. Grant bloodlessly captured Paducah, giving the Union control of the mouth of the Tennessee River. Throughout the war, Paducah served as the center for massive Union supply depots and dock facilities for gunboats and supply ships that supported Federal forces along the Ohio, Mississippi and Tennessee River systems.

The 132nd Illinois arrived at Paducah in June 1864 to find a tense situation shortly after Confederate major general Nathan Bedford Forrest had raided this important Union supply and naval operating base. Forrest seized Paducah to resupply Confederate forces in the region with recruits, ammunition, medical supplies, horses and mules and to disrupt Union domination south of the Ohio River. General Forrest pronounced his operation a success, saying, "I drove the enemy to their gunboats and fort; and held the town for ten hours, captured many stores and horses; burned sixty bales of cotton, one steamer, and a dry-dock, bringing out fifty prisoners." Forrest's raid was successful in terms of the resupply effort and in intimidating the Union, but Forrest returned south, leaving the Union still in control of Paducah.[169]

The 132nd remained at Paducah until expiration of its one hundred days' service, when the regiment returned to Chicago to be mustered out on October 17, 1864. Returning to his home at Earlville, Charles Warren enlisted in Company C, 147th Illinois Infantry Regiment, mustering in on February 11, 1865, as the regiment was organizing at Camp Fry, Chicago, for a one-year term. The 147th Illinois deployed to Dalton, Georgia, arriving on February 27–28 to be attached to 1st Brigade, 2nd Separate Division, District of the Etowah, Department of the Cumberland, until July 1865.

During its duty at Dalton, Georgia, the 147th operated against Confederate guerrillas. Their actions included an expedition to Mill Creek on March 14–16; a skirmish near Dalton on March 14; an expedition to Spring Place on March 20–22 and to Ringgold on March 28–29; movement to Resaca on May 1–2, thence to Calhoun on June 26; to Dalton July 2–3; and on to Marietta, Macon and Albany on July 27–31, where the 132nd was on duty and at Americus and Smithville until November 1865. From there, they moved on to Macon and Hawkinsville on November 4–6 and thence to Savannah on November 25–December 3, where they were on duty until January 23, 1866, under the Department of Georgia. Private Charles Warren mustered out on January 20, 1866.

During 1866, Warren drove a bull team across the plains to Virginia City, Montana, where he was promoted to bullwhacker on August 20, 1866. During the winters, he taught school in Deer Lodge Valley while mining in the placer diggings of Alder Gulch, Last Chance, French Gulch, German Gulch, Silver Bow and Butte, among other locations. From 1869 to 1875, Warren served as deputy sheriff and sheriff of Deer Lodge County, bringing law and order to a part of Montana Territory that attracted many former Confederates, including a number who had served in Quantrill's Raiders. The county then comprised everything from the Big Hole River on the south to the British possessions on the north.

Moving to the new mining town of Butte, Warren continued his mining activities and became the first police magistrate when a city government was organized in 1880. He began to join others in developing the resources to build Butte into "the richest hill on earth." Warren established the Comanche Mining Company, the Charles S. Warren Realty and Mining Company and, with Lee Mantle, the Interstate Publishing Company with a daily newspaper.

A Lincoln Republican since he cast his first vote, Warren never made politics a profession, yet few Montanans served more actively in their political party or in their community. He was elected clerk of the U.S. District Court of Silver Bow County, under Honorable William J. Galbraith, presiding judge, for five years.

General Warren was elected a member of the State Constitutional Convention that met at Helena on July 4, 1889, to frame the constitution of the new state. Upon roll call, he voted aye for women's suffrage, and throughout his career, he never failed to give his support and influence to the political emancipation of women. He was a member of the National Republican Committee for four years and supported the election of Benjamin Harrison to the presidency in 1888. He served as a member of most of the territorial and state Republican conventions for forty-five years and as presidential elector was appointed to the duty of carrying the Montana vote to Washington and casting it for William H. Taft in 1908.

With ranks from major to brigadier general, Warren served on the staffs of territorial governors John Schuyler Crosby, Samuel T. Hauser, Preston H. Leslie and Benjamin F. White. He raised a company and, upon receiving news of the Custer massacre, tendered its services to Governor Benjamin F. Potts early in July 1876, although the governor declined this service. Warren was instrumental in organizing the militia of the Territory of Montana, and during the Nez Perce Indian War of 187, he was adjutant of the Montana Battalion.

General Warren's leadership in patriotic and fraternal organizations in Montana was remarkable. He helped organize and served as commander of Butte's Lincoln Post No. 2, GAR. He was the second departmental commander of the GAR in Montana. He served on the board of managers

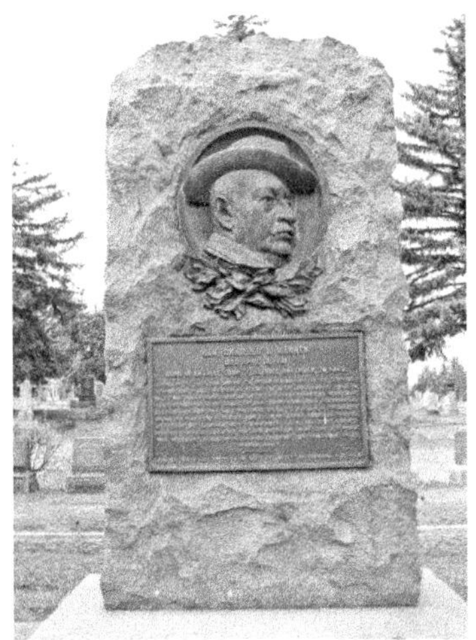

Charles S. Warren's grave monument in Mount Moriah Cemetery in Butte. *Author's collection.*

of the State Soldiers Home at Columbia Falls and as president of the Society of Montana Pioneers in 1907–08.

Warren was a past master of Butte Lodge, Ancient Free and Accepted Masons, a Knight Templar Mason, belonging to the thirty-second degree of the Scottish Rite and Bagdad Temple of the Mystic Shrine. He was a charter member of Butte Lodge of Masons and served as its secretary for the first six years. He was a charter member and first secretary of Fidelity Lodge No. 8, Independent Order of Odd Fellows; a charter member of Damon Lodge No. 2, Knights of Pythias; and a charter member of Silverbow Lodge No. 240, Benevolent and Protective Order of Elks.

On November 15, 1871, General Warren married Mary "Mittie" Avery, a native of Saco, Maine, and they had two children: Wesley W. Warren and Mary Warren Murphey, wife of John Milton Murphey. General Charles S. Warren, known as a man devoid of fear and a man of iron nerve, died in Butte on April 13, 1921, and is interred in Mount Moriah Cemetery, Butte, Montana.[170]

Chapter 23

A Persistent Montana Legend

Jesse and Frank James on the Upper Missouri

Infamous outlaws Jesse and Frank James fought for the Confederacy under Quantrill and Bloody Bill Anderson, and legend has them coming to Montana Territory after the Civil War. This article explores the mystery of whether the James brothers and Cole Younger did or did not spend time on the Upper Missouri.

Did they, or didn't they? A Montana legend portrays Jesse and Frank James living one winter in Montana Territory. The James brothers fought for the Confederacy in the Civil War and after the war moved seamlessly into a life of crime, robbing banks and holding up trains while achieving fame in the eyes of some. Much of their colorful story is well known, yet their possible months in Montana Territory are not. This is their Montana story.

Jesse Woodson James was born in Clay County, Missouri, on September 5, 1847, while his elder brother Alexander Franklin James was born on January 10, 1843. The James family was among the many slave-owning families with ties to the South in the Little Dixie region of Missouri. Clay County counted more slaveholders than any other part of Missouri, and this pro-slavery faction played an active role during the years of turmoil in the mid-1850s between Missouri's bushwhackers and Kansas's Jayhawkers as the issue of slavery in neighboring Kansas Territory was settled.

While Jesse was too young to serve when the Civil War began, by August 1861, Frank James had joined the pro-Confederate regiment of Colonel

John T. Hughes, participating in the fighting on August 10 around "Bloody Hill" in the Missouri State Guard's victory at Wilson's Creek. One month later, Frank was in on the Siege of Lexington when the larger secessionist force captured the town using innovative tactics of maneuvering behind protective wet hemp bales.

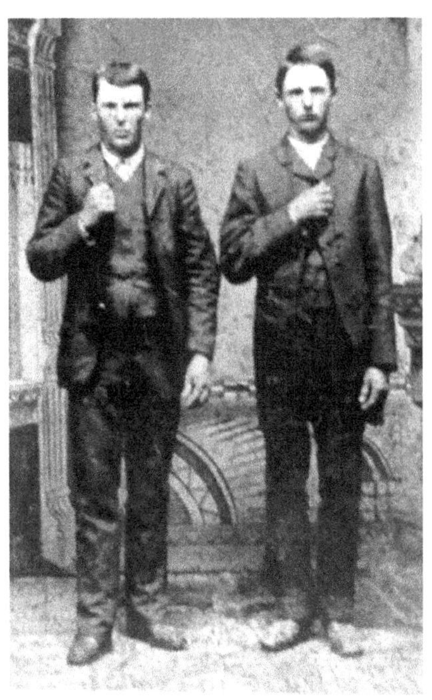

Young Jesse and Frank James during their Civil War years. *Overholser Historical Research Center.*

In the winter of 1861, Frank contracted measles, was captured and paroled to return to his family home in Clay County. While there, he swore an oath of allegiance to support and defend the Constitution of the United States. Yet he did not honor his oath and soon became active in local guerrilla units. By May 1862, he was back in action, joining William C. Quantrill's raiders. As Frank later recounted:

> *I met Bill Gregg, Quantrill's First Lieutenant, in Clay County and with him rowed across the Missouri River to* [Jackson] *county and joined Quantrill at the Webb place on Blackwater ford of the Sni just a few miles from* [Blue Springs, Missouri]. *I will never forget the first time I ever saw Quantrill. He was nearly six feet in height, rather thin, his hair and moustache were sandy, and he was full of life and a jolly fellow. He had none of the air of the bravado or the desperado about him. . . . he was a demon in battle.*[171]

Frank James was in on the action throughout 1863, culminating in Quantrill's raid on Lawrence, Kansas, on August 21, when banks and stores were looted, about two hundred men and boys were killed and a quarter of the town was burned to the ground. In late October, Quantrill, with three to four hundred of his men, including Frank James, headed south to spend the winter in Texas. During that winter of 1863–64, many of Quantrill's men went into regular Confederate units or over to rival guerrilla leader Bloody Bill Anderson.

In the spring of 1864, as Quantrill and his deputy, George Todd, moved back toward Missouri, sixteen-year-old Jesse James probably joined a recruiting party led by Lieutenant Charles F. "Fletch" Taylor in Clay County and including his brother Frank. During the summer of 1864, Taylor was severely wounded, and the James boys joined Bloody Bill Anderson's bushwhackers.

About the same time, a Unionist German immigrant shot Jesse in the breast while he was stealing the farmer's saddle. Jesse was taken across the Missouri River to an inn owned by an uncle, Pastor John Mimms, where he was hidden away until he recovered. By September 20, Jesse returned to action just before Anderson's men engaged in the Centralia Massacre, killing or wounding about twenty-four unarmed Union soldiers and ambushing a pursuing regiment, killing more than one hundred Union soldiers who tried to surrender while scalping more than a dozen.

After both Bloody Bill Anderson and George Todd were killed in October 1864, Jesse and Frank separated. By early December, Quantrill had reconstituted his remaining force. His fifty men posed as the 2nd Colorado Cavalry wearing Federal uniforms and began moving eastward, presumably to Virginia for reasons that were never clear. Frank James moved through Tennessee and into Kentucky with Quantrill's raiders, conducting guerrilla warfare throughout the countryside. On May 10, 1865, Quantrill was mortally wounded, and his remaining men, including Frank James, surrendered.

Meanwhile, Jesse had joined Archie Clement, an Anderson lieutenant, as they intended to move toward Texas to join other Anderson forces there. Clement's men remained in Missouri raiding and conducting guerrilla warfare until May 1865. On May 15, Jesse James was shot through the breast while trying to escape to Mexico. He was found by a farmer and patched up and on May 21 was taken by wagon to Lexington, Missouri, to surrender and take the oath of allegiance. His wound was serious, and it would be almost a month before he could travel by steamboat to Kansas City to rejoin the Mimms family, whose daughter Zerelda "Zee" had nursed Jesse back to health after his similar wound in 1864.

The end of the Civil War found Missouri in chaos. The Confederacy had lost, and the Missouri State Guard of General Sterling Price had been defeated. Most of the Missouri bushwhacker leaders had been killed, and many of the men moved westward.

Jesse and Frank James transitioned from Civil War guerrillas to Reconstruction-era bandits, but the details of their banditry are part of another story. By the late 1860s, the Jameses—joined at various times by Cole, John, Jim and Bob Younger, who shared a passionate allegiance to the South—were gaining national notoriety as bank robbers.

On April 29, 1872, the gang robbed a bank in Columbia, Kentucky. One of the outlaws shot down the cashier, R.A.C. Martin, who refused to open the safe. Other robberies took place, and a year later, on May 27, 1873, the James-Younger gang robbed the Ste. Genevieve Savings Association in Ste. Genevieve, Missouri. As they rode off, they fired in the air and shouted, "Hurrah for Hildebrand!" Samuel S. Hildebrand being an infamous Confederate bushwhacker from the area who had recently been shot dead in Illinois.

On July 21, 1873, a gang wearing Ku Klux Klan masks carried out a train robbery, derailing a locomotive of the Rock Island Railroad near Council Bluffs, Iowa. The robbers took $2,337 from the express safe in the baggage car, narrowly missing a transcontinental express shipment of a large amount of gold and cash. Law enforcement officials concluded that the James-Younger gang had conducted their first train robbery.

After the Rock Island Railroad robbery, the James-Younger gang vanished from the public eye. It was during the following six months that the Montana legend is centered. Did the gang go to the remote Upper Missouri region to cool their tracks in the midst of the thousands of other former Confederates who had sought new lives in Montana Territory? For this trip of 1,100 miles, did they go by Union Pacific Railroad to Corinne, Utah, and then overland to Fort Benton or Deer Lodge—about a two-week trip?

Four months later, on November 23, 1873, a newspaperman who championed their cause, former Confederate John Newman Edwards, published a lengthy article glorifying the James brothers and Cole and John Younger in a twenty-page special supplement to the *St. Louis Dispatch*. Most of this issue, titled "A Terrible Quintet," was devoted to Jesse James, the gang's famed leader, and the article stressed the outlaws' Confederate loyalties.

Examining the clues that the James boys spent time in Montana Territory, several powerful pieces of evidence emerge—personal testimony by credible witnesses and a letter seemingly written by Jesse James from Deer Lodge in late 1873. Among those who claimed to have personal knowledge, the testimony of Charles S. Warren, a Civil War veteran, sheriff of Deer Lodge County, successful businessman and influential political figure in Silver Bow County, stands out. Known as "General" Warren, he was described as "a man devoid of fear and a man of iron nerve." Serving from 1869 to 1875 as deputy sheriff and sheriff of Deer Lodge

County, Warren later told of his personal experience with the James brothers and their gang in Montana Territory.

This is General Warren's powerful story:

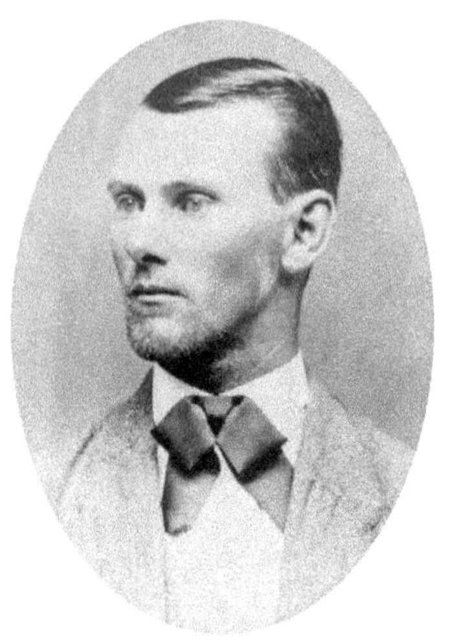

Jesse James as he would have appeared in frontier Montana. *Overholser Historical Research Center.*

> *It was in 1873 or '74, I don't remember exactly which, that the Hon. Thomas Napton, then one of the leading lawyers of Deer Lodge county, said to me: "I would like to have you come to my office, as I would like to talk to you on a business matter." I went along and when we got to his office he said to me: "You have seen the rewards offered for Jesse and Frank James, Cole Younger," and so on. Naming the rest of the gang. Some very big rewards were being offered for the gang in those days, and I replied that I had seen the offers. He asked: "What would you do if Jesse James were to come to this country?" I replied, "I haven't lost any Jesse Jameses and if he comes here as long as he obeys the laws of Montana and Deer Lodge county he will be treated just like any other citizen, for the reason that so many of us had to change our names when we came here."*
>
> *Judge Napton said: "Come back here about 2 or 3 o'clock and I'll have some papers I want you to serve." I was there and was startled at being introduced to Jesse James and Cole Younger. I was immensely surprised at the intelligence of these men, and we were not long in reaching an understanding. I could see at once they wanted immunity, and I simply said: "Mr. Napton will inform you as to the laws of this territory, and as long as you do not break any of them you will not be interfered with. Should there come a requisition for your arrest and return to Missouri, I will submit the paper to Mr. Napton and have him pass on the legality of it. The moment he gets the papers will be an invitation for you to leave the country."*
>
> *I met them many times on the road after that, and I am forced to confess I never knew a whiter crowd of fellows. They stayed in Montana several months and never attempted to do any business. One incident in particular in my acquaintance with these men will serve to show you what sort of fellows they were. I was traveling from Pioneer to Deer Lodge one day with*

> *$20,000 for Donnell, Clark & Larabie's bank, when I met the James boys and Cole Younger on the trail at Rock creek. Jesse said to me, "Sheriff, you've got a big swag with you today. If you think there is any danger we'll ride with you to Deer Lodge." They stayed around some months and then disappeared as mysteriously as they came.*[172]

On December 29, 1873, a letter dated December 20 and bearing Jesse James's signature appeared in the *St. Louis Dispatch*. It insisted that Jesse and Frank were guiltless of all recent crimes, offered alibis for both men and stated they would be willing to surrender if Missouri governor Silas Woodson would ensure them a fair trial and protection against lynch mobs. The letter claimed that Jesse was then living in Deer Lodge, Montana Territory, a story consistent with General Warren's account. Jesse wrote, "We can prove before any fair jury in the state that we have been accused falsely and unjustly." The protection would be from "a mob, or from a requisition from the Governor of Iowa, which is the same thing."

So did Jesse James write this letter from Deer Lodge? It is fascinating that the Deer Lodge Post Office on March 20, 1874, advertised a letter addressed to Jesse W. James, remaining unclaimed. That letter proves that at least one person believed Jesse James was there in the winter of 1873–74.[173]

If the James-Younger gang did spend the winter of 1873–74 in Montana Territory, they must have departed Montana by mid-January to return to Missouri by the end of that month. About 4:45 p.m. on January 31, five bandits armed with navy Colt revolvers and double-barreled shotguns captured the stationmaster and flagged down the Little Rock Express at Gad's Hill, Missouri, a flag stop 120 miles south of St. Louis on the Iron Mountain Railroad line.

Conductor C.A. Alford later described the outlaws to a *St. Louis Republican* reporter as tall men dressed in federal army overcoats and wearing "white cloth masks" with "holes for eyes and nose." One of the bandits had grabbed Alford by the collar and told him, "Stand still or I'll blow the top of your head off!" The passengers were warned that if anyone fired a gun, the conductor would be killed. During this audacious robbery, some $22,000 was stolen from mail, express and passengers. Clues proved that the James-Younger gang conducted this robbery.[174]

The territorial Montana newspapers had been fascinated with Jesse and Frank James since the late 1860s and followed closely their latest activities. Following the killing of Jesse in April 1882, the *Fort Benton River Press* of April 26, 1882, published an article titled "Jesse James in Montana":

> *Anent the recent excitement concerning the killing of Jesse James, it may be of interest to know that famous outlaw and his brother Frank were once in Montana. It was in '70* [sic]. *They fled from Missouri and Iowa to escape arrest and went to Deer Lodge, in the year stated. Soon after that they secured employment in the placer mines at Rock Creek where they worked for some time incognito. Through the medium of a friend in Deer Lodge they communicated with the State authorities of Missouri, offering to return and stand trial on the indictments preferred if they would guarantee immunity from extradition to Iowa, where the writer said, no fair trial could be obtained. The James boys were well known by many people in Montana at that time, and it is said that at least twelve members of Quantrill's gang were living in Deer Lodge while they were in the Territory.*[175]

Note the mention that the James boys "fled from Missouri and Iowa to escape arrest and went to Deer Lodge." Iowa was the scene of the July 1873 Rock Island Railroad robbery. The mention of many of Quantrill's raiders living in Deer Lodge is interesting. Many of Quantrill's men—among them his own younger brother Thompson and Sam Bass gang member James Berry—took refuge on the Montana frontier during and after the war. Thompson Quantrill was known as "a vile, base, worthless, despicable but petty scoundrel."[176]

Jesse James married his cousin Zerelda Mimms on April 24, 1874, shortly after the James boys returned from Montana Territory. Zerelda's eldest brother, Robert W. Mimms, arrived in Montana Territory some time before 1866, and he had served in the Second and Third Territorial Legislative Assemblies, a representative from Edgerton County. By 1874, Squire Mimms, as he was known, was serving as a judge in Helena, Montana; one wonders whether Jesse's wanderings in Montana included a visit with his future brother-in-law.[177]

Other stories about the James brothers in Montana Territory abound to this day, including a family legend among Highwood Mountains ranching families the Pattersons, Harrises and Lepleys that the James boys had visited the area and Frank James taught school for a few months one winter on upper Highwood Creek. Members of these families of the current generation remain convinced that Jesse and Frank James roamed Montana Territory in 1872–74.[178]

Perhaps we'll never know with absolute certainty about the James boys in Montana Territory. Yet the compelling evidence of General Warren, Jesse's letter from Deer Lodge and the *River Press* article in 1882 lend powerful credence to this fascinating Montana legend.

Chapter 24

Killing Booth

Everton Conger Tracks Down Lincoln's Assassin

President Abraham Lincoln was fatally shot on the evening of April 14, 1865, at Ford's Theatre. In the aftermath of President Lincoln's tragic assassination, Secret Service agent Lieutenant Colonel Everton Conger led the pursuit of assassin John Wilkes Booth. Supported by Canadian-born lieutenant Edward P. Doherty, commanding a detachment from the 16th New York Cavalry, Colonel Conger developed the clues and began the chase in this highest-profile manhunt in U.S. history.

The Civil War was ending, but one heinous act would forever change the aftermath. Five days after General Robert E. Lee surrendered at Appomattox, actor and passionate Southerner John Wilkes Booth shot President Abraham Lincoln at Ford's Theatre on Good Friday. The North had won the war, but in the aftermath, would they lose the peace? We'll never know with absolute clarity how post–Civil War Reconstruction would have transpired under President Lincoln. But we do know that it was a disaster for our nation without him.

Overnight, the North went from celebration of Lee's surrender to shock and rage over Lincoln's assassination. The largest manhunt in U.S. history began, and the pursuit of Booth consumed the nation. On April 24, ten days after Booth shot the president, the hunt for the assassin began in earnest, and General C.C. Augur, commander of the Department of Washington, sent the following order to future Montanan colonel Nelson B. Sweitzer, the commanding officer of the 16th New York Cavalry: "You will at once detail a reliable and discreet commissioned officer with 25 men, well-mounted, with three days' rations and forage, to report at once to Col. L.C. Baker, agent of the war department, at 211 Pennsylvania avenue."[179]

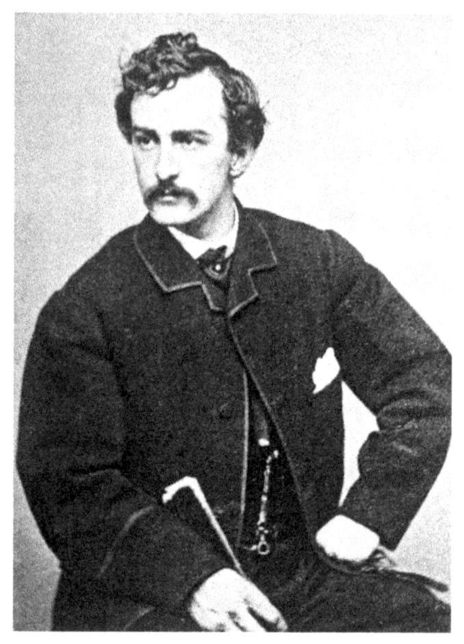

John Wilkes Booth, actor and brutal assassin of President Abraham Lincoln. *Library of Congress.*

In the final year of the Civil War, Colonel Sweitzer and his 16th New York Cavalry had been in continuous action in Northern Virginia and fought a number of engagements against the Confederate cavalry commanded by Colonel John S Mosby.

Colonel L. (Lafayette) C. Baker was the head of the United States Secret Service, reporting directly to the secretary of war. Colonel Sweitzer detailed Lieutenant Edward Doherty to lead the detachment of the 16th New York Cavalry in pursuit of Booth. But Colonel Baker sent his most trusted agent, Lieutenant Colonel Everton J. Conger, to command this critical pursuit force. As Conger's second in command, Colonel Baker sent his own cousin, Lieutenant Luther Baker, to make a personal report.

Edward Doherty, one of many Canadians to serve in the Civil War, was born in 1840 and was living in New York when the war began. He enlisted as a private in Company A of the 71st New York Infantry Regiment and participated in the disastrous First Battle of Bull Run near Manassas, Virginia. Later in the war, he was promoted to first lieutenant in the 16th New York Cavalry, then serving as a guard force, defending Washington, D.C. Fame came to Lieutenant Doherty when he was ordered by Colonel Sweitzer to form a detachment to capture Booth and any collaborators.[180]

Thus, ten days after the assassination, Agents Conger and Baker of the National Secret Service Bureau with Lieutenant Doherty and his twenty-five troopers of the 16th New York Cavalry hastily departed Washington, D.C., for Virginia. By then, Detective Everton Conger had developed the first solid lead on the whereabouts of assassin John Wilkes Booth.

Everton Conger, the son of Presbyterian minister Enoch Conger of Ohio, enlisted in Company F, 8th Ohio Volunteer Infantry, at the beginning of the

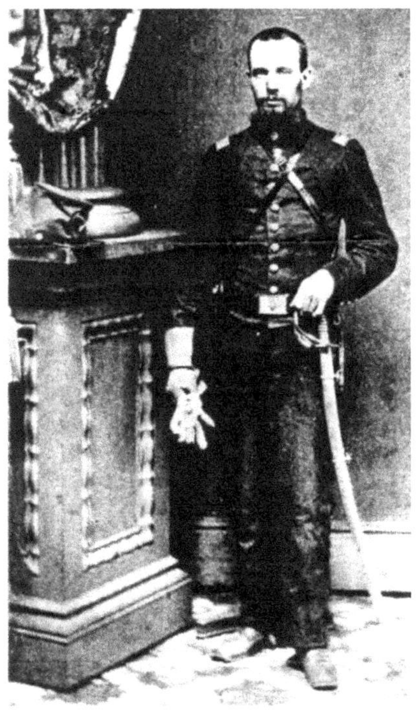

Lieutenant Colonel Everton Conger led the search for and capture of assassin John Wilkes Booth. *Author's collection.*

war. Intelligent and a natural leader, Conger rose rapidly in the ranks. His early military service impressed Brigadier General Rutherford B. Hayes when the two met in West Virginia. After his enlistment expired, Conger returned to Ohio to marry Kate Boren. He then enlisted in the 3rd West Virginia Cavalry. Rising to the rank of lieutenant colonel, Conger was wounded three times during the course of the war and once left for dead overnight on a frigid battlefield one cold October evening. Conger survived and recovered to serve in the 1st District of Columbia Cavalry, where he had de facto command since the colonel of the regiment, Colonel Lafayette C. Baker, was on detached service with the War Department to lead the Secret Service.

No longer able to command in the field, Conger accepted duty as an agent serving secretly under the direct command of the War Department in Baker's Secret Service. Well respected and highly capable, Conger was chosen by Secretary of War Edwin Stanton to lead the mission to locate Booth.

Setting out in pursuit with Lieutenant Baker and Lieutenant Doherty and his 16th New York detachment, including Sergeant Boston Corbett, Conger gathered clues along the way at the Surratt and Mudd homes, both of whom had aided Booth, with Dr. Mudd setting Booth's broken leg. Crossing the Potomac, Conger's pursuit force entered Virginia, still hostile Southern territory.

At Port Royal, Conger learned that two strangers had crossed the river from Port Conway on the ferry on Monday, April 23. One of these strangers was using crutches. Conger also learned that three Confederate soldiers had talked with the crippled man and his companion at the wharf. Conger was able, through information given him by a young woman in a wayside tavern, to trace one of these Confederate soldiers to a hotel in Bowling Green.

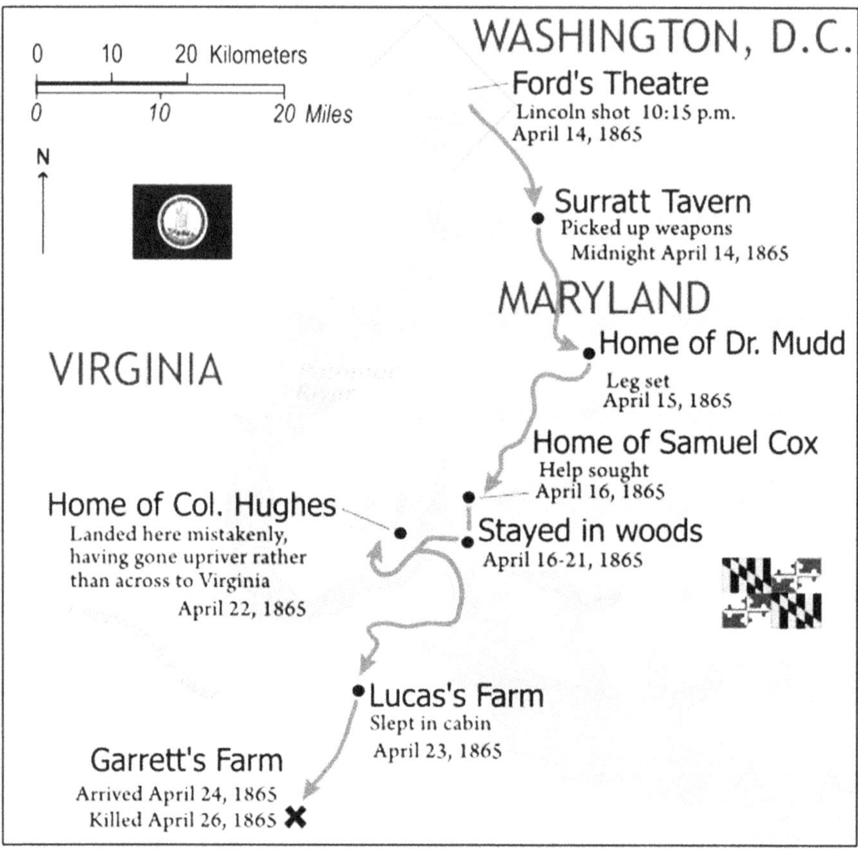

Booth's escape route as he fled into Virginia. *Wikipedia.*

In Conger's later testimony at the trial of the conspirators in Washington, D.C., he related:

> *Posing as confederate soldiers, we rode through the night, stopping at each farmhouse to ask if there were any soldiers there needing assistance to escape to the south. At daybreak, with no clues, we divided into two parties to reconnoiter up and down the river. We finally located a farmer who testified that the day before he had been offered $10 by Booth and a man named Herold to haul them 20 miles to Bowling Green, near Richmond.*[181]

Crossing the Rappahannock River near Port Royal, Conger's force closed in on its target. Conger continued his narrative of the pursuit: "We ferried across the river and in the dusk of the evening galloped to Bowling Green.

Five miles down the road we passed the Garrett plantation where Booth was later killed." At Bowling Green, the pursuers captured William Jett, one of Booth's companions. Interrogating Jett, Conger learned that Booth was at one of the plantations they had passed, the Garrett plantation. There, Booth was resting, delayed by his leg.

Conger proceeded with his account:

> *On the night of the capture* [of Booth] *I found Jett* [Willie Jett, a commissary agent of the Confederate states] *in bed at a hotel in Bowling Green. I told him to get up; that I wanted him. He put on his pants, and came out to me in the front part of the room. I said, "Where are the two men who came with you across the river" he came up to me and said, "Can I see you alone?"*

Conger agreed and asked Lieutenant Luther Baker and Lieutenant Edward Doherty to leave the room. Then Jett admitted, "I know who you want, and I will tell you where they can be found. They are on the road to Port Royal, about three miles this side of there."

"At whose house are they?" Conger asked, and Jett replied, "Mr. Garrett's."

The detachment had passed the Garrett farm that afternoon, and even at that time Booth and David Herold, his companion, were concealed on the farm.

Jett rode with Conger, Baker and Doherty and the 16th New York to Garrett's farm. It was then late at night. Conger continued his narrative:

> *Just before we got to the house, Jett, riding with me said: "We are very near now to where we go through; let us stop here and look around." He and I rode on together. I rode forward to find the gate that went through to the house and sent Lieutenant Doherty to open another. Went back for the cavalry, and we rode rapidly up to the house and barn, and stationed the men around the house and quarters.*
>
> *I went to the house and found Lieutenant Baker at the door, telling someone to strike a light and come out. The first individual we saw was an old man, whose name was said to be Garrett* [Richard H. Garrett, a tobacco farmer]. *I said to him, "Where are the two men who stopped here at your house?"*
>
> *"They have gone," Garrett replied.*
>
> *"Gone where?" I asked.*
>
> *"Gone to the woods," Garrett answered.*

> *"Well sir, whereabouts in the woods have they gone?"*
> *He then commenced to tell me that they came there without his consent; that he did not want them to stay.*

Conger told Garrett he didn't want a long story out of him, he just wanted to know where the men had gone. Garrett wasn't inclined to tell. Then Conger turned to the door and said to one of the men, "Bring me a lariat rope here, and I will put that man up to the top of one of those locust trees." Still Garrett did not seem inclined to tell.

Then one of Garrett's sons came into the house and said, "Don't hurt the old man; he is scared. I will tell you where the men are you want to find." Young Garrett then told Conger the men were in the barn. In Conger's words:

> *We threw a guard around the place in the darkness and I tried to force the door. Booth woke up and wanted to know who was there. I called to him to surrender. He answered that if we would withdraw forty yards he would come out and fight the bunch of us. I told him that we were not there to fight him but to take him prisoner.*

Eventually, Conger ordered a fire started to burn the barn and force Booth and his accomplice David Herold to surrender. He stated that Booth knew that the end was near. Herold surrendered, and then, in the words of Conger, "righting himself on his feet, [Booth] plunged for the door. Against all orders, Sergeant Boston Corbett shot Booth in the neck." The wound proved fatal, and Booth whispered to Conger his final message for his mother: "I did it for my country. Tell my mother that what I did was for the best." Lincoln's assassin was dead.

Of course, Booth's action was not in the best interest of the South, and many southern leaders quickly recognized that fact. Postwar Reconstruction, without President Abraham Lincoln, proved a long downhill slope for the nation, but that is another story.

As Booth lay dying, Agent Conger gathered the assassin's weapons and diary as evidence and, after Booth's death, raced for the capital. In the early morning hours of April 27, 1865, Conger rode through the streets of Washington, D.C., heading for the War Department to report the capture and death of John Wilkes Booth. A relieved and grateful Secretary of War Edwin Stanton announced to a grieving nation that the manhunt was over; President Abraham Lincoln's assassin was dead.

Proud of their war-hero townsman, the citizens of Fremont, Ohio, presented Colonel Conger with an inscribed pair of silver-handled pistols. Congress wrangled over the division of reward money. Finally, Representative Rutherford B. Hayes proposed a compromise bill that Ohioan John Sherman rammed through the Senate. Hayes's plan awarded Conger a large share of the reward—$15,000 of the $75,000 total. Hayes won his case by revealing that it was Conger who had commanded the unit, developed the leads and successfully orchestrated Booth's capture.

For his services, Lieutenant Edward Doherty received a $5,250 reward. He remained in the military until 1870, died in 1897 and is buried in Arlington National Cemetery in Virginia.

After the war, Colonel Conger moved to the small southern Illinois community of Carmi, where he practiced law. He used part of the reward money to build a home that still stands today. The Illinois Historical Society erected a marker at the Colonel Conger House that recounts Conger's unique place in history.

In 1880, then President Rutherford B. Hayes once more played a prominent role in Colonel Conger's life. He appointed Conger an associate justice of the Montana territorial supreme court. Conger's district was the largest in Montana, covering half of the large territory. The strain of his war wounds and serving this vast area of Montana caused Justice Conger to rely too heavily on morphine and alcohol to relieve the constant pain. In June 1883, he was suspended from the bench and an investigation ordered. In January 1884, the suspension was revoked, and he was reinstated and permitted to complete his term until 1887.[182]

Conger spent the rest of his life either as prosecutor or in private practice in Montana until his death in 1918. Colonel Everton J. Conger, the man who tracked down Lincoln's assassin, rests today in Dillon's Mountain View Cemetery.

Epilogue

After thirty years, the arrival of railroads ended the steamboat era on the Upper Missouri. Today, Fort Benton is a small town with a big history—the birthplace of Montana, the head of navigation on the Missouri River and important in every era of Upper Missouri history.

Fort Benton's story centers on the Missouri River as a gateway to the spectacular natural features from the White Cliffs to the great falls of the Missouri and on to the Gates of the Mountains. The story extends to the native Indians and the buffalo that occupied the land long before arrival of American explorers and fur traders. Blackfeet Indians long used the natural ford at Fort Benton to cross the Missouri River into Judith and Musselshell hunting grounds. Lewis and Clark made their fateful decision on the course of the Missouri at Decision Point and proceeded on past the Fort Benton river bottom on their journey to the Pacific.

The story spans the fur trade era of the 1830s–60s when Blackfeet, Gros Ventres, Assiniboine, Cree and Metis traded with St. Louis adventurers who moved up the Missouri to establish trading posts. In 1860, the first steamboats arrived at the long, natural Fort Benton levee delivering trade goods and Indian annuities and taking furs and buffalo robes downriver to eastern markets. That same year, the Mullan Military Wagon Road completed the long overland link between Fort Benton and Fort Walla Walla, on the Columbia River. As the head of navigation on the Missouri River, Fort Benton became the hub for the St. Louis to Fort Benton steamboat trade of 1860–90, bringing thousands of tons of freight and passengers to the frontier.

Early in the Civil War, with strikes at Gold Creek and Bannack in 1862, Fort Benton became a transportation hub. Fort Benton merchant princes formed trading and freighting empires extending from Fort Benton in every direction to the mines and camps throughout Montana and northward up the Whoop-Up and Fort Walsh Trails to Canada. Fort Benton supplied military posts at Fort Shaw and Fort Assinniboine. These were wild and woolly days, and the streets of Fort Benton and its Bloodiest Block in the West were roamed by the rich and famous, scoundrels and killers, former Confederate Rebels and loyal Yankees, merchants and gamblers, Indians and soldiers, Irish Fenians and exiled Metis and eventually by women and children.

During the height of the steamboat era, Fort Benton underwent a building boom with brick buildings replacing original adobe, log or wood frame buildings. The trading firms powered a vast business empire that made Fort Benton the Chicago of the Plains. This was a time of made and lost fortunes and colorful characters.

Railroads brought immense change as Fort Benton transitioned to ranching with tens of thousands of cattle and sheep on the open range and large shipments to markets in the East. In the early 1900s, the fertile lands of north central Montana opened to dryland farming, with homesteaders arriving by railroad. Fort Benton became the trading center for ranchers and farmers in the heart of what is now "Montana's Golden Triangle" agricultural region.

Yankees and Rebels on the Upper Missouri is a tribute to the steamboat era, launched before the Civil War, struggling through the war years and reaching highs and lows in the period of national postwar Reconstruction. This book highlights some of the legends, stories and people arriving to make their mark throughout this period.

Fort Benton became a National Historic Landmark in 1961 and a Historic District on the National Register of Historic Places. Fort Benton is a Preserve America city, on the National Lewis and Clark Historic Trail and the river entry port for the Upper Missouri, now part of the 149-mile National Wild and Scenic River System and the Upper Missouri River Breaks National Monument. Fort Benton is a contributing site on the National Historic Nez Perce Trail in recognition of its military and civilian forces at the Battles of Cow Island and Cow Creek Canyon.

Fort Benton presents four exceptional museums focused on cultural tourism to an international audience. The Museum of the Northern Great Plains features Montana's State Agricultural Museum, the Strand Gallery with the Smithsonian Buffalo, a Homestead Village and a community events center. The Museum of the Upper Missouri tells Twenty Tall Tales of the Upper Missouri, a sampling of Fort Benton's storied past. Old Fort Benton, a combination of the original 1846–47 Block House and reconstructed buildings, forms a trading post with displays interpreting Blackfeet culture and trading days. Old Fort Benton also features the Starr Gallery of Western Art with Bob Scriver bronzes and Karl Bodmer art interpreting Upper Missouri history. Newest is the Upper Missouri River Breaks Interpretive Center that features artifacts like Chief Joseph's surrender rifle, a replica of the cabin of the steamboat *Far West* with the original bell and telegraph, a Murphy freighting wagon and classic scenes from the Upper Missouri. The Interpretive Center's exterior is designed to resemble the White Cliffs of the Missouri.

Today, the city of Fort Benton retains much of its "steamboat days" character. The steamboat levee is now a park with a walking path running the length of the community with interpretive signage. As you follow the levee trail from the Interpretive Center downriver to Old Fort Benton, you walk hallowed ground through the pages of history.

Notes

Introduction

1. Overholser, *Fort Benton*; Lass, *History of Steamboating*; Lass, *Navigating the Missouri*; Lepley, *Birthplace of Montana*; Lepley, *Packets to Paradise*; Lepley, *Blackfoot Fur Trade*; Robison, "Completing the Mullan Road," 131–51.
2. Lass, *Navigating the Missouri*, 192; Wischmann, *Frontier Diplomats*; Sunder, *Fur Trade*; Lepley, *Blackfoot Fur Trade.*
3. Strachan, *Blazing the Mullan Trail*, 53.
4. Gladstone, "View's of Early Fort Benton."
5. Robison, *Montana Territory*.
6. Robison, *Confederates*.

Chapter 1

7. Bowdern, "Joseph LaBarge," 449–69; Overholser, *Fort Benton*; Lass, *History of Steamboating*; Lass, *Navigating the Missouri*; Lepley, *Packets to Paradise*; Lepley, *Birthplace of Montana*; Sunder, *Fur Trade*; "Robison-Wahlberg List." Steamboat passenger lists in newspapers and other sources are incomplete, but those available have been entered into the "Robison-Wahlberg List," an automated file of more than sixteen thousand passengers en route the Upper Missouri; Chittenden, *History of Early Steamboat Navigation*, vol. 2, 249–50.
8. Lass, *Navigating the Missouri*, 193.
9. Robison, *Montana Territory*, 22.

10. Chittenden, *History of Early Steamboat Navigation*, vol. 2, 249; "Robison-Wahlberg List."
11. Schieffelin, "Crossing the Plains," 395–99.
12. See Robison, *Confederates*, 21–23, for Nicholas Wall's story; Chittenden, *History of Early Steamboat Navigation*, vol. 2, 253–58.
13. Lass, *Navigating the Missouri*, 208–9. Partners in La Barge, Harkness & Co. were Joseph and John La Barge, James Harkness, Eugene Jaccard and Charles E. Galpin. See Chittenden, *History of Early Steamboat Navigation*, vol. 2, 287.
14. Lass, *Navigating the Missouri*, 211.
15. Ibid., vol. 2, 258–59.
16. Ibid., vol. 2, 305–14; Overholser, *Fort Benton*, 42–43; Lass, *Navigating the Missouri*, 211–18.
17. Robison, *Montana Territory*, 21–25; Lepley, *Packets to Paradise*, 244; Overholser, *Fort Benton*, 45–49.
18. Petsche, *Steamboat* Bertrand.
19. Lepley, *Packets to Paradise*, 245.
20. Overholser, *Fort Benton*, 49–54.

Chapter 2

21. Nichols, *Guerrilla Warfare*, vol. 2, 109–10; Chittenden, *History of Early Steamboat Navigation*, vol. 2, 251–52.
22. Way, *Way's Packet Directory*, 346.
23. *St. Louis Republican*, March 21–23, April 16, 1863.
24. Typical of these stories was an early account in the *Smoky Hill and Republican Union*, April 4, 1863, under the headline "Bushwhacking on the Missouri. The *Sam Gaty* Boarded and Plundered—The Murder of Two White Men and Fifteen Negroes," published in *Leavenworth Conservative*, March 31, 1863; Nichols, *Guerrilla Warfare*, vol. 2, 109–10. While Gregg was most likely the leader, other accounts name George Todd or "Hicks."
25. *Smoky Hill and Republican Union*, April 4, 1863; Nichols, *Guerrilla Warfare*, vol. 2, 109–10.

Chapter 3

26. Lilly, "Handwritten Account"; Robison, *Confederates*, 58–89.
27 Lilly, "Handwritten Account."
28. Robison, *Confederates*, 81–89.

Chapter 4

29. *Bismarck Daily Tribune*, December 27, 1907.
30. Mills, *Conquest of the Missouri*, 290–308; Thrapp, *Encyclopedia of Frontier Biography*, 944.
31. *Great Falls Leader*, July 17, 1908.
32. Mills, *Conquest of the Missouri*; Overholser, *Fort Benton*; Lass, *History of Steamboating*; Lass, *Navigating the Missouri*; "Robison-Wahlberg List."

Chapter 5

33. *Missouri Daily Republican*, July 22, 29, August 5, 12, 1866.
34. Fort Campbell was an adobe trading post financed by St. Louis–based Robert Campbell in 1846 in opposition to and two miles upriver from the American Fur Company (AFC) post at Fort Benton. The post was sold to AFC in 1860 and was occupied by 1865 by Jesuits who had moved for protection from St. Peter's Mission.
35. *Montana Post*, June 30, 1866.
36. "Robison-Wahlberg List"; *Montana Post*, April 21, 1886; *Missouri Daily Republican*, July 9, 1866; Overholser, *Fort Benton*, 55–57.

Chapter 6

37. Plassmann, "Memories of a Long Life," 184–95; Plassmann, "The 'Far West'"; Plassmann, "Passengers on 'Far West.'"

Chapter 7

38. Brown, "Trip to the Northwest," 103–36 and 246–75; Brown, "John Mason Brown," 41–77.
39. Brown, "John Mason Brown," 41–77.
40. Letter, Andrew Dawson to Aleck [Dawson] from steamboat *Spread Eagle* near Sioux City, May 15, 1861, in Wischmann and Dawson, *This Far-Off Wild Land*, 282.
41. Brown, "Trip to the Northwest," 130.
42. Ibid., 246. Upon reaching the Bitter Root River, Brown declared it "even more beautiful than the Sun," 256.
43. Brown, "Diary, 1862."
44. Ibid.; "Affairs at Fort Benton," 283–84.
45. Letter, John Mason Brown to Andrew Dawson, March 15, 1863, in "Andrew Dawson letters."
46. Brown, "John Mason Brown"; Speed, "10th Kentucky Cavalry."
47. "45th Kentucky Mounted Infantry Webpage."
48. Ibid.

Chapter 8

49. *Natrona County Tribune* (Wyoming), November 25, 1915.
50. "Bucknum Family History."
51. Charles K. Bucknam, Civil War Pension Records, Overholser Historical Research Center, Fort Benton, MT.
52. Hubbard, *Minnesota in Three Centuries*, 422–23.
53. "Bucknum Family History."
54. *Benton Record Weekly*, September 1877.
55. Ibid., October 1877.
56. Ibid., December 1877.
57. *Great Falls Tribune*, February 14, 1932.
58. Choteau, one of the nine original counties in Montana Territory, had its name amended to Chouteau County by the Montana legislature in 1903.
59. "Bucknum Family History"; *Natrona County Tribune* (Wyoming), November 25, 1915.

Chapter 9

60. Leeson, *History of Montana*, 1028; *Great Falls Tribune*, March 11, 1925.
61. U.S. Civil War Soldiers Records. Private Stephen Spitzley.
62. Record of Service of Michigan Volunteers in the Civil War, 1861–1865, vol. 27, interactive.ancestry.com/18555/dvm_PrimSrc000301-02083-1?backurl=http%3a%2f%2fsearch.ancestry.com%2fsearch%2fdb.aspx%3fdbid%3d18555%26path%3d&ssrc=&backlabel=ReturnBrowsing.
63. "Robison-Wahlberg List."
64. *Great Falls Tribune*, November 15, 1889.

Chapter 10

65. Biographic sketches of Montana's William "Bill" Bent are provided in *Progressive Men of Montana*, 1471–72; Noyes, *Land of Chinook*, 88–99; Centennial Book Committee, *Thunderstorms and Tumbleweeds*, 296; "Nephew of Kit Carson Dies; William Bent, Pioneer of Old West, Passed Away at Harlem. Son of Man Who Built Early Day Fort on Arkansas River, Brother to Former Provincial Governor of New Mexico, Crosses the Great Divide," *Great Falls Tribune*, November 19, 1919.
66. U.S. Civil War Soldiers, Confederate William Bent.
67. *Progressive Men of Montana*, 1471–72.
68. Miller, *History of the Fort Peck Assiniboine*, 55; Centennial Book Committee, *Thunderstorms and Tumbleweeds*, 22–23.
69. Choteau County Marriage License No. 57, William Bent married Lizzie Canoe, April 6, 1891, Chouteau County Clerk and Recorder, Fort Benton, MT.
70. Noyes, *Land of Chinook*, 94–98.
71. Ibid.
72. *Helena Weekly Herald*, February 17, 1887.

Chapter 11

73. Stout, *History of Montana*, 978–79.
74. U.S. Civil War Soldiers Records, Private Daniel Dutro.
75. Stout, *History of Montana*, 978.
76. *Fort Benton River Press*, July 1, 1885.

77. *Dupuyer Acantha*, December 10, 1896.
78. *Fort Benton River Press*, March 10, 1897.

Chapter 12

79. Quaife, *"Yellowstone Kelly,"* 2–3. Quotes in this article are from this source.
80. Ibid., 20.
81. Ibid., 20–21.
82. Ibid., 40–47.
83. Mills, *Conquest of the Missouri*, 158–62.
84. *San Francisco Call*, March 2, 1909.
85. Keenan, "Yellowstone Kelly," 27.

Chapter 13

86. Robison, "On Being a Black American."
87. Robison, *Confederates*.
88. *Fort Benton Illustrated Almanac 1878*.
89. *Great Falls Tribune Montana Parade*, June 24, 1956, in Montana African-Americans Vertical File in the Great Falls Public Library. Regrettably, deceased Mrs. Florence Franklin's manuscript has not been located. Sadly, also, no photograph of Mattie Castner has ever been located.

Chapter 14

90. U.S. Federal Census Montana, Choteau County, Fort Benton.
91. *Fort Benton River Press*, July 5, 1882.
92. "Ed Simms Tells How Blind Man Follows Ball Game His Eyesight Gone, He Is One of Great Falls' Most Enthusiastic Fans. Played the Game Himself Back in Texas When a Young Man," *Great Falls Tribune*, December 17, 1911. Mrs. Henrietta Johnson was one of seventy-six blacks in 1880 living in Fort Benton, where she worked as chambermaid at the Grand Union on its opening on November 2, 1882. She later moved on to the town of Great Falls as it began to grow in the late 1880s.
93. "Robison-Wahlberg List."

94. *Great Falls Tribune*, December 17, 1911.
95. Thomson, *Early Settlers*, 239–40.

Chapter 15

96. "Mrs. Maria Dutriueille" in Works Progress Administration, *Great Falls Yesterday*, 377–79. This account of the life of Maria Adams Dutriueille does not state whether her family were free blacks but gives no indication of slavery and every indication that she and her sisters were raised as a family unit.
97. Works Progress Administration, *Great Falls Yesterday*, 377, states that the packet steamer was the *Big Eagle*, yet no steamboat by that name is recorded in Way, *Way's Packet Directory*.
98. Stiles, *Custer's Trials*, 334–35.
99. Merington, *Custer Story*, 253.
100. Works Progress Administration, *Great Falls Yesterday*, 377.
101. Manion, *General Terry's Last Statement*, 23–24.
102. Ibid., 81–90.
103. *Helena Weekly Herald*, July 18, 1878, carried a passenger list for the *Nellie Peck* with only "Miss Maria Adams," yet Mary Adams likely accompanied her sister—perhaps working as a cook on the trip.
104. Choteau County Assessment Book No. 2, 1879, 17. No issues of the *Benton Record Weekly* exist between March 23–29 to report Mary's death. The May 16 *Benton Record* carries the first notice to creditors signed by Maria Adams, "administratrix of the estate of Mary Adams, deceased," dated at Fort Benton, May 13, 1879. The *Bismarck Tribune* of December 28, 1877, reported that Mary and Mariah Adams owned Bismarck dwellings valued at $600. The *Bismarck Tribune* of October 14, 1881, carried notice that Mary Adams, died on March 22, 1879, owned real estate valued at $300 in Burleigh, Dakota Territory.
105. U.S. Federal Census 1880, Fort Benton, Choteau County, MT; Choteau County Assessment Book No. 2, 1879–80, 1, 20.

Chapter 16

106. Lewis and Clark County, MT, marriage license recorded incorrect names: "Duke Dutrielle and Mary Adams." *Benton Record*, May 16, 1879.

107. "Dutriueille Family Papers," Montana Historical Society SC 1584; Choteau County Assessments Book No. 2, 5.
108. Works Progress Administration, *Great Falls Yesterday*, 377–79.
109. *Fort Benton River Press*, September 10, 1884.
110. T.E. Collins was defeated by Republican John E. Richards in the 1892 governor's race. Duke Dutriueille returned to the Republican Party and remained active in politics through the rest of his days in Helena.
111. *Independent*, September 24, 1892.
112. *Belt Valley Times*, January 19, 1911; *Great Falls Tribune*, January 19, 1911; Kennedy and Strober, *Belt Valley History*, 227.

Chapter 17

113. Gallery of Outstanding Montanans.
114. Mattie Castner's name, date of birth and slave owner are conflicted. Her biography in Works Progress Administration, *Great Falls Yesterday*, 74–75, recorded her name as "Mattie Bell," birth date as "April 10, 1855," and her owner as "Robert Settser," yet this author believes her name, as she emerged from slavery, was Mattie Bell Bost and her owner was Reuben Setzer. The 1860 U.S. Census for Catawba County, North Carolina, recorded no "Settser" families but many "Setzer" families. It recorded no slave owner "Robert Setzer" but did have a "Reuben Setzer." Mattie's birth has been reported variously from 1848 to 1855—her gravestone records "Age 71" at her death on April 1, 1920. The 1900 census recorded that Mattie was born in March 1851. Analysis of the 1860 census revealed just two female slaves near Mattie's age (ages twelve and fifteen) in any Setzer family, that of Reuben Setzer. Mattie's name has been recorded variously as Mattie Bell, Mattie Bost Bell and Mattie Bell Bost. Historian Tom Stout recorded Mattie Bell Bost Castner in his biographic entry for Mattie and her husband, John K. Castner, and this author believes that is most likely Mattie's correct name. See Stout, *History of Montana*, vol. 3, 724–25.
115. *Benton Record*, May 16, 1879; "Robison-Wahlberg List."
116. U.S. Federal Census 1880, Montana Territory. The "Sire" name may have been with another spelling—Cyr, Sear, Sears, Sayre, Seers or Siria.
117. Stout, *History of Montana*, 724–25; "Robison-Wahlberg List"; *Belt Valley Times*, September 2, 1915.

118. Stout, *History of Montana*, 724–25; *Belt Valley Times*, September 2, 1915; *Fort Benton River Press*, December 27, 1882.
119. *Great Falls Tribune*, April 27, 1894; Works Progress Administration, *Great Falls Yesterday*, 74–75.
120. *Butte Inter Mountain*, October 21, 1903.
121. Works Progress Administration, *Great Falls Yesterday*, 74–75.
122. *Belt Valley Times*, December 30, 1915.
123. *Belt Valley Times*, January 20, 1916; Works Progress Administration, *Great Falls Yesterday*, 74–75; *Great Falls Tribune*, April 6, 1920.
124. *Great Falls Tribune*, April 3, 1920; *Great Falls Leader*, April 7, 1920.

Chapter 18

125. U.S. Federal Census and Slave Schedules, 1850 and 1860. The only other female slave of the right age in the 1860 census belonged to Thomas W. Ringgold, who had a total of seven slaves. In 1860, a total of fifty-four slaves belonged to Ringgold masters in Maryland; Maryland Constitution of 1864: Art. 24.
126. U.S. Federal Census, 1870, Washington, D.C.
127. Powell and Shippan, *Officers of the Army*, 417.
128. *Helena Weekly Herald*, March 20, 1873; "Robison-Wahlberg List."
129. Rust, *Lost Fort Ellis*.
130. *Helena Weekly Herald*, August 28, 1873.
131. Rust, *Lost Fort Ellis*; Rockwell, *U.S. Army in Frontier Montana*.
132. *Helena Weekly Herald*, January 9, 1879; *Benton Record Weekly*, April 4, August 8, 1879; Choteau County Assessment Book No. 2, 14.
133. Voynick, *Yogo*, 85.
134. *Great Falls Tribune*, undated article.
135. *Benton Record Weekly*, November 5, 1880.
136. *Great Falls Tribune*, December 5, 1906, May 19, 1935; Montana Historical Society library vertical file, Ringold file, *Fergus County Democrat*, October 1906; Hay, "I Remember Old Yogo," 62–69.

Chapter 19

137. U.S. Federal Census and Slave Schedule, 1850, Gaston County, North Carolina.

138. Ibid.
139. Wallin, "Aunt Adeline."
140. Ibid.
141. Wikipedia, "Battle of Fredericktown."
142. Wallin, "Aunt Adeline."
143. U.S. Civil War Soldiers Records, Private Alfred F. Skaggs.
144 Wallin, "Aunt Adeline."
145 Ibid.
146. Ibid.
147 *Lewistown Daily News*, January 9, 1941.
148. Robison, "Adeline Hoffman."

Chapter 20

149. Farwell, *Encyclopedia of 19th Century*, 415.
150. Heitman, *Historical Register*, 562; "Frontier Guard."
151. *Washington (D.C.) Evening Star*, April 19, 1861.
152. Ibid., April 26, 1861.
153. *Kansas State Journal*, May 9, 1861.
154. "Miscellaneous Documents and Histories."
155. *Benton Weekly Record*, August 12, 1883.
156. *New York Times*, June 2, 1878.
157. Ibid., October 13, 1883; *Benton Weekly Record*, August 18, 1883.
158. *Benton Weekly Record*, October 27, 1883.
159. *Cincinnati Enquirer*, March 19, 1905, June 27, 1913.

Chapter 21

160. Swiggett, *Bright Side of Prison Life*.
161. Ibid.
162. Wikipedia, "Camp Ford."
163. Swiggett, *Bright Side of Prison Life*.
164. Ibid.
165. Ibid.
166. Ibid.
167. Miller, *Illustrated History*, 167–70.

Chapter 22

168. Stout, *History of Montana*, 1–2.
169. "Paducah in the Civil War."
170. Stout, *History of Montana*, 1–2.

Chapter 23

171. Yeatman, *Frank and Jesse James*, 35.
172. *Montana Standard*, March 8, 1942. Thomas L. Napton, from a prominent slave-owning family in Missouri, served as a lieutenant in the 2nd Missouri Infantry Regiment, Confederate army. He and several of his brothers came to Montana after the war and settled in the Deer Lodge area.
173. *New North-west* (Deer Lodge, MT), March 21, 1874.
174. Spell of the West, "Missouri Outlaws."
175. *Fort Benton River Press*, April 26, 1882. Montana territorial newspapers, including the two early Fort Benton newspapers, devoted considerable coverage to the activities of the James gang, reflecting the large number of Missourians who settled in territorial Montana.
176. Connelly, *Quantrill*, 30.
177. *St. Louis Republican*, April 24, 1874.
178. Oral histories, John G. Lepley by author, various dates, 2010–13.

Chapter 24

179. "Did Booth Kill Himself?" *Rocky Mountain American*, March 12, 1940.
180. Mayer, "U.S. Civil War." Colonel Sweitzer and at least four men of the 16th New York Cavalry later migrated to Montana Territory, although it is not known whether any of these four were among Lieutenant Doherty's detachment.
181. "E.J. Conger Ran Booth to Earth. Story of Capture and Death of Lincoln's Assassin Is Told," *Spirit Lake Spotlight*, January 6, 1941. Conger's testimony that follows is from this source.
182. "Did Booth Kill Himself?" *Rocky Mountain American*, March 12, 1940; Sanders, *History of Montana*, 596.

Bibliography

Online Resources

"The 45th Kentucky Mounted Infantry Webpage." www.oocities.org/johnmasonbrown.

Gallery of Outstanding Montanans. "Mattie Bost Bell Castner." mhs.mt.gov/Portals/11/education/Montanans/castnertext.pdf.

Kansaspedia, Kansas Historical Society. "Frontier Guard." www.kshs.org/kansapedia/frontier-guard/16898.

"Miscellaneous Documents and Histories Regarding the Fourteenth U.S. Infantry During the Civil War." 1-14th.com/14thInfantry/3-CivilWar/h31overview.html.

Paducah, Kentucky. "Paducah in the Civil War." www.civilwaralbum.com/misc11/paducah1.htm.

Robison, Ken. "Adeline Hoffman." Historical Black Americans in Northern Montana. blackamericansmt.blogspot.com/2015/01/adeline-hoffman-from-slave-to-servant.html.

The Spell of the West. "Missouri Outlaws." www.jcs-group.com/oldwest/outlaw/missouri.html.

Wikipedia. "Battle of Fredericktown." en.wikipedia.org/wiki/Battle_of_Fredericktown.

———. "Camp Ford." en.wikipedia.org/wiki/Camp_Ford.

Newspapers (Montana Unless Otherwise Noted)

Belt Valley Times
Benton Record
Bismarck Tribune (ND)
Cincinnati Enquirer (OH)
Dupuyer Acantha
Fergus County Democrat
Fort Benton River Press
Great Falls Leader
Great Falls Tribune
Helena Herald
Helena Independent
Helena Radiator
Kansas State Journal (KS)
Missouri Republican (St. Louis, MO)
Montana Post
Montana Standard
Natrona County Tribune (WY)
New North-west (Deer Lodge, MT)
New York Times (NY)
Smoky Hill and Republican Union (MO)
St. Louis Republican (MO)
Washington Evening Star (Washington, D.C.)

Other Sources

"Affairs at Fort Benton, from 1831 to 1869. From Lieut. Bradley's Journal." *Contributions to the Historical Society of Montana* 3 (1900): 283–84.

"Andrew Dawson letters, 1860–1864." MF 99H Montana Historical Society.

Bowdern, T.S. "Joseph LaBarge Steamboat Captain." *Missouri Historical Review* 62 (Summer 1968).

Brown, John Mason. "Diary, 1862." Mss/A/B878a, Filson Historical Society.

———. "A Trip to the Northwest." *Filson Club History Quarterly* 24 (April 1950): 103–36 and (August 1950): 246–75.

Brown, Meredith Mason. "John Mason Brown during the Civil War: Indian Country and Fighting Morgan's Raiders." *Register of the Kentucky Historical Society* 111 (Winter 2013): 41–77.

"Bucknum Family History." Overholser Historical Research Center, Fort Benton, MT.

Centennial Book Committee, comp. *Thunderstorm and Tumbleweeds 1887–1987.* East Blaine County, MT, 1989.

Chittenden, Hiram Martin. *History of Early Steamboat Navigation on the Missouri River: Life and Adventures of Joseph La Barge.* 2 vols. New York: Francis P. Harper, 1903.

Connelly, William Elsey. *Quantrill and the Border Wars.* Cedar Rapids, IA: Torch Press Publishers, 1910.

"Dutriueille Family Papers." Montana Historical Society SC 1584.

Farwell, Byron. *Encyclopedia of 19th Century Land Warfare.* New York: W.W. Norton, 2001.

The Fort Benton Illustrated Almanac 1878. Fort Benton, MT: [Benton Record, 1878].

Gladstone, William. "View's of Early Fort Benton." *Rocky Mountain Echo,* December 8, 1903.

Hay, Kenneth W. "I Remember Old Yogo and the Weatherwax." *Montana the Magazine of Western History* 25, no. 2 (Spring 1975): 62–69.

Heitman, Francis Bernard. *Historical Register and Dictionary of the United States Army 1789–1903.* Vol. 2. Washington, D.C.: U.S. Government Printing Office, 1903.

Hubbard, Lucius F., et al, eds. *Minnesota in Three Centuries 1855–1908.* Vol. 3. New York: Publishing Society of Minnesota, 1908.

Keenan, Jerry. "Yellowstone Kelly from New York to Paradise." *Montana the Magazine of Western History* 40 (Summer 1990): 15–27.

Kennedy, Ethel Castner, and Eva Lesell Strober. *Belt Valley History, 1877–1979.* Great Falls, MT: Advanced Litho Printing, 1979.

Lass, William E. *A History of Steamboating on the Upper Missouri.* Lincoln: University of Nebraska Press, 1962.

———. *Navigating the Missouri: Steamboating on Nature's Highway, 1819–1935.* Norman, OK: Arthur H. Clark Company, 2008.

Leeson, Michael A. *History of Montana, 1739–1885.* Chicago: Warner, Beers & Co., 1885.

Lepley, John G. *Birthplace of Montana: A History of Fort Benton.* Missoula, MT: Pictorial Histories, 1999.

———. *Blackfoot Fur Trade on the Upper Missouri.* Missoula, MT: Pictorial Histories, 2004.

———. *Packets to Paradise: Steamboating to Fort Benton.* Missoula, MT: Pictorial Histories, 2001.

Lilly, John C. "Handwritten Account of John C. Lilly." Overholser Historical Research Center, Fort Benton, MT.

Manion, John S. *General Terry's Last Statement to Custer*. El Segundo, CA: Upton and Sons, Publishers, 2000.

Mayer, Andre. "The U.S. Civil War and the Role 5 Canadians Played in It: From Confederate Blockade Runners to the Man Who Captured Lincoln's Assassin." *Canadian Broadcasting Corporation (CBC) News*, April 8, 2015.

Merington, Marguerite, ed. *The Custer Story: The Life and Intimate Letters of General Custer and His Wife Elizabeth*. New York: Devin-Adair Company, 1950.

Miller, David R., et al. *The History of the Fort Peck Assiniboine and Sioux Tribes, 1800–2000*. Poplar: Fort Peck Community College and the Montana Historical Society Press, 2008.

Miller, Joaquin. *An Illustrated History of the State of Montana*. Chicago: Lewis Publishing Co., 1894.

Mills, Joseph Hanson. *Conquest of the Missouri Being the Story of the Life and Exploits of Captain Grant Marsh*. Chicago: A.C. McClurg & Co., 1909.

Nichols, Bruce. *Guerrilla Warfare in Civil War Missouri*. Vol. 2, 1863. Jefferson, NC: McFarland & Company, 2007.

Noyes, Al J. *In the Land of Chinook or The Story of Blaine County*. Helena, MT: State Publishing Co., 1917.

Overholser, Joel. *Fort Benton, World's Innermost Port*. Fort Benton, MT: privately printed, 1987.

Petsche, Jerome E. *The Steamboat* Bertrand*: History, Excavation, and Architecture*. Washington, D.C.: National Park Service, 1993.

Plassmann, Martha Edgerton. "The 'Far West,' Famous Missouri River Steamer—The Part It Played in Tragic Expedition Against the Sioux Indians." *Sanders County Signal*, June 30, 192.

———. "Memories of a Long Life." Unpublished manuscript [author's collection].

———. "Passengers on 'Far West' Afforded Thrilling Experience When Sioux Tribe Is Transferred." *Big Timber Pioneer*, July 7, 1924.

Powell, William Henry, and Edward Shippan, eds. *Officers of the Army and Navy (Regular) Who Served in the Civil War*. Philadelphia: L.R. Hamesly & Co., 1892.

Progressive Men of Montana. Chicago: A.W. Bowen & Co., circa 1903.

Quaife, M.M., ed. *"Yellowstone Kelly": The Memoirs of Luther S. Kelly*. New Haven, CT: Yale University Press, 1926.

Robison, Ken. "Completing the Mullan Road from Mullan Pass to Fort Benton: A Harbinger of Change." In *The Mullan Road: Carving a Passage through the Frontier Northwest, 1859 to 1862*. Edited by Paul D. McDermott. Missoula, MT: Mountain Press Publishing, 2015.

———. *Confederates in Montana Territory: In the Shadow of Price's Army*. Charleston, SC: The History Press, 2014.

———. *Montana Territory and the Civil War: A Frontier Forged on the Battlefield*. Charleston, SC: The History Press, 2013.

———. "On Being a Black American in Territorial Fort Benton—Parts I, II, III." *Fort Benton River Press*, July 24, 2005, May 4, December 29, 2009.

"The Robison-Wahlberg List of Upper Missouri Steamboat Operations." Overholser Historical Research Center, Fort Benton, MT.

Rockwell, Ronald V. *The U.S. Army in Frontier Montana*. Helena, MT: Sweetgrass Books, 2009.

Rocky Mountain American. "Did Booth Kill Himself?" March 12, 1940.

Rust, Thomas. *Lost Fort Ellis: Frontier History of Bozeman*. Charleston, SC: The History Press, 2015.

Sanders, Helen Fitzgerald. *History of Montana*. Vol. 1. Chicago: Lewis Publishing Company, 1913.

Schieffelin, William H. "Crossing the Plains in '61." *Recreation Magazine* 2, no. 6 (June 1895).

Speed, Thomas. "10th Kentucky Cavalry Regimental History." In *The Union Regiments of Kentucky*. Louisville, KY: Courier-Journal Job Printing Company, 1897.

Spirit Lake Spotlight. "E.J. Conger Ran Booth to Earth. Story of Capture and Death of Lincoln's Assassin Is Told." January 6, 1941.

Stiles, T.J. *Custer's Trials: A Life on the Frontier of a New America*. New York: Alfred A. Knopf, 2015.

Stout, Tom. *History of Montana*. Vol. 3. Chicago: American Historical Society, 1921.

Strachan, John. *Blazing the Mullan Trail: Connecting the Headwaters of the Missouri and the Columbia Rivers and Locating the Great Overland Highway to the Pacific Northwest*. Printed from the *Rockford Register*, April 1860–April 1861. N.p.: Edward Eberstadt & Sons, 1952.

Sunder, John E. *The Fur Trade on the Upper Missouri, 1840–1865*. Norman: University of Oklahoma Press, 1965.

Swiggett, Captain S.A. *The Bright Side of Prison Life: Experiences, In Prison and Out, of an Involuntary Sojourner in Rebeldom*. Baltimore, MD: Fleet, McGinley & Co., 1897.

Taylor, Quintard, and Shirley Ann Wilson Moore, eds. *African American Women Confront the West, 1600–2000*. Norman: University of Oklahoma Press, 2003.

Thomson, Janet, ed. *Early Settlers of Great Falls, Montana, 1884–1920*. Vol. 2. Great Falls, MT: Create Space Independent Publishing Platform, 2012.

Thrapp, Dan L. *Encyclopedia of Frontier Biography*. Vol. 2, G–O. Spokane, WA: Arthur H. Clark Company, 1988.

Voynick, Stephen N. *Yogo, the Great American Sapphire*. Missoula, MT: Mountain Press Publishing Company, 1985.

Wallin, Chadbourne M. "Aunt Adeline, Near 100, 'Doc' to Early Miners." *Jordan Tribune*, August 7, 1939.

Way, Frederick, Jr. comp. *Way's Packet Directory, 1848–1983*. Athens: Ohio University, 1983.

Wischmann, Lesley. *Frontier Diplomats: Alexander Culbertson and Natoyist-Siksina among the Blackfeet*. Spokane, WA: Arthur H. Clark Company, 2000.

Wischmann, Lesley, and Andrew Erskine Dawson. *This Far-Off Wild Land: The Upper Missouri Letters of Andrew Dawson*. Norman, OK: Arthur H. Clark Company, 2013.

Works Progress Administration, comp. *Great Falls Yesterday: Comprising a Collection of Biographies and Reminiscences of Early Settlers*. Great Falls, MT, 1939.

Yeatman, Ted. *Frank and Jesse James: The Story Behind the Legend*. Nashville, TN: Cumberland House Publishing, 2000.

Index

C

D

G

H

I

J

N

O

P

Q

R

S

About the Author

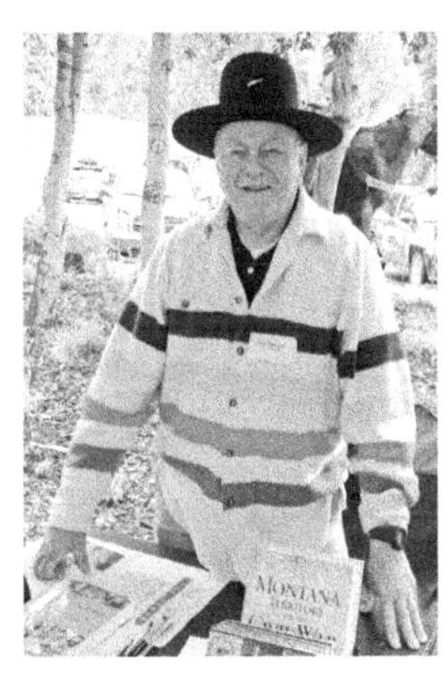

Ken Robison is a chronicler of neglected western history who lives in Great Falls, Montana, with his wife, Michele. Ken, a Montana native, is historian at the Overholser Historical Research Center in Fort Benton. He serves as historian for the Great Falls/Cascade County Historic Preservation Commission and is active in historic preservation throughout Montana. His books include *Montana Territory and the Civil War: A Frontier Forged on the Battlefield*; *Confederates in Montana Territory: In the Shadow of Price's Army*; and *Life and Death on the Upper Missouri: The Frontier Sketches of Johnny Healy*. He has contributed to *Montana, a Cultural Medley: Stories of Our Ethnic Diversity* and *The Mullan Road: Carving a Passage through the Frontier Northwest, 1859 to 1862*. Ken is a retired navy captain after a career in naval intelligence. The Montana Historical Society honored him as "Montana Heritage Keeper" in 2010.

Visit us at
www.historypress.net

This title is also available as an e-book

www.ingramcontent.com/pod-product-compliance
Lightning Source LLC
LaVergne TN
LVHW052335100826
845147LV00020B/1072

9781467135627